MediaWiki 1.1
Beginner's Guide

Install, manage, and customize your own
MediaWiki-based site

Mizanur Rahman

Jeffrey T. Orloff

PUBLISHING

BIRMINGHAM - MUMBAI

MediaWiki 1.1
Beginner's Guide

First published: March 2010

Production Reference: 1220210

Published by Packt Publishing Ltd.
32 Lincoln Road
Olton
Birmingham, B27 6PA, UK.

ISBN 978-1-847196-04-0

www.packtpub.com

Cover Image by Louise Barr (lou@frogboxdesign.co.uk)

Credits

Author

Mizanur Rahman

Jeffrey T. Orloff

Reviewers

Richard Carter

Jens Olofsson

Acquisition Editor

David Barnes

Development Editor

Dhiraj Chandiramani

Technical Editor

Ajay B Chamkeri

Indexer

Monica Ajmera Mehta

Editorial Team Leader

Aanchal Kumar

Project Team Leader

Lata Basantani

Project Coordinator

Joel Goveya

Proofreader

Lynda Sliwoski

Graphics

Geetanjali Sawant

Production Coordinator

Melwyn D'sa

Cover Work

Melwyn D'sa

About the Authors

Mizanur Rahman graduated in Computer Science from North South University, Bangladesh. His main interests cover a wide area centered on algorithms, distributed and mobile computing, and new web technologies. He has been programming since 1999. He has been a Research Assistant at the Department of Computer Science, North South University, designing and developing web-based solutions for different software for the university. His area of interest includes Java, PHP, AJAX, and other related technologies. He is a moderator of phpXperts—the largest PHP user group in Bangladesh. He is a certified Internet programmer from the largest online testing site, `www.Brainbench.com`, including a master certificate in PHP. He is currently working as a Senior Software Engineer at Relisource Technologies Ltd, a USA-based software company located in Dhaka, Bangladesh. He is also the technical reviewer of two previous Packt publication books, *vBulletin* and *Smarty*. You can reach him at `mizanur.rahman@gmail.com`.

I would like to thank my wife Lily and my son Adiyan for their continuous support to complete the book. I want to dedicate my work to my son. I would like to thank my parents and my relatives for their support.

I would like to thank Hasin Hyder and David Barnes for giving me the opportunity to work with Packt Publishing. I would also like to thank all my friends and colleagues for being with me all the time. And finally, I would like to thank Tohin Kashem and Jehad Sarkar, two of my senior colleagues, for their invaluable support throughout my professional career.

And last but not the least, all the people who have worked with me on this book. I am thankful to my reviewers, Nikhil, Peter, and Marc for their valuable inputs. A very special thanks to Nikhil for his great work on the book. A special thanks to Rajlaxmi and Akshara, my technical editors, and others who worked with me in different phases of the book. Without the support of these people, I couldn't have completed the book.

Jeffrey T. Orloff has been working with computers since the days of the IBM personal computer. His first foray into the world of computers was a book on programming games in Basic. Since then, he has spent time working with network security, free/open source software, and web technologies. Working as a freelance writer, he has been published in ComputerWorld and IBM developerWorks as well as numerous blogs. He currently keeps a blog titled Insatiable Techknowledgy (http://www.insatiabletechknowledgy.com).

Jeff has worked as a technology coordinator for the School District of Palm Beach County for over five years. In addition to his work with educational technology, Jeff served as a consultant to SafeWave.org in helping them build the iLAND5 social network for children. He currently serves as a chief consultant for Sequoia Media, Inc., focusing on the IT side of social media and web content delivery.

I would like to thank my family for all of their support in this endeavor. My wife Jackie for picking up all the slack around the house while I was writing and editing. To my daughter Priscilla for being so patient and helpful and to my son Jeffrey for insisting I take breaks to throw the baseball out in the yard.

I would also like to thank David Barnes for bringing me into the Packt family. It has been a great project to be a part of! I would also like to thank Neil Salkind for his work in helping get everything started. Finally, I need to thank all of the people at Packt who put so much time into making sure this book can be the best possible source of information it can be!

About the Reviewers

Richard Carter is senior web designer at Peacock Carter, a web design agency based in the North East of England.

He has had years of experience with MediaWiki as both an end user, and as a consultant for companies and organizations, large and small, looking to use MediaWiki for a huge range of purposes.

Richard has written two books, *MediaWiki Skins Design* and *Magento 1.3 Theme Design*, and is currently working on a third.

> My thanks go to the author, who has truly written to the publisher's mantra of "community experience distilled", and to those at Packt who continue to produce these books. Finally, thank you to MediaWiki's team of developers who, I'm sure we can agree, have produced an incredibly useful piece of software!

Jens Olofsson is a freelance marketer and web designer. His formal education includes a Bachelor of Social Science in Marketing as well as numerous university courses within web design, programming and graphical design. His practical work involves mainly commission work but also other projects. He has experience working with various companies and their marketing activities—both on the Internet, as well as in more traditional channels. You may contact him on `http://www.jfomedia.se`.

Table of Contents

Preface

MediaWiki was developed specifically to power the most widely known wiki in the world, Wikipedia. It's success has led it to become the wiki engine of choice for web developers looking to create a large, collaborative community where anyone can create, edit, and delete content.

While MediaWiki is meant to be a completely open platform where anyone can contribute, thanks to a large developer community, extensions have been created to lock down a MediaWiki wiki to restrict what visitors can do. Other extensions and administrative tricks you will learn will allow you to increase the functionality of MediaWiki in ways you never thought possible.

What this book covers

Chapter 1, *About MediaWiki*, introduces you to a history of wikis and how wikis were developed to create collaborative communities.

Chapter 2, *Installing MediaWiki*, explains about the essential software required to install and run MediaWiki. It teaches you how to bring the MediaWiki installation files to our web server so we can install the software. It also teaches how to create a database that MediaWiki will use to store configuration information about the wiki as well as the content that drives visitors to the wiki.

Chapter 3, *Getting to Know Your Wiki*, teaches you about how MediaWiki organizes pages and gives you the first couple of steps in transforming MediaWiki into your wiki. It also teaches you how a page differs from an article, to avoid confusion throughout the book.

Chapter 4, *Creating Content*, teaches you how to go about making our content more attractive to the reader through different formatting techniques.

Chapter 5, *Advanced Formatting*, teaches you about lists, tables, and other formatting techniques that we can use to not only make our wiki look better, but also to better manage it and display our content.

Chapter 6, *Putting the Media in MediaWiki*, teaches how we can use multimedia to enrich our wiki's content.

Chapter 7, *Organizing Your Wiki's Content*, teaches how to organize our content by creating namespaces that allow us to group pages with similar purposes together, and we learn how to use categories to group pages with similar content together. It also teaches you about redirecting, moving, and swapping pages around so that we can ensure when a visitor comes to our site, they find the information they are looking for because the page titles will match up with page's content.

Chapter 8, *The MediaWiki Administrator*, teaches you that through proper management of the user groups, we can take away privileges and provide users with extra privileges. It also teaches how we can control the type of files we allow our users to upload to our wiki if we have enough trust in our user base.

Chapter 9, *Multi-user Environment*, teaches how to modify our profiles and change the editing preferences. It also shows how the administrators, or sysops, can view a page's history to view previous edits made to the page.

Chapter 10, *Advanced Customization*, teaches how to modify the look and functionality of our wiki so that it not only has the appearance that we want, but also the functionality.

Chapter 11, *Maintaining MediaWiki*, teaches you how to back up our database using phpMyAdmin, and our filesystem by copying important files, so that in the event of a disaster we could restore our wiki back to its functional state. We also learn how to restore our wiki from these backups, most importantly, we see that we need to test our backups frequently by restoring them to see if everything is working.

Chapter 12, *Integrating MediaWiki*, teaches how MediaWiki can be integrated with some of the leading web applications to build powerful sites for your visitors. Specifically, we saw how extensions allow us to display WordPress comments on a related wiki page and authenticate to our wiki with a Joomla! username.

What you need for this book

MediaWiki requires you to have access to a web server. Throughout the course of this book, it is assumed that you will be using a hosting account through a web service provider. If you are installing MediaWiki on a local server of your own, that is fine as well.

Additionally, you will need to have PHP version 5.0 or later and either MySQL 4.0 or later, or PostgreSQL version 8.1 or later.

Who this book is for

If you are a Web Designer, IT Administrator or Executive, or a Programmer and wish to gain a solid foundation in the MediaWiki software application, then this book is for you.

Conventions

In this book, you will find several headings appearing frequently.

To give clear instructions of how to complete a procedure or task, we use:

Time for action – heading

1. Action 1

2. Action 2

3. Action 3

Instructions often need some extra explanation so that they make sense, so they are followed with:

What just happened?

This heading explains the working of tasks or instructions that you have just completed.

You will also find some other learning aids in the book, including:

Pop quiz – heading

These are short multiple choice questions intended to help you test your own understanding.

Have a go hero – heading

These set practical challenges and give you ideas for experimenting with what you have learned.

You will also find a number of styles of text that distinguish between different kinds of information. Here are some examples of these styles, and an explanation of their meaning.

Code words in text are shown as follows: "At the bottom of the page, type `{{templatename}}` substituting your template for `templatename`."

A block of code is set as follows:

```
#Add other file extensions to upload
$wgFileExtensions = array('png','jpg','jpeg','ogg','doc','xls','ppt',
'mp3','pdf');

#Ogg handler extension
require( "$IP/extensions/OggHandler/OggHandler.php" );
```

New terms and **important words** are shown in bold. Words that you see on the screen, in menus or dialog boxes for example, appear in the text like this: "Click on **Show preview** to see your new template. If you are satisfied, click on **Save page**."

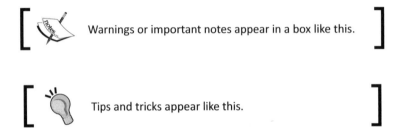

Warnings or important notes appear in a box like this.

Tips and tricks appear like this.

Reader feedback

Feedback from our readers is always welcome. Let us know what you think about this book—what you liked or may have disliked. Reader feedback is important for us to develop titles that you really get the most out of.

To send us general feedback, simply send an e-mail to feedback@packtpub.com, and mention the book title via the subject of your message.

If there is a book that you need and would like to see us publish, please send us a note in the **SUGGEST A TITLE** form on www.packtpub.com or e-mail suggest@packtpub.com.

If there is a topic that you have expertise in and you are interested in either writing or contributing to a book on, see our author guide on www.packtpub.com/authors.

Customer support

Now that you are the proud owner of a Packt book, we have a number of things to help you to get the most from your purchase.

> **Downloading the example code for the book**
>
> Visit http://www.packtpub.com/files/code/6040_Code.zip to directly download the example code.
>
> The downloadable files contain instructions on how to use them.

Errata

Although we have taken every care to ensure the accuracy of our content, mistakes do happen. If you find a mistake in one of our books—maybe a mistake in the text or the code—we would be grateful if you would report this to us. By doing so, you can save other readers from frustration and help us improve subsequent versions of this book. If you find any errata, please report them by visiting http://www.packtpub.com/support, selecting your book, clicking on the **let us know** link, and entering the details of your errata. Once your errata are verified, your submission will be accepted and the errata will be uploaded on our website, or added to any list of existing errata, under the **Errata** section of that title. Any existing errata can be viewed by selecting your title from http://www.packtpub.com/support.

Piracy

Piracy of copyright material on the Internet is an ongoing problem across all media. At Packt, we take the protection of our copyright and licenses very seriously. If you come across any illegal copies of our works, in any form, on the Internet, please provide us with the location address or website name immediately so that we can pursue a remedy.

Please contact us at copyright@packtpub.com with a link to the suspected pirated material.

We appreciate your help in protecting our authors, and our ability to bring you valuable content.

Questions

You can contact us at questions@packtpub.com if you are having a problem with any aspect of the book, and we will do our best to address it.

1
About MediaWiki

It is amazing to see how far the web has come in such a short period of time. Just a few years ago, websites were limited to static pages where information was delivered at the hands of the site's webmaster. As technology progressed, websites no longer relied on just a few pages of HTML to share information. They grew into dynamic application platforms where content changed instantaneously and groups of people around the world could collaborate to build huge sites with tons of information for their visitors. Few technologies embrace this type of collaboration and information sharing like wikis do.

In this chapter we shall:

- Find out what a wiki actually is and how they came to be
- Learn what we can use wikis for
- See how wikis compare to other web technologies
- Be introduced to MediaWiki and its features
- See how MediaWiki compares to other wiki engines

So let's get on with it.

Before we get started

It is important that you understand what this book will cover and what you should expect to have learned after reading it and following along with the examples.

This book is a step-by-step guide for getting a wiki up and running using the MediaWiki wiki engine. You will be given directions and examples, that will teach you how to install, configure, manage, and secure a fully-functional wiki.

MediaWiki is a robust wiki engine that is capable of creating large **wiki farms** where one or more servers host multiple individual wikis. People who create a wiki on one of these farms don't have to worry about the installation of the software, the administration of the server, or even the wiki software itself. All they have to do is create their content and build their site. MediaWiki also allows for integration with directory services such as **Lightweight Directory Access Protocol (LDAP)**. Using LDAP, network administrators can host a wiki on their local/wide area network and integrate their users' network login credentials with their wiki to create a more seamless environment.

As this is a beginner's guide, this book will not cover such advanced topics; however, the foundation you build by reading it will prepare you for exploring more advanced configurations and uses of MediaWiki.

 Throughout this book, we will use the term **wiki engine**. A wiki engine is the software that runs a wiki system.

An introduction to wikis

Many people first became familiar with the term wiki when they were introduced to Wikipedia. While it is the most popular wiki to date, the wiki's roots go back further than Wikipedia.

The history of the wiki

Although development of the first wiki began in 1994, roughly seven years before Wikipedia, it was not introduced until March 2005 by Ward Cunningham. WikiWikiWeb, as Cunningham called it, is written in Perl and derived its name from an airline employee in Honolulu telling Cunningham to take the Wiki Wiki Shuttle. The Hawaiian word *wiki* means quick so Cunningham was being told to take the quick shuttle. Cunningham later explained that he chose the name wiki wiki as, "an alliterative substitute for quick and thereby avoided naming this stuff quick-web."

WikiWikiWeb wasn't just a catchy name that Cunningham had thought up, it had a purpose. As a programmer heavily involved in the Portland Pattern Repository, Cunningham developed the wiki as a way for programmers to quickly create and share ideas with other programmers who contributed to the Portland Pattern Repository. With this new tool, programmers could collaborate with one another on projects without the need for a webmaster to upload new or edited content because the wiki lets the participants do all of this from their own web browser.

 The term wiki also has a backronym associated with it that expands to read *what I know is*.

After Cunningham deployed WikiWikiWeb as a supplement to the repository site, he began inviting other programmers to contribute content. The plan was to have interested parties write web pages about the people, projects, and patterns that have changed the way they program. Cunningham wrote to his colleagues, "Think of it as a moderated list where anyone can be a moderator and everything is archived. It's not quite a chat, still, conversation is possible."

With that, the ball started rolling and WikiWikiWeb still exists today as the largest wiki related to a single topic. You can visit the original wiki, although it has evolved over time, by going to `http://c2.com/cgi/wiki?WikiWikiWeb`.

Wiki Wiki Web

This website and the software it runs on were created by WardCunningham for the PortlandPatternRepository. It is home to an InformalHistoryOfProgrammingIdeas as well as a large volume of material recording related discourses and collaboration between its readers.

The content is written by the users - people like you and me. Anyone can change any page or create new pages. Read the TextFormattingRules to find out how, and then go to the WikiWikiSandbox to try it yourself. Please use the WikiWikiSandbox if you want to experiment with how editing works. If you make a page you don't want to keep, just replace its text with the word "delete".

Some starting points:

- NewUserPages
- TipsForBeginners
- OneMinuteWiki
- TextFormattingRules
- StartingPoints

As word spread about the success of Cunningham's wiki, others quickly adopted this technology for their websites. Soon, clones of the original wiki engine were starting to emerge in just about every programming language available.

Just about the time wikis were really starting to emerge as a viable tool, the Web 2.0 attitude took over many of the design concepts for the web. Developers and designers started looking at technologies that could help promote interactivity and participation from their visitors, not just the web masters. The freedom to collaborate and participate made wiki engines a perfect fit for the Web 2.0 paradigm because of the following reasons:

- A wiki is a piece of application that is used for collaborative participation
- Users are the primary contributors to wikis
- Users have the ability to edit existing content
- Users do not have to register for the site before contributing; making the wiki a truly open platform
- User participation determines the site's success

While wikis remained popular within the programming and technical community, it wasn't until the introduction of one wiki in particular that the concept really took off with the average user.

Introducing Wikipedia

Since 1999, Jimmy Wales had been running a site called *Nupedia* as a free content encyclopedia with content written by experts. To make the content comparable to that found in professional encyclopedias, everything submitted underwent an extensive peer review process before it was published. In January 2001, Wales decided to create an encyclopedia with far less restrictions than his current Nupedia project. This encyclopedia would take on the slogan of **the free encyclopedia that anyone can edit**. To allow contributions and edits from the public, Wales and Nupedia editor Larry Sanger turned to a technology that the programming community had been using for years, the wiki.

While Nupedia ceased operations in 2003, its counterpart, Wikipedia, has grown into the largest wiki in the world with over 6 million articles written in 140 different languages!

Wikipedia is what introduced much of the world to the wiki. Not only is it the world's largest wiki, but it runs on the MediaWiki engine that we are going to install and configure over the course of this book.

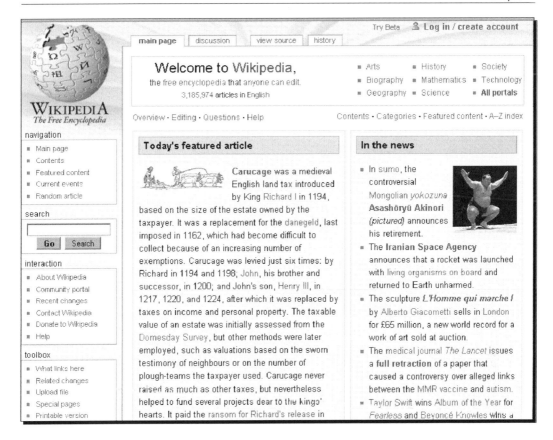

What can you do with a wiki?

We have seen how wikis have been used by programmers and how a wiki engine was used to create the Wikipedia, but you may be asking, "How can I put a wiki to use?" You may even have a few ideas of what you would like to do with a wiki but are a bit unsure if it will work. The good news is, we will cover many different uses for wikis throughout this book with real examples of how they are put to use. The bad news is, a wiki is not a solution for all situations, but we will cover that as well.

When wikis are not the best choice

Let's go ahead and get this part out of the way so we can focus on building a wiki with MediaWiki. While wikis can do great many things, they were not developed to be the sole means of providing content to the World Wide Web. The key to a successful wiki is making sure that the community of users is willing, and able, to create and edit content for the wiki. Even with willing participants, there are many cases in which a wiki may not be the technology of choice.

Strict access control

Even as the focus of the web tends to shift more towards user-created content and a social web, there are times when you need to restrict who can create or edit certain content. As wikis were developed to allow anyone to create, publish, and edit content, for a scenario when access needs to be controlled, a wiki is not the best option. Although there are wiki engines such as PmWiki and MoinMoin that allow for some levels of access control, at its core, MediaWiki is an open access system that allows anyone, registered or not, the ability to contribute to the site. We will address how to control this in the following chapters.

 If you are looking for a way to restrict access to your wiki, we will be discussing some MediaWiki extensions that will help you prevent access to certain pages, or the entire wiki.

E-commerce

While a wiki about a certain product or business may compliment a company's web presence by providing customers with a user manual or customer-based support site, wikis are not designed to handle e-commerce. There are many different open source e-commerce programs that can provide a better environment for online sales. Remember, wikis are about content and collaboration.

Static content sites

If a website has no plans to include collaboration or interactivity then a wiki is not a good solution. A wiki is most successful when the community surrounding it is able to contribute content to the site. If the content that will be posted on the site will be maintained solely by a web master and is static, HTML or a content management solution may be a better choice.

Users are unwilling to learn something new

Wikis use different markup languages to format text as bold, italics, and so on. For instance, MediaWiki requires users to learn wikitext. While many of the markup languages are easy to learn, as we will see in the following chapters, if your community or organization has a large group of people who don't want to learn this, the wiki won't be successful.

What are wikis good for?

Okay, so we have covered when you would not use a wiki. Now, let's tackle the more relevant question, when is wiki a good solution? After all, you bought this book because you want, or need, to implement a wiki.

Wikis can be used for a great many things. A wiki can be used for brainstorming ideas, developing frequently asked questions (FAQs), knowledge management, course management, collaborating on projects, a knowledge base, or providing reference material. Of course, the previous list is not complete by far. Creative individuals have thought of many different ways to implement a wiki.

While it is easy to say that a wiki has many different uses, it is better to show how they are used. The following examples show how different organizations and companies use wikis to share information. Each example not only uses a wiki, but they have chosen MediaWiki as their wiki engine. As this book is about MediaWiki, we will be highlighting how MediaWiki is a solution in each instance.

Community information sharing

The best example of how a wiki can share information with a large community is Wikipedia. With over 6 million articles, imagine how long it would take for a webmaster, or even a team of webmasters, to post each piece of content. As the wiki software allows users to post their own articles, a large amount of content can be shared almost immediately after it was created.

The ability to edit and delete articles also makes Wikipedia so successful. One of the problems that Nupedia faced was not only having content written for the site, but having it edited and verified for accuracy. Using a wiki, Wikipedia can rely on the experts in the community to enforce accuracy over the site's content.

Project collaboration

Think about how easy work would be if you had the ability to view a document's edit history with a simple click or being able to make sure you are not the only one in the office referring to version 2 of a document while the rest of the team is working from version 4. While a word processor has tools to minimize this, not everyone has the same software at home that they do at work. Again, a wiki engine like MediaWiki makes this all possible. Co-workers can share and collaborate without having to e-mail documents back and forth, and you don't have to worry about lost or forgotten USB drives because with a wiki, all content is hosted and can be accessed from your web browser. Even if you use Firefox at work, and Safari at home, you will be able to work on documents without having to convert the files.

As a wiki is an ideal platform where people can easily share notes, ideas, design requirements, and other lightweight assets, it makes for a great addition to a project management plan. In fact, this is what the original WikiWikiWeb was designed for.

WikiMedia is the choice for many organizations who use a wiki in a similar manner. Advanced Gaming Systems created an internal wiki to help facilitate the development of "The Next Harpoon" game. AOE media GmbH, the leading TYPO3 consultant group, also uses MediaWiki as an internal tool for collaborating on projects.

Many organizations who do not want information to be seen by people outside their group will install MediaWiki on their company or organization's intranet. This way, the openness of a wiki can be maintained while protecting proprietary information.

Creating a user manual/FAQ page

Have you noticed how software and hardware companies no longer include thick user manuals in their packaging? As technology allows them to include their documentation on the installation media, they are able to save money on shipping and printing costs. However, many free/open source software companies don't provide installation media for their users. Instead, the files are downloaded and the user manual is often not included. Many of these companies have turned to MediaWiki as a way to create documentation for their software.

Blender modeling software is a great example. While the home page for Blender (http://www.blender.org) was created in standard HTML, the user manual (http://wiki.blender.org/index.php/Doc:Manual/Introduction) makes use of MediaWiki. Providing the user manual and/or FAQs page for a software package not only is a cost-saving solution, but it also keeps free/open source software projects true to the community philosophy. Using software such as MediaWiki allows the community to create and modify the user manual. The Writer Guide (http://wiki.blender.org/index.php/Meta:Guides/Writer_Guide) of this manual explains how community members can contribute. The following screenshot shows the Blender User Manual in MediaWiki:

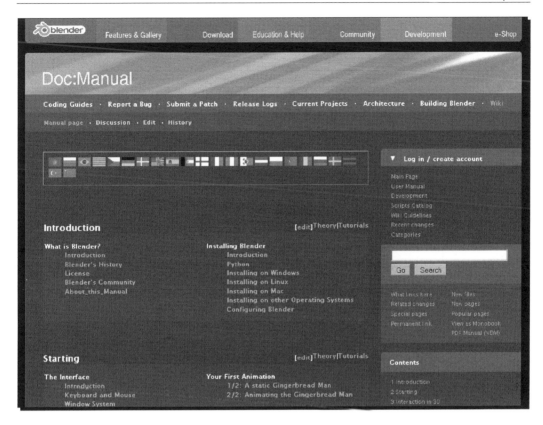

Building an entire website

Now, we are not talking about hosting a standalone wiki such as Wikipedia, and we are not talking about certain parts of a website like the user manual. There are organizations that have built their entire website, from the home page to the download page, entirely with MediaWiki.

If you have visited the MediaWiki home page then you have already seen a perfect example of this. If that example is much too obvious, then let's take a look at the site for the enterprise-grade network management software, openNMS (www.opennms.org). As the openNMS group spans the globe, it makes perfect sense to create a site that anyone, anywhere can contribute to, making it a true community and a true free/open source project. The following screenshot shows the openNMS home page created with MediaWiki:

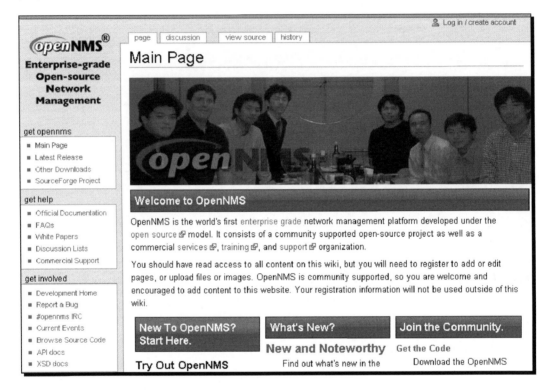

Company policies and documents

For many companies, creating an employee manual can be a nightmare. As laws and regulations change, so do human resource policies, IT policies, and just about every other governance that pertains to employees. Printing these manuals can be costly to begin with, and making sure that each employee has the updated version takes quite a bit of effort and manpower for a large organization.

So what would allow a large group to create and maintain a site filled with content? A wiki of course. With a solution like MediaWiki installed on an company's intranet, the human resources department can host the employee manual and all of the forms that they require workers to fill out, information technology departments can post software installation procedures and acceptable usage policies, and the finance department can provide employees with updated information on direct deposit. The possibilities are as wide open as the number of companies who use MediaWiki for this very reason. Big organizations like Intel, Gyanasoft, and Aperture Technologies are some of the best examples of how big organizations use MediaWiki for this exact purpose. Even smaller companies like Pepper Computer, Inc. make use of MediaWiki for employee documents.

Learning management

With such a focus on collaboration and discussion, wikis are a great platform for learning management. While it lacks the grading and testing features that a large scale learning management system(LMS) like Moodle has, MediaWiki can help someone put together an extremely informative course. While companies may elect to use MediaWiki as a free training resource for their products, one site that really shows off the power of MediaWiki as a learning management tool is ECGpedia.

ECGpedia is an online course for nurses and doctors about electrocardiographs. The site (www.ecgpedia.org) provides students with the full course, reference materials, the textbook, and a large library of case studies. To better help students understand such a complex subject, ECGpedia makes use of MediaWiki's ability to let users post multimedia files using one of the many extensions available. If you visit the site, you can see a flash movie of a beating heart that coincides with a normal rhythm.

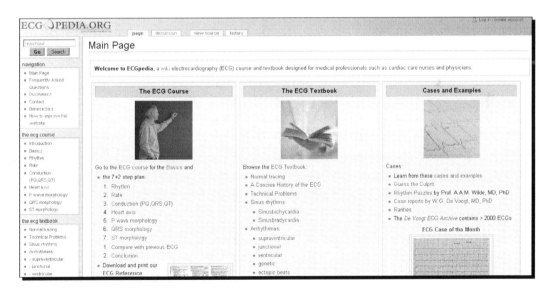

Comparing wikis to content management systems, blogs, and forums

If you have been working with web technologies for a while, you may be asking if someone couldn't just use some other form of community software like a **Content Management System** (**CMS**), forum, or blog for any one of these examples. The short answer is yes. These technologies could be substituted for a wiki in many of the examples mentioned above. However, if you think that a CMS, forum, or blog is an easier or more robust solution, take the time to compare them against a wiki to see how easy and powerful a wiki can really be. Let's look at a few differences:

Feature	Blog	Forum	CMS	Wiki
Posting or editing content	Blogs usually only allow the blog owner to post content. Visitors are usually restricted to only commenting on posts from the blog owner. Often many times these comments need to be approved before they appear on the site.	Registered members can post content, however posting may require approval first. If a posting is closed, further comments are not allowed. Original posts cannot be changed by anyone other than the author.	Only those with certain accounts, such as administrators or editors, can post content. Visitors can only view content.	Anyone can add or edit content without the need for an administrators approval. Even unregistered members can be given permission to add and edit.
Method of contribution	As the blog owner is the author of the content, he or she is the main contributor. Permissions can be given to certain authors as well. Most contributions are limited to commenting on other people's posts.	Anyone participating is a contributor, however replies must focus on the original posting. Topics are generally moderated.	Only privileged members can contribute and/or edit.	Everyone has the ability to contribute by creating new articles, editing inaccurate content, or adding to existing content.

Wikis by nature are simple to use and simple to manage. There is no need for an administrator to create user accounts and grant permissions since users can create their own account. Once we get into writing and editing articles, you will see how easy it is for your users to start using wikitext as well.

MediaWiki

Now that we know the history of the wiki, and understand how wikis can serve many purposes, let's take a look at the most powerful wiki engine available—MediaWiki.

MediaWiki came to life to solve issues that Wikipedia was having with its wiki engine, UseModWiki. As Wikipedia grew and its content and traffic increased, it began to outgrow the Perl-based UseModWiki. To address page load problems and provide greater functionality, Lee Daniel Crocker went to work on a PHP-based application that utilized a MySQL database for the backend while Magnus Manske went to work on the user interface.

In June 2003, Jimmy Wales, co-founder of Wikipedia, announced the creation of the Wikimedia Foundation to manage all projects related to Wikipedia. In August of the same year, MediaWiki was introduced and is now the wiki engine that runs all of the projects under the Wikimedia Foundation, including the flagship Wikipedia.

MediaWiki's features

One of the reasons that MediaWiki is the wiki engine of choice for many organizations is that it has so many features available for both users and administrators. Let's take a look at a few:

- **Easy navigation system**: MediaWiki provides an easy navigation system with options such as a search feature, a **Go** button that takes you directly to a page you have searched for, **Random page**, **Special pages**, and a **Printable version** for articles.

- **Editing, formatting, and referencing**: MediaWiki provides an easy way to edit, format, and reference pages with other pages. It also gives us the option to track changes. As wikis are deployed in multi-user environments, the ability to see who created or edited a piece of content is a key feature to manage the content properly.

- **Look and feel change**: Users can change the look and feel of a wiki site using MediaWiki. They can use a variety of skins and make style changes for their individual pages.

- **File uploading**: MediaWiki gives you an option to add file upload capabilities to your pages as we saw with ECGpedia. It also gives you flexibility to decide the allowable file extensions that can be uploaded by users and also a list of file extensions to be blocked.

- **Multilanguage support**: MediaWiki supports many languages and UTF-8. So you can implement MediaWiki in different languages. Many sites such as Wikipedia use the multilingual feature, which allows you to read and write different languages using the same piece of software.

- **User management**: MediaWiki has a built-in user management system where you can create new logins and assign user privileges if you require greater access control. You can also customize privileges for user types in order to fit your security needs.

- **Syndication**: MediaWiki supports web syndication by providing RSS syndication for many special pages such as **Special pages | Newpages** and **Special pages | Recentchanges**. Syndication helps you to grow your site rapidly in the web world.

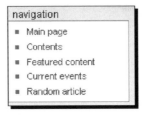

MediaWiki and other wiki engines

Of course, MediaWiki is not the only wiki engine to choose from. If you visit a site called Wikimatrix (www.wikimatrix.org) you will see a long list of wiki engines that are available to you. Now, MediaWiki was created specifically to run the largest wiki in existence. It is the choice of large corporations such as Intel and Novell and small to medium-sized businesses such as Moby Games. Many free/open source projects rely on MediaWiki as an integral part of their online presence. However, if you still don't know if MediaWiki is the right choice for you, let's look at how it stacks up against some of the other wiki engines. The list below introduces us to some of the other popular wiki engines:

- **DokuWiki**: DokuWiki is a simple wiki engine written in PHP and can be used to create any type of document. It is simple and standards compliant. It is suitable for small companies, development teams, and user groups. Instead of using a database, DokuWiki's data is saved in a plain text file or a flat file. The syntax is very simple yet powerful enough to create any type of content. Key features includes simplified editing, linking, support for image and other files, and plugins support to extend wiki functionality.

- **PhpWiki**: PhpWiki is a clone of original WikiWikiWeb. It was the first wiki software written in PHP and was released in 1999. It supports a majority of the databases. The installation process is very simple and gives you what you look for in an out of the box solution. It supports plugins in order to increase functionality. It is suitable for free-form discussion-based site creation and also for collaborative development sites.

- **PmWiki**: PmWiki is a PHP-based wiki that does not require any database and uses flat files like DokuWiki. It is very easy to install it and extend its functionality. It supports a template system in order to change the look and feel of the website as well as the functionality to a great extent. It also provides an access control system in order to protect site pages or groups of pages by enabling a password-protected mechanism. It also gives ample opportunity to customize the site as well as extend its functionality using plugins.

- **QwikiWiki**: QwikiWiki is another wiki system written in PHP and does not require any SQL database in order to operate. It uses cookies and its own filesystem in order to process and manage files. It has some key features such as file uploading, a template system, and an access control system.

- **Wikipage**: It is small, but a wiki standard, easy-to-use system. Wikipage is more secure than TipWiki. It has password-protection support for access control, multilanguage, and multisite support. Other common features include file uploading, table support, and so on.

- **TWiki**: TWiki is a flexible, powerful, and easy-to-use enterprise collaboration platform and knowledge management system. It is a structured wiki written in Perl. It is typically used to run a project development space, a document management system, a knowledge base, or any other groupware tool, on an intranet or on the Internet. It does not require any database since the data is stored in filesystem. It has a large plugin system with more than 200 plugins available to use such as spreadsheet, image gallery, slide shows, drawings, charts, graphs, and so on.

- **Kwiki**: Kwiki is perhaps the simplest to install, most modular, and easiest to extend. It is written in Perl and also available in CPAN. Other than providing basic wiki features, Kwiki by default offers slide shows, page backups, privacy options, and blog capabilities that are not found in any other wiki. It supports a plugins system in order to extend functionality.

◆ **MoinMoin**: MoinMoin is written in Python and has been derived from the **PikiPiki** wiki engine. This wiki uses a flat file and folder in order to save data. It does not require any database for operation. It is extensible and customizable. It supports subpages, Unicode, RSS feed, a template system, theme support, an access control list, and an anti-spam feature.

While flat files are easy to compress, databases provide you with much more scalability and are easier and faster to search. Also, wiki engines that rely on flat files often require a script to run that writes the file. If you are planning to deploy one of these wiki engines on a hosted website, make sure your hosting provider allows you to run scripts on the server.

How MediaWiki fits your needs

While the wiki engines mentioned in the previous section have some great features and qualities, MediaWiki is still a better choice due to the extensive feature set and flexibility it offers. Let's take a moment to see how MediaWiki can best fit your needs:

◆ **Simple editing**: Every page contains an **edit** link on the top navigation bar that only needs to be clicked to open the editing screen. When you finish making changes, you can post them by clicking the **Save page** button, so your changes go live on the site.

◆ **Use of simple markup**: Editing in HTML is difficult if you do not know HTML tags. While WYSIWYG editors take away the need to be fluent in HTML, there are cases when you need to work with HTML markup. With MediaWiki you don't have to remember complex tags; it has its own type of syntax that is made up of a few simple markup rules. This makes editing simpler and the proper HTML tag conversion is done by the system. MediaWiki will solve this problem by writing the HTML for you. These rules are designed to make wiki markup easy for general users to write and adopt.

◆ **Recording histories**: MediaWiki will save a copy of your old pages and let you revert to an older version of a page if you need to. In fact, MediaWiki will display a comparison, called a **diff**, which shows you the exact changes you or someone else has made to your page over time. So if someone edits an article in a way that is inaccurate or inappropriate, you can easily change it back.

◆ **Simplifying creating links**: MediaWiki stores your entire website's content in an internal hypertext database. MediaWiki knows about every page you have and about every link you make. When you are using MediaWiki, you don't have to worry about the location of files or the format of your tags. Simply name the page, and MediaWiki will automatically create a link for you. You can create links within your wiki or to some other wiki as well as to the web world.

- **Simplifying creating new pages**: MediaWiki links you to pages that don't yet exist. Click on a link that points to a nonexistent page, and the wiki will ask you for the initial content to be placed in the page. If you write this content, then the wiki will create the page right then and there. All links to that page (not just the one you clicked) will now point to the newly-created page. This is the simplest way of creating a new page in MediaWiki. You don't even have to bother to create the page, save it, and then link it from another page.

- **Simplifying site organization**: MediaWiki uses a database in order to manage the hypertext of the site. As a result you can organize your page however you want. Many CMS require you to plan classifications for your content before you actually create it. This can be helpful if you are looking for a rigid structure. With MediaWiki you can organize your page into categories and namespaces if you want. Instead of designing the site structure, many wiki sites just let the structure grow with the content and the links inside their content.

- **Tracking all your stuff**: As MediaWiki stores everything in a database that knows about all your links and all your pages it is easy for MediaWiki to show **backlinks**, a list of all the pages that link to the current page. It also stores your document history so that it can list recent changes to the document and even a list of recent changes to pages that link to the current page.

- **Encouraging discussions**: Using the **discussion** page feature, users can communicate and collaborate on an individual page's content and/or edits. The discussion page, or talk page as it is commonly called, is also editable by users to facilitate communication among the community.

Summary

In this chapter, we were introduced to a history of wikis and how wikis were developed to create collaborative communities. As we investigated how wikis are used, we saw examples of how different companies and organizations use wikis in different situations, and each of these examples highlighted the MediaWiki engine. To show how MediaWiki is a viable solution for any wiki needs, MediaWiki's features were explained and it was compared to some of the other popular wiki engines. In the next chapter, we will learn how to install MediaWiki on our server through FTP, cPanel, and through a proprietary application installer.

2
Installing MediaWiki

Now that we have a pretty good idea of how we can put MediaWiki to use, we have to get ready for the next step. As MediaWiki is a software package, we will learn how to install it. Not only are we going to cover how to install MediaWiki on your web server, but we are going to make sure that your web server has the required hardware and dependencies installed as well.

As this is a beginners' guide, we are going to assume that most of you are installing MediaWiki on a server provided by a web hosting company. As you may well know, different web hosting companies use different configurations for their servers. In this chapter, we will cover some of the most commonly used methods for getting MediaWiki onto the server such as through the use of a **script library** called **Fantastico**, **cPanel**, and an **FTP client**.

Once we have uploaded MediaWiki to the server, and are ready to install, we will cover all of the steps that need to be taken prior to installing the MediaWiki software. By the end of this chapter you will have a working installation of MediaWiki that we will reference throughout the rest of this book.

For demonstration purposes, I will be creating a new wiki alongside you that is dedicated to free/libre/open source software at `http://www.flosspropopulo.com`.

In this chapter, we shall:

- Cover all of the software requirements for a MediaWiki installation
- Learn what is the minimum hardware that is required to run MediaWiki
- Prepare to install the software using a script library
- Download a copy of MediaWiki for installation
- Upload the MediaWiki files through cPanel and FTP
- Prepare necessary directories on the server
- Create the database for the MediaWiki installation
- Run the installation script

If you are ready, let's get to it.

MediaWiki requirements

In order to install MediaWiki, you have to make sure that the server has some other software already installed on it. If you were installing MediaWiki on your own server, you would need to download and install each of these packages on your own.

To make life easier for their clients, most web hosting companies have their servers prepared with all of these packages. If you are having another company host your MediaWiki site for you, you will need to make sure that the server you choose has the necessary software installed on it. Without some of these, MediaWiki will simply not work.

The good news is, the software that is required is pretty much standard on any Linux hosting package. If something is not a part of the hosting package, check with your hosting provider. Many times, they will install these to keep their customers happy.

Hosting providers and Service Level Agreements

There are many different hosting providers out there. If this is the route you are going, then you should have no trouble finding a host who will meet your needs. Make sure to do your research and read the fine print. There are some hosts who have hidden charges for things like excessive bandwidth, installation of outside software, and other things. While this practice is common, be sure you know what your Service Level Agreement allows for, so that there are no surprises down the road.

PHP

PHP is a recursive acronym for **PHP: Hypertext Preprocessor**. PHP is a *server-side scripting language* that helps people create dynamic web pages. Server side means that all of the processing and compiling of the code happens on the server itself, not on the client requesting the web page. As it is server side, the web server needs to have the PHP engine installed so that the server can handle these requests and deliver web pages that utilize PHP.

Remember that PHP itself is a programming language. In fact, it is the language that MediaWiki is written in! When you are researching web hosts, you need to make sure that the PHP engine is installed on the server so it has the ability to serve MediaWiki pages to your visitors.

There are other server-side scripting languages that are similar to PHP in what they do. Microsoft's **Active Server Pages**, or **ASP.NET**, and Sun Microsystems' **Java Server Pages** are languages that deliver dynamic web pages like PHP, however, they are not a substitute for PHP as they will not compile code written in this language. Only the PHP compiler can translate code written in the PHP language into code that your computer can read. Likewise, other compilers for other computer languages only translate their language into computer readable code.

Software version

In order to run MediaWiki, any old version of PHP just won't do. At a minimum, you need to make sure your server is running PHP version 5.0. While this is the minimum, it is recommended that the server runs PHP version 5.1.x or later, for optimal performance.

Extensions

In order for MediaWiki to work properly, certain PHP extensions must be installed as well. The Perl Compatible Regular Expressions, Session, and Standard PHP Library are the only extensions required by MediaWiki and all three are enabled by default in PHP. You can check with your hosting provider to make sure that they are using a default installation of PHP, just to be sure.

Database

We have seen in Chapter 1 that one of the advantages that MediaWiki has over some of the other wiki engines is that it stores articles, user information, and other data in a database. Reliance on a database means that you have to make sure that your web server has a database installed on it as well.

MediaWiki supports four databases: MySQL 4.0 or later, PostgreSQL 8.1 or later, Ingres 2006 or later, and SQLite. While any one of these databases will work with MediaWiki, it is recommended that you use MySQL. This database is commonly installed on web servers and is the one we will be using.

Database management

Databases can be tricky to use and require knowledge of a special language, **Structured Query Language (SQL)**. In order to work with SQL, many users choose to install database management software on their server as well. One of the most popular packages for MySQL is **phpMyAdmin** which can be downloaded from `http://www.phpmyadmin.net`. If your hosting provider does not have a database management tool already installed for you, ask them about having something like this installed. It is such a powerful tool that even advanced database administrators rely on it.

Web server

This is kind of redundant. After all, we would hope that if we are paying for a web server, it would have server software installed on it. Instead of worrying about whether or not your host is going to have web server software installed, let's instead look at the choices.

MediaWiki has been tested, and runs using IIS 6.0, Cherokee, and lighttpd. While it runs in these environments, you should choose Apache as the web server software to run your wiki on. Apache is the preferred web server of most developers, so there is much more support out there for installations on an Apache web server.

If your hosting provider allows you to choose Microsoft hosting or Linux hosting, opt for the Linux hosting. More often than not, Microsoft hosting packages have IIS installed as their web server software while the Linux packages generally use Apache.

Hardware requirements

In this book, we will cover how to install MediaWiki on a server through a hosting provider. Any hosting service worth anything will provide you with hardware that exceeds the minimum requirements for MediaWiki, so that shouldn't be a concern, right? Let's hope not, but there are some issues that needs to be addressed when it comes to hardware, so it is important that we cover this here.

The bare minimum

MediaWiki requires you to have at a minimum, 258MB of RAM and 40MB of available storage space on your hard drive. However, this will not hold up if the website has a large volume of traffic and you certainly cannot allow any files, not even pictures, to be uploaded if operating with the bare minimum.

One final decision

Before you install MediaWiki, you have one more decision to make, where you are going to install the software. Before anyone answers "On our web server of course!", let me explain. When installing any software that you will use on your web server, you have the option of installing it in the root folder, in a subdomain, or in a subdirectory.

The root folder is the foundation of your website; it is the folder that your domain name and IP address will point to. If you install MediaWiki here, whenever someone enters your domain name, MediaWiki is what they will see. This may sound perfect if you are creating a site that is a dedicated wiki, like Wikipedia. After all, your visitors will only have to type in your URL and voila, they will arrive directly at your wiki. Some hosting providers do not allow you to install certain software packages directly to the root folder. If you have trouble with this, you have two options—ask your hosting provider to install MediaWiki for you, or install to a subdomain or subdirectory. It is a good idea to check with your hosting provider about your MediaWiki installation before you pay them any money. Some will go out of their way to help you while others may not provide much assistance at all.

Subdomains

A subdomain is part of the larger domain. If you registered `mywebsite.com`, it would be your domain. Subdomains are one level lower on the hierarchy. If you were going to install MediaWiki on a subdomain, you may create one called `wiki`. The files would then be installed at `wiki.mywebsite.com`. Any links to your wiki would also use this address.

Sites use subdomains for a variety of reasons, the most common being organization. If a website has multiple installations, for instance, they may have `wiki.mywebsite.com`, `blog.mywebsite.com`, and `store.mywebsite.com`. Now, the owner of that site can install the necessary software in each location. If you wish to install MediaWiki into a subdomain on your site, check first with your hosting provider for instructions on how to set one up.

Subdirectories

Subdirectories are simply folders created in the root folder of your domain. Unlike the subdomain, a subdirectory is listed after the domain name: `mywebsite.com/wiki`. This is the most common way to organize a site because it is the most convenient. Unless you are an experienced webmaster, this is the route you should take if you are not installing MediaWiki into the root folder.

Installing to the root folder

MediaWiki does not recommend installing directly to the root folder of your website because automated programs will eventually request certain files as they would an article. For instance, googlebot crawls different websites and collects content from these sites to build the searchable index used by Google's search engine.

To prevent MediaWiki from responding to these requests as if the files were articles, the developers recommend installing the software to a subdirectory, or even a subdomain, and then redirecting your domain, the way Wikipedia is set up. Unfortunately, if you are using a shared web host, you will not have access to the files on the server that need to be configured in order to set up a redirect for MediaWiki. Most hosting providers will set this up a redirect for you if you request it. If they won't, you may have to install to the root.

Pop quiz – MediaWiki requirements quiz

Well, you have skated along far enough. Time for you to start using your head and getting involved! What better way to do this than to test your knowledge with a quick quiz.

1. Which programming language does MediaWiki require?

    a.   ASP.NET

    b.   Visual Basic

    c.   PHP

    d.   Fortran

2. Which web server has MediaWiki **not** been successfully tested on?

    a.   BadBlue

    b.   IIS

    c.   Apache

    d.   Cherokee

3. What is a good tool to manage your databases with?

    a.   SQL

    b.   A monkey-wrench

    c.   Perl extensions

    d.   phpMyAdmin

If you have finished your quiz, we can get ready to move the installation files for MediaWiki to our web server. As stated in the introduction of this chapter, there are many different ways we can bring these files to our server. We are going to cover three different methods—using a script library, uploading MediaWiki using cPanel, and uploading the files via FTP. This should cover any scenario you, as a beginner, may face.

Using the Fantastico installer

Fantastico is the script library that we will be using to install MediaWiki. A script library is by far the easiest method of installing any software on your web server because it will create the database tables for you, install the software, make any adjustments to file and folder permissions, and make any configuration changes on your web server. All of this is automated, you only need to provide a bit of information to the installer and it takes care of the rest.

> While Fantastico is the most popular script library, it is not the one used by all web hosts. If your hosting provider uses a different script library, you will need to make slight adjustments if using this method to install MediaWiki. If you are unsure or you don't want to the risk by making changes, use one of the methods listed later in this chapter.

Installing MediaWiki with Fantastico

If you are following along, you should have created an account with a hosting provider and registered a domain name for your site. As the installer script for MediaWiki is included in the library, your web server meets the minimum requirements for installation.

Time for action – installing the software

This is the moment we have been waiting for. After we complete the following steps, you will have a working installation of MediaWiki. If you are installing MediaWiki into a subdomain, create that before you start the installation process.

1. Log into your hosting account.

2. Open your web browser and point it the address provided to you by your hosting provider. If you don't know what this is, go back and check the e-mails that your provider sent you when you purchased hosting from them.

3. Access your script library.

4. Click on the location of the script library. This will open a categorical list of all the programs available to you as shown in the following screenshot:

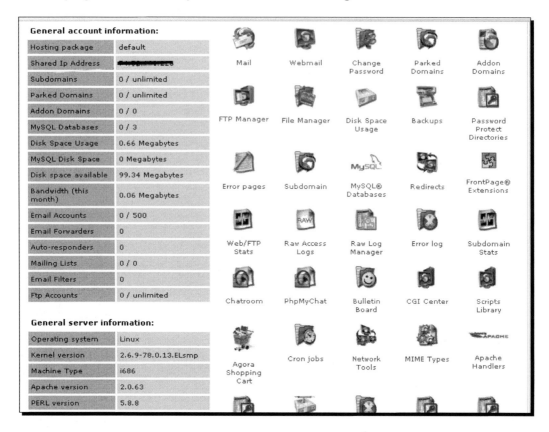

5. Under the **Wiki** category at the bottom of the page, locate **MediaWiki** and click on it. This will start the installer script that will take you through the rest of the process.

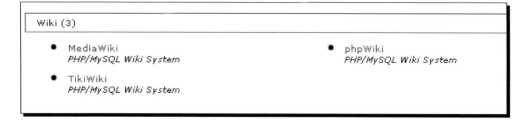

6. The next screen begins the installation process. Here, you will need to provide the installer script with some necessary information as shown in the following screenshot:

❑ First, you need to supply a username for the site's **administrator** where it reads **Admin User**.

❑ Next, you will need to supply a password for the administrator under **Admin Pass**. To make sure it is correct, you will type the same password under **Admin Password (Again).**

❑ Now, enter the e-mail address for the administrator. MediaWiki will use this as the default address to send administrative messages and information about the installation process.

❑ Lastly, choose the **Installation URL**. By default, MediaWiki will create a subdirectory, or folder, called **mediawiki**, as the installation location. You can change this to anything you want but it is best if you name it something related to your wiki. If you have created a subdomain, you will have the option to choose it here as well.

❏ Click on the **Install** button and when the installation is finished, you will see something similar to the following screenshot:

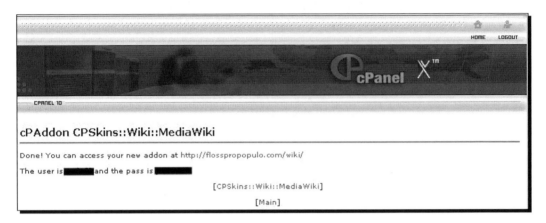

What just happened?

With a few simple clicks, MediaWiki was successfully installed onto your web server. Really, it was just that easy! While the installation using Fantastico may seem too good to be true, other script installers can be as equally painless. If you are using another installer, you may find small differences between the steps provided here and what you see. A good example is that many installers allow you to name the database that is installed with MediaWiki where Fantastico did not. If you used a script installer, you have two choices at this point: you can either skip ahead to the *Completing the installation section* later in this chapter, or you can read along to see how MediaWiki can be installed using cPanel and FTP.

Username and password choices

When choosing your username and password, make sure that you keep security in mind. While it may be tempting to use "Admin" or "Administrator" as the username, it is generally not considered a best practice because it is too easy for someone else to guess. Your password should also be something that is hard to guess. Security best practices dictate that your password should be a **strong password**, which is made up of a combination of lower case letters, uppercase letters, numbers, and special characters. You can test a password's strength by visiting The Password Meter website at: `http://www.passwordmeter.com/`.

Downloading MediaWiki

Before we can go ahead and install MediaWiki with either cPanel or FTP, we need to get ourselves a copy of the software. We do this by downloading a file called `mediawiki-*.tar.gz`, where * is the latest version number. You can obtain this file by opening your web browser and entering `http://www.mediawiki.org/wiki/Download` in the address bar. Once you are there, click on the **Download MediaWiki 1.15.1** link:

When you click this link, you will be asked if you want to open the file or save it. Make sure the **Save File** option is selected and then click **OK**.

Uploading files using cPanel

We have already seen cPanel to some extent when we learned how to install MediaWiki using Fantastico. Now, we are going to use the same tool to move the recently downloaded MediaWiki files to our web server. While this alternate method of installation may require a bit more knowledge, it gives you more control over the process. If you are installing to a subdomain, it is necessary that you create that before you start moving the files over.

Time for action – uploading MediaWiki files with cPanel

To perform this series of steps, you need to log in to your cPanel account provided to you by your web hosting company. Once you are logged in, you need to find the icon for **File Manager**. If you refer back to the screenshot under the *Time for action – installing the software section*, you can see that it is in the second row.

1. Click the File Manager icon to launch the program. This will open up a new window listing all of the files and folders on your web server. Locate the subdirectory or folder, named `public_html`, and click on the folder, not the folder name, to open it.

2. If you are moving the files to a subdirectory, click on **Create New Folder**. In this example, I am going to install in a folder called `wiki`. When you click on the **Create** button, the new folder will appear in the list to your left.

3. Open the `wiki` folder by again clicking on the folder, not the name.

4. Now we will move the files over to the server. Do you remember where you saved it after downloading? Hopefully so, because when you click on **Upload File(s)**, you will see the following screenshot. Here you need to click on **Browse** to locate and select your `mediawiki-*.tar.gz` file. Once you have done this, click on **Upload**.

**File uploads are restricted to prevent account issues caus
exceeding your file system quota**

Current available free-space: 36.29 MB
Maximum file size for upload: 31.29 MB
Required free space after upload: 5 MB (Default 5MB)

Please select files to upload to /home/flosspro/public_html/wiki

	Browse…		Browse…
	Browse…		Browse…
	Browse…		Browse…
	Browse…		Browse…
	Browse…		Browse…
	Browse…		Browse…

Overwrite existing files: ☐

Upload

The upload process may take some time depending on your network connection. Once it is complete, you will receive a message telling you that the file has been uploaded successfully.

5. Now that the compressed files are uploaded to the server, we need to extract them. Make sure you are in the directory where you uploaded your MediaWiki file. Click on the file `mediawiki-*.tar.gz`. On your right, you should see a list of options; click on **Extract File Contents**. This will extract your files to a folder named `mediawiki-*`. As this is not the right folder, you will need to move the files and subfolders to the directory that you set up for MediaWiki.

File Type: Zip archive data, at least v1.0 to extract

Show File Contents
Extract File Contents
Delete File
Edit File
Change Permissions
Rename File
Copy File
Move File

Like we saw in the Fantastico installation, we are only halfway done. Once we learn how to send the files to our web server using an FTP client, we will continue with the installation. You can skip ahead to that section, or you can read along.

What just happened?

You just uploaded and extracted the MediaWiki software package to your web server using cPanel's File Manager. If you are feeling a little impressed with yourself, you have every right to. If you opted for this method over using a script installer, you gave yourself a bit of a head start as well. When it comes to bringing in third-party enhancements and extra themes to use with MediaWiki, you will be an old hand at it! All of the extras we learn about in later chapters require us to upload files to the server, so having this practice will make it a much less intimidating process later on.

If after installing MediaWiki you find that there are errors that prevent you from accessing your wiki, see the resources listed in Appendix C, *Where to turn to*. You will find multiple avenues of support to help with any installation problems.

Uploading MediaWiki files with an FTP client

For our third and final method of installing MediaWiki, we will use an FTP client. FTP stands for **File Transfer Protocol** and the client is a program that manages the file transfer for us. If you do not have an FTP client, you will need to download one to follow along here. I would suggest getting a copy of Filezilla, which can be downloaded at `http://filezilla-project.org/`. Filezilla can be used on Windows, GNU/Linux, or on Mac. On the scale of difficulty, this method is on an even keel with using the cPanel File Manager.

Time for action – uploading the files

Unlike using cPanel, uploading files with an FTP client requires you to extract the `mediawiki-*.tar.gz` file before you move it to the web server. Use your favorite file archiving tool, such as **WinZip** or **7-Zip**, to extract the files to your computer. Make a note of where they are because in a moment, we are going to start uploading them.

You may be required to create an FTP account on your web server before we get started. If you are unsure how to do this, check with your hosting provider. They should be able to walk you through the steps.

Now that we have extracted the files and our FTP account is ready to go, let's connect our web server with our FTP client and complete the following steps:

1. In your FTP client, navigate to the folder where you will be installing MediaWiki in the **Remote site** section. If you want to install it to a subdirectory but haven't created it yet, you can do so now using your FTP client.

2. In the **Local site** section—your computer—navigate to the folder where you extracted the `mediawiki-*.tar.gz` file.

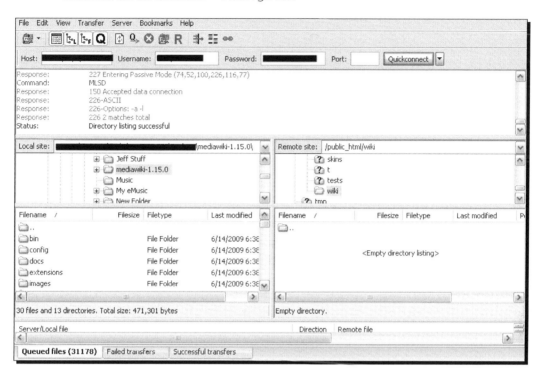

3. Now, simply copy all of the files from the MediaWiki folder on your computer to the target directory on your web server. This may take a little time.

What just happened?

That's it, you have just completed the third method of getting the MediaWiki files onto your web server! Using the FTP client gives you more control over the file transfer, like using cPanel did. Unlike cPanel, FTP allows you to place the files into the directory you want them in. It doesn't create a subdirectory that you have to move your files out of after they are extracted since you take care of the extraction on your local computer.

Completing the installation

Now that we have covered the three ways in which we can get the MediaWiki installation files onto our web server, we will go ahead and complete the process. No matter which method you chose, everyone should now follow along together because the remaining steps will be the same for all of us.

We will be:

♦ Creating the database

♦ Changing permissions on the `config` folder

♦ Finishing up the installation process through our web browser

Time for action – getting everything ready

In these next steps, we will work with the database and the permission settings on our web server. These are the final steps before we actually install the software that we put on the server.

Do you remember that when we compared MediaWiki to other wiki engines, we stated that one of the advantages of MediaWiki is that it stores articles, images, and other files in a database rather than a flat file? This next step is where we create the database that will be home to everything that will make our wiki great, the content!

If you moved the installation files over to your web server using a script installer like Fantastico, your database may have been created already. To check this, we will be using the MySql Databases section on cPanel. If you are using some other site management application, you will need to access your databases using their method. Again, most site management tools are similar so you can apply the steps here to what your hosting provider uses.

1. Click on the MySql Databases icon to bring up the database management screen. If your database was created, write down the name of it as you will need it later.

2. If you have no database for MediaWiki listed, you will need to create it now. Under the section named **Current Databases**, find the textbox next to **New Database** and enter the name for your database. You can use whatever you want, but it should be something that describes what data is being held there. For this demonstration, I will be using `MediaWiki`. Once you have entered your new database's name, click on **Create Database**.

3. Now, go back to the database screen. Under the **Current Users** section, enter the name and password for the database administrator in the text boxes marked as **Username** and **Password**. When you are done, click **Create User**.

4. Now we have to add the user we just created, to the database. Go back to the database screen and under **Add Users to Your Databases**, make sure that the correct username is matched with the database. Make sure that the **Privileges** are set to **ALL** and click the **Add User to Database** button.

When you have completed these steps, go back to the **MySQL Account Maintenance** screen and you will see something similar to the following screenshot:

```
CPANEL 10

                        MySQL Account Maintenance

                          Current Databases:

        flosspro_MediaWiki  Delete  Check  Repair

                          Users in MediaWiki
        ██████████████████(Privileges: ALL PRIVILEGES)  Delete

        Connection Strings

              $dbh = DBI->connect("DBI:mysql:flosspro_MediaWiki:localhost",
        Perl  "flosspro_mediawa","<PASSWORD HERE>");

              $dbh=mysql_connect ("localhost", "flosspro_mediawa",
              "<PASSWORD HERE>") or die('Cannot connect to the database
        PHP   because: ' . mysql_error());
              mysql_select_db ("flosspro_MediaWiki");


        New Database: [                    ]  [ Create Database ]


                          Current Users:
                    ████████████████  Delete

        Username: [                    ]
        Password: [                    ]  [ Create User ]
```

Have a go hero – use phpMyAdmin

Using the database manager provided by your host is the easiest way to set up your database. If you really want a challenge, use phpMyAdmin to set up your database and user. This tool is a must for web developers and once you get used to the interface, you will quickly see how easy and powerful this program is. You can download phpMyAdmin from http://www.phpmyadmin.net.

Setting permissions

Now that the database is set up, we need to set the permissions of the config folder on our web server to be writable. During the installation process, certain setup files will be written to this folder. If we skip this step, the installation will not work properly.

1. Using your web host's control panel, open your file manager and locate the directory where you uploaded your MediaWiki files to. Once you have located this, expand the directory to see the files and folders it contains.

2. Locate the folder named `config`. This folder should have permissions set to **777**. If it is something else, like **755**, you will need to change it. In cPanel, click on the folder and where the options are listed on the right side of the screen, select **Change Permissions**.

3. Set the permissions to **777**. This allows the User, the Group, and the World to read, write, and execute in the `config` folder. Click on the **Change** button to set the permissions.

After you click on the **Change** button, you will see the permissions for this folder change:

You can also use your FTP client to change permissions to your website as well. Try both methods and use whichever one you feel is comfortable.

What just happened?

By completing the previous steps, you altered your web server to accept changes made during the installation process by allowing the software to write important files to the `config` folder. We also successfully created a database that will be used to store your wiki's content.

The hard work is now done. From here on, we only need to sit back and let the installation run. Oh, we will have to provide some information here and there (you still have your database name and user information written down, right?) but compared to what we just did, it will be a breeze.

Time for action – finishing up

So far, we have moved all of the installation files to our web server, set the permissions on the `config` folder so we can write to it, and created a database for MediaWiki content and other details. All that is left is to run the installation much like we would if we were installing a copy of `OpenOffice.org` or GIMP on our computer at home.

The entire process is done through our web browser so before we get started, open your web browser and type the location of your wiki in the address bar. As I am creating a wiki in the root of my domain, I would type in `http://www.flosspropopulo.com`. If, however, I was installing to a subdomain named `wiki`, the address would be `http://wiki.flosspropopulo.com`. Of course, if the installation was going to be in a subdirectory named `wiki`, I would type `http://www.flosspropopulo.com/wiki`.

1. After bringing up MediaWiki in your browser, you should see the following on your screen:

Click on the link that says **set up the wiki**.

2. After clicking on the link, the installation script will automatically check to make sure the server has all of the required programs and settings. If everything is okay, and you can proceed with the installation, the message **Environment checked. You can install MediaWiki** will be shown in bright green at the bottom of the section named **Checking environment....** If there is something missing or wrong, it will show a red error message instructing you to fix certain things before continuing the installation process. You may receive warning messages and still be okay to continue. This is normal and depends upon how your web host has configured the server you are using.

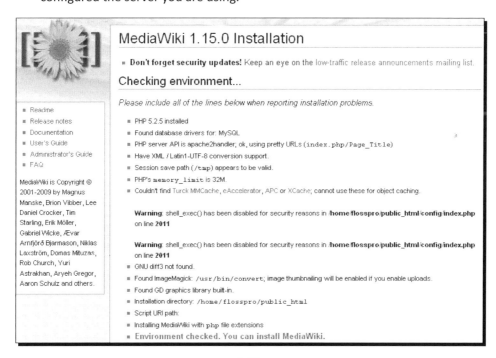

3. Scroll down to the section that says **Site Config**. This is the main installation process file so make sure the information you enter is accurate. You will need to provide the following:

- **Wiki name**: This is a mandatory field and cannot be **MediaWiki** or contain a **#**. For the example used in this book, I will enter **Floss Pro Populo**. You would enter your wiki's title.

- **Contact e-mail**: This is the e-mail address of the wiki administrator. It is used to send information such as error reports and password reminders.

- **Language**: Choose the language you wish to support. The default is **en-English**.

- **Copyright/license**: This describes how you wish to license your content. If you are unsure, leave the default, **No license metadata** checked.

- **Admin username** and **Password**: These are the login credentials for the **Sysop** account. The Sysop is a user with very high-level system privileges such as locking and removing pages, blocking IP addresses, and performing various setup tasks. You might be familiar with the terms **owner** and **administrator** for a site. Sysop is a synonymous term for administrator and owner. Remember this information and keep it safe!

- **Shared memory caching**: If you have any shared memory set up for the server to cache pages, you can enter the information in the shared memory option field. It is highly unlikely that this is the case, so most likely, you will be leaving it set to **No caching**. This topic will be covered later on in the book.

Site config

Wiki name:	[ ] Must not be blank or "MediaWiki" and may not contain "#"
	Preferably a short word without punctuation, i.e. "Wikipedia". Will appear as the namespace name for "meta" pages, and throughout the interface.
Contact e-mail:	[webmaster@flosspropopulo.cc]
	Displayed to users in some error messages, used as the return address for password reminders, and used as the default sender address of e-mail notifications.
Language:	[en - English ▼]
	Select the language for your wiki's interface. Some localizations aren't fully complete. Unicode (UTF-8) is used for all localizations.
Copyright/license:	⊙ No license metadata ○ Public Domain ○ GNU Free Documentation License 1.2 (Wikipedia-compatible) ○ GNU Free Documentation License 1.3 ○ A Creative Commons license - choose
	A notice, icon, and machine-readable copyright metadata will be displayed for the license you pick.
Admin username:	[WikiSysop]
Password:	[ ] Cannot be blank
Password confirm:	[ ]
	An admin can lock/delete pages, block users from editing, and do other maintenance tasks. A new account will be added only when creating a new wiki database. The password cannot be the same as the username.
Object caching:	⊙ No caching ○ Memcached
Memcached servers:	[ ]
	An object caching system such as memcached will provide a significant performance boost, but needs to be installed. Provide the server addresses and ports in a comma-separated list.

4. The next section is titled **E-mail, e-mail notification and authentication setup**. These configuration settings enable general e-mail setup, user to user e-mail system, and e-mail notification system setup. The installation file itself contains good explanation for each of these options. In the demonstration, we will be leaving all of the settings as defaults in this section. If you wish to disable any e-mail communication for your site, simply select **Disabled**.

5. Just like anything else, MediaWIki saves the best, or at least the most important, for last. That's right, I'm talking about the **Database config** section. Do you remember when I said, "Write down your database, database admin username, and password"? You will need this to complete the next steps. If you need to get that information again, obtain it from your web host's control panel. Once you have that, we will need to enter it into the following:

- **Database name**: The name of the MySQL database you created earlier.

- **DB username**: The username you set up earlier for accessing your wiki MySQL database.

- **DB password**: The user password you had set up for your database user.

- **Database table prefix**: This may be optional, but it is recommended that you have a database table prefix. Providing a table prefix allows you to install more than one wiki using the same database. For advanced users, this option also gives you the opportunity to create MediaWiki tables under an existing database with the tables distinguished by our desired prefix.

- **Superuser account**: This option provides a root password for the database. You can provide the information if you have it. If you don't, then leave the box unchecked and the field empty.

- There are four areas that you will leave as the defaults. The first two you see, **Database type** and **Database host** should be left alone. Also, the last two, **Storage engine** and **Database character set** should be left as they are.

Database config

Database type: ⦿ MySQL

Database host: `localhost`

If your database server isn't on your web server, enter the name or IP address here.

Database name: `wikidb`

DB username: `wikiuser`

DB password: Must not be blank

DB password confirm:

If you only have a single user account and database available, enter those here. If you have database root access (see below) you can specify new accounts/databases to be created. This account will not be created if it pre-exists. If this is the case, ensure that it has SELECT, INSERT, UPDATE, and DELETE permissions on the MediaWiki database.

Superuser account: ☐ Use superuser account

Superuser name: `root`

Superuser password:

If the database user specified above does not exist, or does not have access to create the database (if needed) or tables within it, please check the box and provide details of a superuser account, such as **root**, which does.

─ MySQL specific options ─────────────

Database table prefix:

If you need to share one database between multiple wikis, or between MediaWiki and another web application, you may choose to add a prefix to all the table names to avoid conflicts.

Avoid exotic characters; something like `mw_` is good.

Storage Engine   Select one:
⦿ InnoDB
◯ MyISAM

InnoDB is best for public web installations, since it has good concurrency support. MyISAM may be faster in single-user installations. MyISAM databases tend to get corrupted more often than InnoDB databases.

Database character set   Select one:
⦿ MySQL 4.1/5.0 binary

6. After providing all the information, you are just a click away from finishing the installation. Click the **Install MediaWiki**! button to start the process. If something is wrong, then the server will come back to the setup page with an error message telling you that something wasn't complete. If all the information provided is correct then in a few seconds, you will see a success message in green at the bottom of the page proclaiming **Installation successful!**

7. We're not quite done yet. During the installation process a file named LocalSettings.php is created by the server and is located under the config folder. To ensure that this file is created, we had to change the config folder's properties to make the folder writable. Before clicking the link to view the wiki homepage, move the LocalSettings.php file to the root folder using your FTP program or a file management program like cPanel. After doing so, you have to click on the link that reads **this link** and you will be taken to your wiki's **Main page** as shown in the following screenshot:

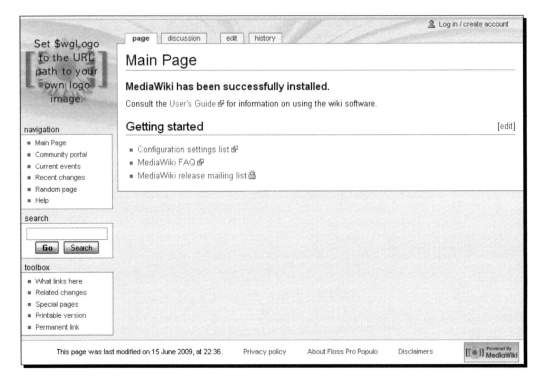

What just happened?

That's right, that just happened! You successfully installed MediaWiki. By creating the database, we were able to set up a home for all of the wiki's settings and the eventual content that it will contain. Changing the permissions on the config folder allowed us, or the installer at least, to write files essential to the installation file—the LocalSettings. php. Finally, we provided the information the installer needed to tie everything together. We now have the main page to our wiki ready to be configured.

Summary

We learned quite a bit in this chapter about installing the MediaWiki software on our web server.

Specifically, we covered:

- The essential software required to install and run MediaWiki. Without PHP, a database like MySQL, and a web server such as Apache, we cannot run MediaWiki on our server.

- The bare minimum hardware requirements that our web server must have to install, and properly run, MediaWiki.

- How to bring the MediaWiki installation files to our web server so we can install the software. We covered three specific ways of doing this, by using an installer script called Fantastico, by using cPanel, and by using an FTP client.

- How to create a database that MediaWiki will use to store configuration information about the wiki as well as the content that drives visitors to the wiki.

- How to change the permissions on one of the web server's folders. This was done to allow the installer access to the folder during installation.

Once we covered all this material, we were able to successfully install the MediaWiki software on our server.

Now that we've learned about the installation requirements and steps, we are ready to cover how to set up your new wiki which will be the topic of the next chapter.

3
Getting to Know Your Wiki

Now that we have MediaWiki installed on the server, we get the chance to really get hands-on with it and make some changes. Before we start creating pages, we need to learn a few things about the layout of MediaWiki. Also, we need to take some preliminary steps to customize the wiki not only to make it our own, but also to make sure that no one gets in to deface it while we are still learning the ins and outs of the software.

In this chapter we will learn:

- How to navigate the Main Page
- What the different menus do
- How to log in to our wiki
- How to create a new user account
- How to make some basic customization changes to the look of our wiki

So if you are ready, let's get started.

Navigating the Main Page

Before we begin to write the content for our wiki, we need to understand the navigation system used by MediaWiki. By having a solid understanding of this, we will be able to better organize our content and give our visitors a great first impression that will have them coming back for more.

Now that the installation is complete, when we visit our site we are taken directly to the **Main Page** of our wiki. Compared to a standard website, the Main Page serves the same function as the **home page**. The Main Page introduces the visitor to our wiki and the type of content the wiki provides. It gives visitors a way to log in to our wiki, a way to create an account, and a way to navigate their way around the wiki itself. Of course, our wiki contains no content yet. To get a better understanding of what the Main Page does for the visitor, let's take a look at the Main Page for Wikipedia found at `http://en.wikipedia.org/wiki/Main_Page`.

Pretty impressive, huh? Now let's compare it to our Main Page. Type the URL of your wiki into the address bar of your web browser. While it may not be loaded with content such as **Today's featured article**, and **Did you know**, the structure of our Main Page is similar to that of Wikipedia's.

We have divided the page in to six different sections for you. As you read on, we will discuss each of the sections of the Main Page:

1. Navigation
2. Search
3. Toolbox
4. Body
5. Footer
6. Account area

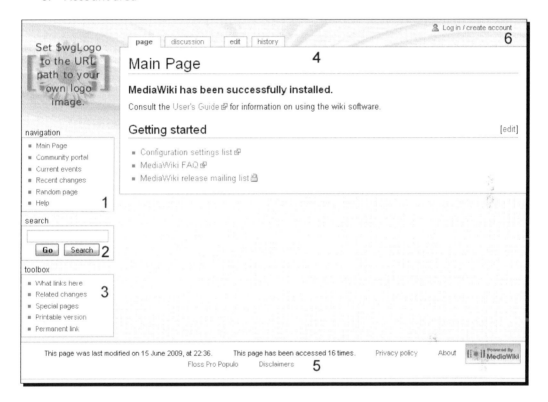

By the end of this book, your wiki will begin to fill up with content as well. Once you have completed the last section, take time to compare the Main Page for your wiki against Wikipedia's again. I am sure you will be pleased with the results.

Have a go hero

If you haven't noticed how the default Main Page is set up differently than Wikipedia's, take a moment to go back and look over the screen shots.

Now that you see how the Main Page can be customized, go out and find some MediaWiki wikis and see how they are set up. Did they keep the default organization, or did they customize the Main Page to better suit their site?

You can check out the examples from Chapter 1, but you should search for some new ones on your own. Here are two that you can start with:

Joomla! Official Documentation: `http://docs.joomla.org/Main_Page`

Information Technology documentation for the University of South Florida: `http://wiki.acomp.usf.edu/index.php/Main_Page`

Navigation

The first section you see on the Main Page is the **navigation** box that is populated with links to pages that are commonly found in most wikis. As we learn to configure our wiki in the upcoming chapters, we will see how we can make changes to this section by adding and removing links to different pages. You may even notice that certain links on the Wikipedia Main Page are different, or are located in different locations, than those on our Main Page.

For now, we will look at the pages that MediaWiki automatically fills in links to for you in the navigation section:

- **Main Page**
- **Community portal**
- **Current events**
- **Recent changes**
- **Random page**
- **Help**

As we have discussed the **Main Page** already, let's begin with the **Community portal**.

 As we have no content in our wiki, we will refer to Wikipedia for examples of each page linked to in the navigation section.

Community portal

Remember that the main focus of a wiki is collaboration and community. With this in mind, it makes perfect sense that a wiki would have a special page dedicated for providing information to the community called the **Community portal**. The community portal is a great place to provide how-to's and guidelines for contributing to the wiki, post news, provide to-do lists, and give your visitors other resources related to the community.

Remember, your community can be the general audience you have built if you are creating a public wiki, or it can be the employees at your work if you are creating a wiki that will be kept private. The following screenshot shows the Wikipedia community portal:

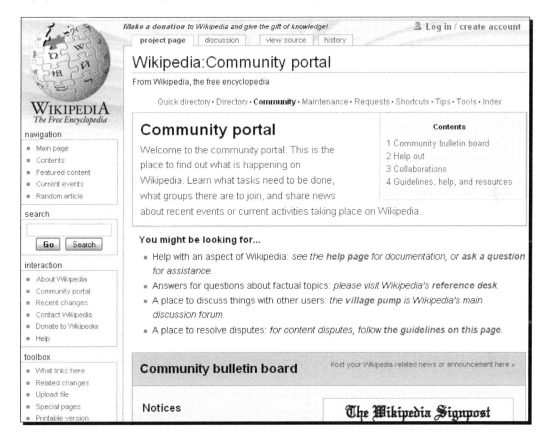

Current events

The **Current events** link takes you to a page that can be used to list both onsite and offsite news. Current events pages may provide visitors with headlines for the day, a calendar, upcoming events, or maybe even a special call for content. It is important to remember that if you decide to use a current events page on your wiki, you have to keep it current! Don't let old events linger on this page. The following screenshot shows the current events page for Wikipedia:

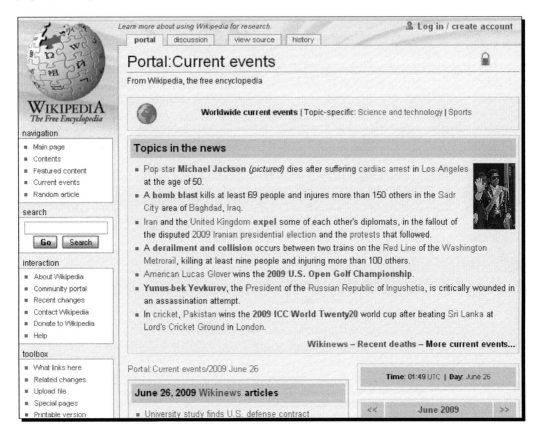

Recent changes

The **Recent changes** link will take you to a page that lists all edits that have recently taken place to pages on your wiki. As the sysop of the wiki, you will find this page extremely helpful as you can track edits, monitor articles for mistakes, watch for inaccurate content, and keep an eye out for vandalism to your wiki.

The Recent changes page is not only helpful to sysops and administrators though. Contributors to the wiki can keep an eye on pages that they have created as well to see what kind of changes have been made to their content.

The Recent changes page also represents the first special page that we encounter. Special pages are created to perform a specific function in the software. Special pages are unique in that they cannot be edited like other pages in the wiki. These pages can also have their access restricted to users with specific privileges such as sysop or administrator. We will learn more about Special pages later in the book.

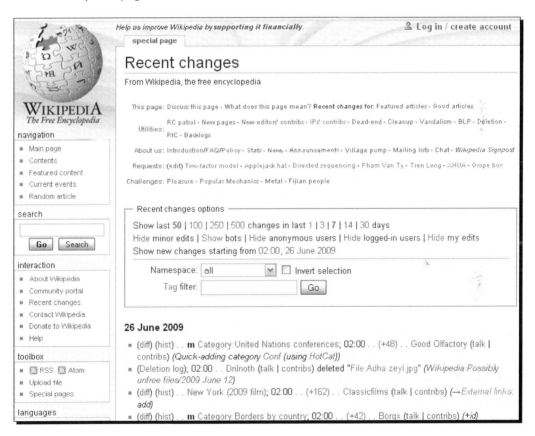

Random page

The **Random page** link is pretty self-explanatory. Clicking on this link will take you to a random page within the wiki. While it does not perform any specific purpose, it gives your visitors a way to explore your wiki by visiting pages they may never have searched for.

Help

The **Help** page allows you to create articles that help guide your visitors. You can provide information on how to create an article, how to upload multimedia, how to create links, or any other topic that you feel your visitors may need help with. Again, Wikipedia provides an excellent model for creating a help page as seen in the following screenshot:

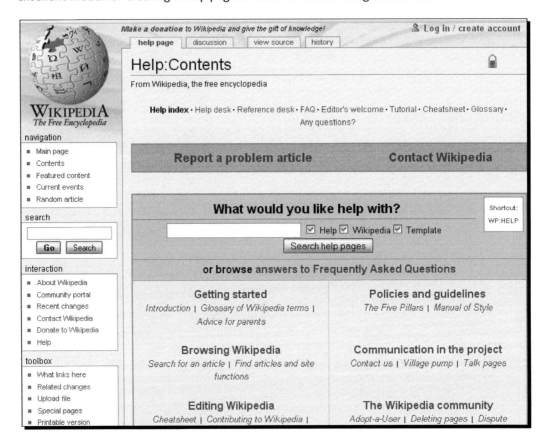

Pop quiz – the navigation box

Let's see how much you learned about the links in the navigation box.

1. Which link takes us to a special page that is unknown to the visitor?

    a. Random page link

    b. Recent page link

    c. Main Page link

    d. Community portal link

2. This page is considered the home page for your wiki:

    a. Main Page

    b. Community portal

    c. Landing page

    d. First page

3. Which page is generally not used to provide information about your wiki?

    a. Help page

    b. Community portal

    c. Random page

    d. Current events page

 Looking closely at the examples, you may have noticed that the navigation box in Wikipedia is much different than ours. While MediaWiki populates the sections on our Main Page with links that are commonly used, links, as well as sections, can be added or removed.

Search

If you want people to visit and use your wiki, it needs to be user-friendly. To accomplish this, MediaWiki's developers included a **search engine** to the default installation. Instead of the traditional placement of the search box in the upper-left corner, MediaWiki places it directly under the navigation box. The search box is made up of three components, the textbox, the **Search** button, and the **Go** button. To search for all pages related to a topic, visitors need only enter the terms into the textbox and click on the **Search** button. MediaWiki then searches all content for the term(s) entered and responds back with a list of pages that it found. The following screenshot shows the **Search results** for the term **wiki**:

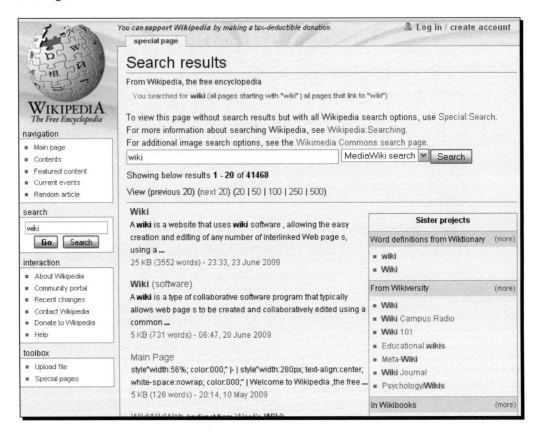

The **Go** button works a bit differently. If a visitor knows the title of a specific page, he or she can enter this into the textbox and then click on the **Go** button. This will then take the visitor directly to that page much like the **I'm Feeling Lucky** button used by Google's search engine.

 The **Go** button is a great feature if you know the title of the page you want, but you don't know the URL. If you don't know the title, Wikipedia has a neat function built into it. When you begin typing your search term, you are provided with the titles of pages based on your text entry. Not all MediaWiki wikis have this feature. We will learn more about how to do this in Chapter 9.

Toolbox

The third section on the Main Page is the **toolbox**. The links in this section will be used more when you become more familiar with MediaWiki. For now, let's take a look at the five links that are here: **What links here**, **Related changes**, **Special pages**, **Printable version**, and **Permanent link**.

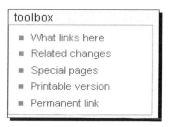

What links here

The name **World Wide Web** exists because of one thing, the ability to create links between websites to create a *web*. Wikis are built on the same premise. Pages throughout the wiki link to one another, creating a large web of information. Clicking on the **What links here** link, you can see all of the different pages, from inside your wiki, that link to your current page.

At the most basic level, the **What links here** section allows us to find content related to the current page. After all, if it is linking to it, it must have some mention of it somewhere in the text. While this serves the wiki's community, there is another purpose to the **What links here** section that the creator of the wiki will find to be important.

When a piece of content (such as a page or article) links to another piece of content, what is known as a **backlink** is created. Those familiar with **Search Engine Optimization (SEO)** know that backlinks can help the search engines such as Google rank pages higher in the results. Seeing how many backlinks a page in your wiki has will help you know what type of content is more popular to your visitors, and will help you plan your SEO strategy much more effectively.

Related changes

The **Related changes** feature will show you, or your visitors, any recent changes to pages that are linked *from* the current page. Unlike the **What links here** feature, this one deals with outgoing links.

Visitors to your wiki can check to see if any pages they have referenced have been altered and authors can check to see if they need to update their pages to reflect changes made to content they refer to. As with any of the other tools that allow you to see changes made to content, this gives the sysop another opportunity to review content that has been changed to make sure it is accurate. The following screenshot shows the various options available on the Related changes page:

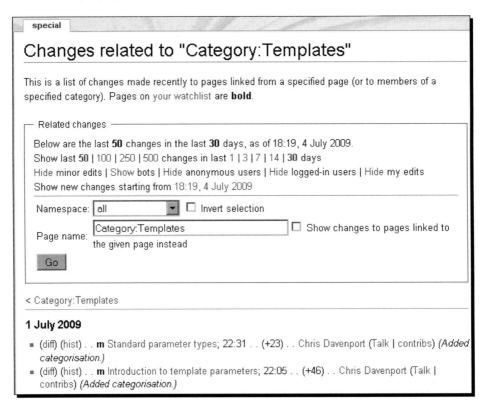

The previous screenshot shows us what the **Related changes** page for the Main Page looks like on a wiki that has some content written for it, the Joomla! Official Documentation site. Notice from the screenshot that the page allows you to customize your results a bit as well. You can choose the number of results shown, how many days to go back, and even hide edits that are insignificant or your own.

Special pages

We mentioned Special pages when we introduced the Recent changes page earlier in this chapter. Clicking on this link will take us to a page that, as you may have guessed, gives links to all of the special pages created by the system. We will cover Special pages in greater depth when we get to Chapter 6.

 Remember that even registered users cannot make changes to Special pages.

Printable version

While it would be ideal if people could read information that they need directly from their computer screen, this is not often the case. In an effort to save toner and paper, and enhance readability, MediaWiki has a **Printable version** link for visitors who need a paper copy of an article. When you click on this link, you are provided with a scaled down version of the page you are currently on that is formatted to fit a piece of letter-sized paper. You can easily print the page by clicking on **File | Print** from the browser's main toolbar.

Permanent link

Bloggers reading this book may already know what a Permanent link, or **permalink**, is but for those who don't, the explanation is simple. When content is moved, or edited in the case of a wiki, the link often changes. A visitor who stores this link may come back to find that the content they are looking for is different, or even gone. Permanent links use a string of characters in the URL that may designate the date, time, or author id for the specific page. It is then possible through the Permanent link feature to find the exact content, and version, that the visitor is looking for. Even if the page has been deleted in MediaWiki, the visitor who clicked on the permalink will be taken to a page that informs them of the date it was deleted, who deleted the page, and the content that was there.

This is a great feature to have in a wiki where you anticipate multiple authors, edits, and dynamic content.

Pop quiz – the toolbox

Let's see how much you learned about the toolbox.

1. Special pages are unique pages within MediaWiki that give non-registered users the ability to edit content?

    a. True

    b. False

2. The Related changes feature shows you:

    a. A list of pages that have changed and link to the current page

    b. A list of pages that have changed that the current page links to

    c. A list of all pages that have changed in the past 14 days

    d. A list of the last 25 pages that have changed

3. The toolbox link that allows you to link to content whose URL has changed is the:

    a. Special pages

    b. Related content

    c. Special link

    d. Permanent link

4. The Printable version feature allows you to print a highly graphical display of the current page that includes the navigation box, the tool box, and the footer:

    a. True

    b. False

Body section

The body section is where the meat of your wiki exists. This, of course, is the content. If you look at the body of the Main Page, you will see a very basic, generic article. At the top of the article, you will see four different tabs: **article**, **discussion**, **edit**, and **history**. If you are logged in as a registered user, you will see two additional tabs, **move** and **watch**. Each one of these tabs takes us to a different part of the page.

◆ **page**: This takes us to the main content of the page. The page contents can be edited by other users.

◆ **discussion**: This section of the page allows the community to discuss topics surrounding the page and article content. Maybe users will talk about current or future changes, who will revise the document, or even what other content will be created that is related to this article.

◆ **edit**: This section allows a user to edit the content of the article.

- ◆ **history**: This shows all of the changes to the article.

- ◆ **move**: This tab is seen only to logged in users. This allows the page to actually be renamed. If the newly chosen name is already in use, you will not be able to "move" the page.

- ◆ **watch**: Clicking on the **watch** tab will add the current page to your **watchlist**. When you click this tab, it also changes to read unwatch. Likewise, you can click on the **unwatch** tab if you no longer wish to watch the page. This tab is also only seen by registered users. Users will be notified about changes to pages on their watchlist.

The word **Main Page** underneath the tabs is known as the **title** of the article. Below the title and horizontal line is the **main body** section of the page.

What is the difference between a page and an article? I know that some of you may be scratching your heads wondering just this. After all, the two seem to be interchangeable. An article is basically the content found on a page. It consists of the title and body of the Body section. A page, on the other hand, houses everything related to the article and the wiki alike. The page contains the article, the navigation and tool boxes, tabs, login, and other information.

Pop quiz – the body

Time for another quiz! Let's see how well you understood the previous section.

1. The Page contains the Article among other things.

    a. True

    b. False

2. Extra tabs are shown above the Article when a registered user logs in.

    a. True

    b. False

3. Which is not a tab found above the Article:

    a. Watch

    b. Ignore

    c. Edit

    d. Discussion

4. If you wanted to be notified of changes to a Page, which tab would you use?

    a. Edit

    b. Discussion

    c. History

    d. Watch

Footer

Like all websites, the footer contains information that is important to the site, but not considered content that draws visitors to your site.

The footer contains links such as **About**, **Disclaimers**, and the **Privacy policy**. Visitors can also see the last time the page was modified and how many times it has been accessed.

Have a go hero – make some changes

We are going to learn how to create and edit articles in Chapter 4, *Creating Content*. However, if you are itching to get some pages up this is the perfect opportunity.

As the About page is already created by MediaWiki so when you click the link in the footer, the page shown in the following screenshot appears:

Now you can click on the **edit this page** link or the **create** tab to get started.

Account section

On the top, right-hand side of the Main Page you will find the heart of your wiki's community, the **Log in/create account** section. Although we created a sysop account when we set up our wiki, let's take a moment and create a standard user account. Once we are done, we will log in and see some of the changes to the Main Page.

Time for action – creating a user account

We are going to create a sample user account to see exactly what our visitors will see when they log in to our wiki. This account will come in handy later on when we want to test certain features and extensions added to our wiki because it will allow us to view the wiki from a member's perspective rather than the sysop.

1. Click on the **Log in / create account** button in the top, right-hand corner of your screen. You will be taken to the Log in/create account page similar to the one shown in the following screenshot:

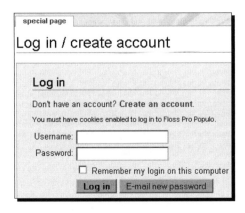

2. As we are going to create a new account, we will click on the **Create an account** link.

3. You are now taken to the **Create account** page. Fill out the necessary information requested on this page. Before you click on the **Create account** button, make sure that the password for this account is not the same one as your sysop account. In fact, make it as different as possible. This is just a good security practice for anything that requires passwords.

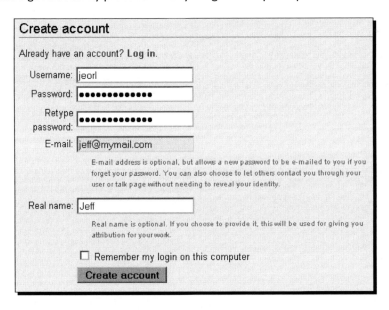

4. Now that you are set, go ahead and click on the **Create account** button.

Once your account is created, you are taken to a special page titled **Login successful**, and MediaWiki automatically logs you in to the system. Like most other sites that require registration, you are sent a confirmation e-mail and you are prompted to change your preferences. While it is a bit too soon to start making changes to the preferences, I do encourage you to take a look around this section to see what you can do.

 The confirmation e-mail will be sent to the e-mail address that you provided when you installed MediaWiki. There is no need to set up a separate e-mail server for this to work.

What just happened?

We just took a bit of a side trip to show how easy it is for your users to create accounts for themselves. To demonstrate this, we created a basic account that we will use later for testing purposes.

Looking at the screenshot under the *Footer* section more carefully, we can see that when we log in to the wiki, the links where the **Log in/create account** section is, changes. These links are provided to registered users and can be changed based on how we set up the site. We will approach these features later on in Chapter 8.

Have a go hero – explore the user preferences

While we will discuss some of the user preferences in following chapters, this is a great time to get a preview of what your users can do with their wiki account. Click on the **my preferences** link found on the **Login successful** page.

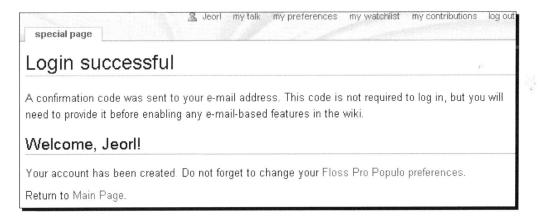

When you get to the Preferences page, navigate to the different sections using the tabs. Once you are done exploring, we will get back to learning about the Main Page!

The logo

As we move into the subsequent chapters, we begin to transform MediaWiki into our own wiki. The one item that defines this more than anything is the logo. When building a new website, the logo is often the first task that is taken on because it gives the site its identity. To really take the first steps into establishing this wiki as our own, we are going to go ahead and change the logo to one that represents our site.

If you already have a logo, that's great. However, in order to replace the default MediaWiki logo, you have to make sure that the image is 135 pixels by 135 pixels. If you do not have a logo as of yet, you will need to create something to use in this chapter. In Chapter 11, we will cover different hacks for MediaWiki. Among these will be how to set up MediaWiki to allow different sized images.

There are many free/open source programs that you can use to resize or create your logo. I would suggest using **GNU Image Manipulation Program** (or the **GIMP**) if you are used to Adobe Photoshop. If you prefer something along the lines of Adobe Illustrator or CorelDraw, then **Inkscape** would be a better choice for you. Both of these programs are free of charge and can be downloaded from `http://www.gimp.org` or `http://inkscape.org` respectively.

We are going to cover two different methods of changing the logo. The first method requires two less lines of code to be written into the `LocalSettings.php` file so it is a bit easier. The second method requires a bit more code, and a bit more navigating of the file system. The trade off is that the second method organizes your wiki how MediaWiki expects it to be.

Time for action – changing the logo method one

Enough talk, let's make some changes! What we will be doing here is uploading an image file to our server and then altering a PHP file in MediaWiki so that it knows where to pull the new logo from. MediaWiki recommends that the logo be 135 pixels by 135 pixels in size, so if you haven't already done so, modify your logo to fit these parameters.

Let's get started.

1. Open up your FTP client, cPanel, or the file manager that your hosting company provides you. If possible, try using a different method for uploading than you did when we installed MediaWiki. This will give you more exposure to different tools.

2. Upload your logo file to the `/images` folder on your server. Usually, this is found under `public_html` if you are using a shared host. If you are using your own server, you should be able to locate this folder under `/var/www/html`.

3. Locate your `LocalSettings.php` file. This too should be in the `public_html` folder. Copy this file renaming it to `LocalSettings2.php`. We do this so in case we mess up we can always restore the original file.

4. Open the `LocalSettings.php` file for editing using a text editor such as Notepad for Microsoft Windows or eMacs for GNU/Linux. You may need to download this file first depending on which tool you are using.

5. Scroll to the bottom of the file and add the following line of code:

   ```
   $wgLogo = "/images/yourlogo.png";
   ```

   Make sure to change `yourlogo.png` to the filename of your actual logo.

6. Save your newly edited `LocalSettings.php` file. If you downloaded it prior to editing, upload the file back to the original folder.

7. Open your browser and enter your wiki's URL into the address bar. You should now see your logo in place of the placeholder that used to be there.

You can see the new logo appears right above the **navigation** box. Now, let's look at the second method we can use to change the logo with something that better represents your site.

What just happened?

By uploading a new image file for our logo and telling MediaWiki where to look for it, we are able to change the logo that appears on our wiki. The first method we used was very basic, but it calls for us uploading our image file to the same folder where our visitors will upload images.

Time for action – changing the logo method two

The previous method was pretty simple right? This method is pretty easy as well, it just requires you to dive a bit deeper into the filesystem and type a bit more code into the `LocalSettings.php` file. This method is recommended by MediaWiki because it keeps the logo file in folder where the system expects it to be. The previous method had us uploading the logo file into the same folder where users too will upload their image files.

1. Upload the file for your logo to the `\skins\common\images` folder using one of the file transfer tools mentioned in the first method.

2. Locate your `LocalSettings.php` file and copy it. Rename the file to `LocalSettings2.php`. In the event something goes wrong, we can revert back to the original file.

3. Open the `LocalSettings.php` file for editing using a text editor such as Notepad for Microsoft Windows or eMacs for GNU/Linux. You may need to download this file first depending on which tool you are using.

4. Scroll to the bottom of the file and add the following lines of code, each on a separate line:

    ```
    $wgStylePath        = "$wgScriptPath/skins";
    $wgStyleDirectory   = "$IP/skins";
    $wgLogo             = "$wgStylePath/common/images/yourlogo.png";
    ```

    Make sure to change `yourlogo.png` to the file name of your actual logo.

5. Save your newly-edited `LocalSettings.php` file. If you downloaded it prior to editing, upload the file back to the original folder.

6. Open your browser and enter your wiki's URL into the address bar. You should now see your logo in place of the placeholder that used to be there.

What just happened?

The second method used to change the logo requires a couple of additional lines of code, and we have to navigate a bit deeper into our filesystem on the server when we upload our image. However, using this method, we are keeping our wiki in line with how MediaWiki organizes files and folders.

Summary

Congratulations, you have done something important! In this chapter, we learned about how MediaWiki organizes pages and you took the first couple of steps in transforming MediaWiki into your wiki.

Specifically, we covered:

- The components of the Main Page
- What the different links in the navigation box do by covering each feature individually
- What the features in the toolbox do
- That special pages are not able to be edited by our visitors as they are created by the system
- How users create accounts and how they log in to our wiki
- Two different methods for changing the logo on our wiki

We also discussed how a page differs from an article to avoid confusion throughout the book.

Now that we've learned the basics, we can start learning how to create content and really customize our wiki.

4
Creating Content

We've done well so far learning about MediaWiki as a software package. In the previous chapter we actually started working with our own wiki by changing the logo. Now, we are going to begin creating actual content for our wiki. This chapter is especially important because content is the reason your wiki exists in the first place.

If you are creating a wiki on a particular subject that you will be hosting for anyone on the web to see, you need to make sure that your content is engaging enough to build a large community that sees the importance of your wiki and is compelled to contribute as well. The content you create in the beginning is the foundation that will set the tone for your visitors.

Maybe you are creating a wiki whose primary audience is looking to find out more about a particular product or service. The content you provide your visitors may determine whether or not they make a purchase or take part in whatever service you are providing.

Perhaps your wiki is a collection of internal documents for your company. Again, clear, well-written content that is easy to access and find can determine whether or not your wiki project is a success. If all the buzz around the water cooler is how easy the wiki has made it for employees to find important company information, you can smile and give yourself a pat on the back.

While we won't be able to give you lessons on how to craft content like a Nobel Prize winning author, in this chapter we will teach you how to:

- Plan a new page
- Create a new page using the edit tab
- Create a new page through a link
- Create a new page using the search feature
- Create a new page using the URL
- Delete a page
- Format content
- Use HTML to format content
- Create links to other content

So let's get going!

Planning for new content

Before we get started writing new content for our wiki, we need to think about a few things first. While we may be tempted to jump right in and start writing, for the greater good of our wiki we need to set a few ground rules for any content we create. In fact, this would make for a great page called *Contributor Guidelines,* don't you think?

- Always search the site for a page before you begin to create it. As your wiki grows, and the community expands, it becomes more and more possible that someone else had the same idea for a page as you. Searching for this page allows you to see what, if any, similar pages already exist. If there is nothing that mirrors the page you are thinking of creating, then go right ahead. If the page you were thinking about does exist, then you have one of two options. First, you can edit the existing page by making it better or by adding to it. The other option is to create a new page with a different title that approaches the subject in a different way. For example, on the FLOSS Pro Populo site, a page about MediaWiki would exist since it is a Free/Libre/Open Source software package that is quite popular. Seeing that this page has already been written, I may choose to create a new page called MediaWiki Hacks as this isn't covered in the existing page.

- Review changes before you save them using the **Show changes** button. This provides you with a side-by-side comparison of what has been modified so you can make sure that the changes you made are correct.

◆ The page name you provide becomes the title of the page so make sure that it is meaningful. Also, you must make sure that your page name, or title, uses valid characters. Characters such as [,], {, }, |, #, <, and > are used by MediaWiki internally. As the MediaWiki software processes wiki syntax before it formats text, anything it sees with these characters will be converted and executed according to their syntax rules (such as creating a link). Characters that can be used are: A-Z, a-z, 0-9, !, @, $, *, (,), -, _, +, =, `, and ,. MediaWiki does allow you to define valid title characters using the `DefaultSettings.php` file. We will cover this later when we discuss *MediaWiki administration* in Chapter 7.

 The forward slash (/) is another valid character for MediaWiki titles. However, it is used to indicate any subpages for a particular page. If you decide to activate subpages, then it is not recommended that you allow the forward slash to be used in a page title.

◆ Make sure that your title/page name does not use a **namespace**. Namespaces, in MediaWiki, are groups of pages that have a similar purpose. Their main job is to separate content. There are 18 built-in namespaces:

  ❑ Main
  ❑ Talk
  ❑ User
  ❑ User talk
  ❑ Project
  ❑ Project talk
  ❑ File
  ❑ File talk
  ❑ MediaWiki
  ❑ MediaWiki talk
  ❑ Template
  ❑ Template talk
  ❑ Help
  ❑ Help talk
  ❑ Category
  ❑ Category talk
  ❑ Special
  ❑ Media

Remember namespaces, because they will come up in later chapters!

Creating a new page

Now that we know the rules for creating content, we are going to cover three different ways to create a new page. However, we are going to start small so the first piece of content that we actually create will be a simple edit of the Main Page to welcome visitors to our wiki.

Editing the Main Page

As we are building the wiki from the ground up, we might want to start by changing the Main Page so it doesn't read, "MediaWiki has been successfully installed." It is important to think about what you want your Main Page to say before you start writing it because more often than not, this will be the first thing your visitors see when they come to your wiki.

Time for action – editing the Main Page

The Main Page is the easiest page to create because we are actually editing a page that already exists, and it is the first page we see when we open our wiki. As this book is all about building our skills from the ground up, let's get our feet wet by creating content for the Main Page.

1. Type the URL for your wiki into the address bar of your browser. For example, to access the sample wiki we are building you would type `http://www.flosspropopulo.com`. When the Main Page appears, log in to your wiki using your sysop account. You can edit the Main Page by logging in as the user we created in the previous chapter, however, there is a reason why I want you to use the sysop account. Don't worry, all will be revealed shortly.

 By default, MediaWiki allows any visitor to edit a page, even if they do not create an account or log in. If you, or a visitor, does not log in to the wiki, the IP address will be logged in the edit history of the page.

2. Click on the **edit** link at the top of the Main Page. Clicking on the **edit** button to the right will only edit the **Getting Started** section.

3. Type your welcome message for your visitors in the text. Notice that we have changed the text between the `<big>'''  '''</big>` tags, but not the tags themselves. This is because we wanted the formatting in the welcome message to remain the same.

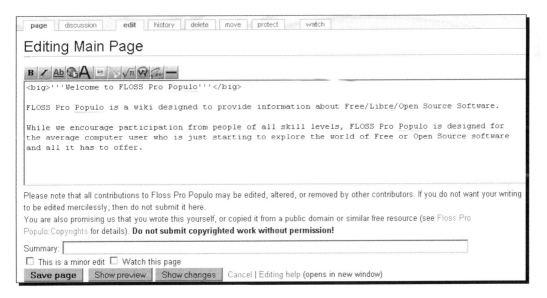

4. Practice what we preach and click on the **Show changes** button. Now, we can see how our changes compare to the original text. If you wish to see how the page will look as it is formatted, you can click the **Show preview** button.

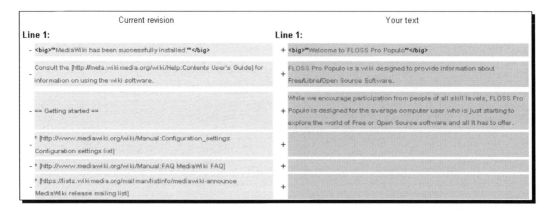

5. If everything is up to par, then go ahead and click the **Save page** button and marvel at what you have accomplished!

What just happened?

In the preceding task, we just edited the content of the Main Page to something more fitting for our individual wiki. While a simple task indeed, we were able to familiarize ourselves with how content is created so that the upcoming lessons will be easier to understand.

Have a go hero

Now that you have seen how easy it is to edit an existing page, give it a try on your own. The About page on your wiki is currently an empty page. Locate the **About** button at the bottom of your page and click on it to add some content telling your visitors what your wiki is all about. While you are at it, change the **Privacy Policy** and **Disclaimers** pages as well.

Protect the Main Page

You may remember that I had you log in to the wiki as the sysop. The reason is as the sysop user, you can prevent others from making changes to the page you are working on using the **protect** tab. As the Main Page is what the visitors first see when they visit our site, we don't want any vandalism to occur here. Think about how your visitors would feel if they went to your wiki for some solid information and were greeted with something completely inappropriate. To guard against this, we will change the settings so that only administrators (or sysops as they are also known) can edit and move this page.

Time for action – protect the Main Page

Protecting the Main Page is a simple task. Follow along with the following steps and you will have taken the first step towards guarding against vandalism.

1. Click on the **protect** tab. If you don't see this tab, log out and log back in under your sysop account.

2. You should now be on the **Change protection level for "Main Page"** screen. In the first box, under **Edit**, select **Administrators only**.

3. Make sure that **Administrators only** has been selected under **Move**. This should happen by default when you selected this option under **Edit**.

4. Select the amount of time you want the page to be protected for. If you don't want the date to expire, leave it set to **infinite**.

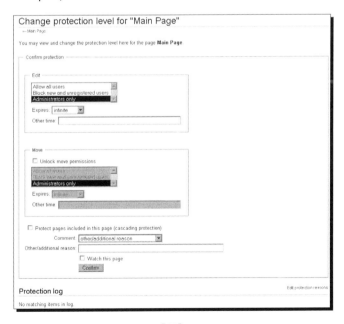

5. If you wish, provide a reason for protecting the page in the **Comment** section. This is like commenting code, making use of this feature can be helpful in managing your wiki.

6. Click on **Confirm**.

If you should ever need to edit this page, you can simply click on the **unprotect** tab when logged in as the sysop.

 If you only wish to prevent users from moving a page (renaming the page), you can protect this as well. Before you are able to select **Administrators only**, you have to first check the **Unlock move permissions** box. This allows you to then select any of the options in the menu.

What just happened?

In order to prevent users from altering our Main Page, we protected it from editing and moving. This way, we have greater control over what our visitors first see when they visit our wiki.

Create a new page using the search feature

Editing a page is rather easy in MediaWiki. Now you will see that creating a page is just as simple. The first way we are going to create a new page is by using the search box we learned about in the previous chapter.

The ability to perform a search is nothing new to websites. Actually, it is considered a best practice to include a search option on your website. While the search option included in MediaWiki works in much the same way as other search options when content exists, it differs greatly when the page, or content, you are looking for does not exist. When MediaWiki cannot find the content you are searching for, it gives you the option to **create this page**.

Time for action – create a new page using the search feature

To create a page using the search box, think of a title for a page you would like to create. For our example, I am going to create a definition for the term "FLOSS". We are going to use this term to create our page. Once you have an idea for your page, follow along with the directions provided below:

1. Type the title of the page you will create in the **search** box and click on the **Go** button.

2. Under the section that reads **No page title matches**, click on the **create this page** link.

3. Write your article.

4. Enter a summary of your article in the **Summary** textbox at the bottom of the page.

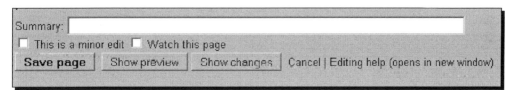

5. Check the **Watch this page** box. This will allow you to see if anyone should edit your page at a later date. If the content changes, you can go back and review it to make sure it is accurate.

6. Click on the **Show preview** button to make sure that your article and page look the way you anticipated. If there is anything that needs to be changed, you can edit it directly.

7. If everything appears correctly and you are happy with your page, go ahead and click on the **Save page** button.

After clicking on the **Save page** button, you will be taken to your newly-created page.

What just happened?

After searching for our new page produced no results, we were given the option to create a new page. After writing the new page's content, we previewed the results to make sure we were happy with the content and we published the page to our wiki.

In the section of this chapter called *Planning for new content*, one of the guidelines suggested is to search for a new page before you write it. After completing this task, you can see why this is the recommended method of creating a new page. If no results appear, you have the option of creating the new page. If the wiki finds a page with your title already in existence, you can move on to creating another page.

Unlike the Main Page that we recently edited, we did not protect this page. In the wiki which we are creating as a demonstration, we want to encourage community members to collaborate on all of the content. Someone may have a better way of defining F/L/OSS, or they may wish to add to the definition. By leaving this article open for editing, anyone can do just that. There may be instances where you wish to protect your article from unregistered users making edits. You can do this by choosing the option to **Block new and unregistered users** under the **protect** tab. Of course, you may wish to protect the page from any and all editing by community members. After all, if your wiki is meant to host employee manuals, or human resource documents, you may not want people making changes to the content. If this is the case, feel free to protect your page in the manner you see fit.

Have a go hero

The beauty of MediaWiki's collaboration is that you can discuss pages with other community members. Maybe you want to request additional content, or you want to make sure that someone reads over a certain section for accuracy. You can make these requests, and leave other notes using the **discussion** tab on your page.

Now that you have created a new page, add some items to the discussion section that you feel are appropriate to your page. While you are at it, take a peek at the **history** tab to see what it looks like!

Compare selected revisions

- (cur) (prev) ⦿ 21:17, 22 September 2009 FLOSSuser (Talk | contribs | block) (435 bytes) (rollback | undo)
- (cur) (prev) ⦿ 22:48, 14 September 2009 Jeff (Talk | contribs | block) m (419 bytes) *(Minor edit - added my signature)* (undo)
- (cur) (prev) ○ 16:02, 23 August 2009 Jeff (Talk | contribs | block) m (399 bytes) *(moved Top Software by Operating System to Top 3 Applications by Operating System)* (undo)
- (cur) (prev) ○ 21:00, 9 August 2009 67.35.121.150 (Talk | block) (399 bytes) (undo)
- (cur) (prev) ○ 18:32, 9 August 2009 67.35.121.150 (Talk | block) (175 bytes) (undo)
- (cur) (prev) ○ 18:05, 9 August 2009 67.35.121.150 (Talk | block) (125 bytes) (undo)
- (cur) (prev) ○ 18:02, 9 August 2009 67.35.121.150 (Talk | block) (180 bytes) *(Created page with 'Some of the top FLOSS packages by operating system... {| |Windows |Mac |GNU-Linux |- |OpenOffice.org |AbiWord |Emacs |- |ClamWin |Skim |Celestia |- |Audacity |Freemind |Firefox ...')*

Compare selected revisions

(Latest | Earliest) View (newer 50) (older 50) (20 | 50 | 100 | 250 | 500)

Creating a new page using a wikilink

Now that we have created the first new page in our wiki, we need to continue adding content relevant to our topic. What better way to do this than to create new pages that are linked to from our current page. These links between pages in our wiki are called **wikilinks**.

Creating pages through wikilinks is a great way to establish a web of information for your users. These links allow them to easily follow a trail of related information. The following steps will walk us through this process. With this in mind, it is easy to see why this method of creating a new page is the best because we already have at least one page linking to it, and therefore our visitors have another means of finding the page.

Time for action – creating a new page using a link

When creating a new page using a wikilink, we have to have an existing page open. Let's start by finding a topic in the page we just created that would serve as a good page. Once you have determined what you are going to create your next page about, we can get started.

It is important to let you know that we are going to jump ahead a bit in this section and cover a bit of wiki syntax. To create a link to another page, you will need to enclose the text in a set of double brackets. For example, if we wanted to create a link around the word *wiki*, we would type [[wiki]]. Don't worry about the syntax just yet; we will cover it further later on in this chapter.

Syntax is set of rules that define how to properly combine words and symbols in a programming language. For example, using double brackets to enclose a link in wikitext is considered proper syntax.

1. Open the page you are going to link from and click on the **edit** tab.

2. Locate all instances of the term you will be using as a link and type double brackets around them. For example, in the demonstration, I will be linking to an article about Richard Stallman so I located the reference to him in the text and changed it to `[[Richard Stallman]]`.

3. Click the **Save page** button. You will now be taken back to the page you were editing. Every instance where you created a link will have changed its font color from black to red.

4. Click on the link you have created. This will take you to the editing page where you will be greeted with a message that reads:

    You have followed a link to a page that does not exist yet. To create the page, start typing in the box below (see the help page for more info). If you are here by mistake, click your browser's back button.

5. Write your article and then click the **Save page** button. Remember to preview it first though!

That's it, you are done! Creating content keeps getting easier and easier, doesn't it?

What just happened?

In a standard website, when we click on a link whose page doesn't exist, we are given an error message. Due to MediaWiki's collaborative nature, when we do this in our wiki, we are given the opportunity to create a new page of content.

We were introduced to the wiki syntax that allows us to create an in-text link to another page. These links, as we saw, appear in a red-colored font until the new page is created. Using this link, we were able to create a new page, write the content, and then publish this new page into our wiki. On our newly-created page, we can also click on the **What links here** button and see how web of internal links is beginning to form.

What's cool about this feature as well is that you can create links in your articles for future pages. Who knows, someone else in the community may take the initiative and create a page from one of these links!

Creating content on the fly is extremely easy with a wiki. This is what makes it such a good tool for collaboration. There are no special permissions or intricate steps required to create a new page as is needed with a content management system. With MediaWiki, just type and go!

Creating a new page using a URL

This method of creating a new page is by far the easiest. However, while it may reinforce the idea that content is easy to create when using MediaWiki, it doesn't directly follow the guidelines we set up earlier in this chapter. Using this method, we have no way of telling if there is already a page that exists in our wiki that is similar to the one we are creating. Of course, we could always do a search prior to creating our page, but in this case, it would be easier to just click the **Create this page** button.

Time for action – creating a new page using a URL

When you have one of your pages open in your web browser, the URL in the address bar should read something similar to `http://www.yourwiki.com/index.php/page_title`. We are going to use this URL to create a new page. While most hacks may take a bit of skill and know-how, this one is extremely easy, so follow along:

1. In the address bar of your web browser, remove the title of the current wiki page (in our example, the word `page_title` would be deleted).

2. Type the title of your new page after `index.php/` in the address bar.

3. Hit the *Enter* key and you will be taken to a page that looks similar to this:

4. Now, click on the **create** tab and you will be taken to the Editing page. Simply write your content in the space provided, preview, and click on **Save page**.

What just happened?

We just looked at the third way we can create a new page. Simply by altering the title portion of the URL, we are taken to the Editing page for this new page. Again, this method of creating a new page is the easiest way we have seen, however it is a bit unorthodox because we are assuming that there are no pages that are similar to the one we are creating. The ideal way to create a new page is to use the Search method. This is because it allows you to see if any similar pages have already been created. You then have the option to create your page, or edit the existing one.

Pop quiz – creating pages

We have seen the three ways to create a new page in MediaWiki so let's test our knowledge with a short quiz.

1. According to the text, the best way to create a new page is through:

    a.   A wikilink

    b.   A URL

    c.   The search option

    d.   Editing a page that already exists

2. Which method of creating a new page was not discussed in this chapter?

    a.   Using a URL

    b.   Using the Wiki:New feature

    c.   Using the search box

    d.   By creating a link to the new page

3. According to the book, why is using a wiki for collaboration better than a content management system?

    a.   Wikis are more robust and powerful

    b.   Wikis are a newer technology

    c.   Wikis envelop web 2.0 standards

    d.   Wikis make content creation easier

4. When creating a new page, you should first search for similar pages and pages of the same title?

    a.   True

    b.   False

Deleting a page

There will come a time when a page in your wiki is either outdated, or inadvertently created. When this happens, you will need to delete the page to get it out of your wiki. This process is just as easy as it is to create a new page.

Time for action – deleting a page

Deleting a page wipes it out of your wiki but it still remains in the database. If you really want to rid your wiki completely of a page, you will need to remove it from the database as well.

To delete a page, you need to be logged in under your sysop account. Once you are sure you are the sysop, we can get started.

1. Navigate to the page you wish to delete. You can use the search box for this or you can simply type the URL in the address bar if you know it.

2. Once the page is up, locate the **delete** tab and click on it.

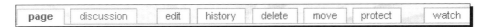

3. Read the warnings that MediaWiki gives you. If you are still sure you need to delete the page, select the **Reason for deletion**.

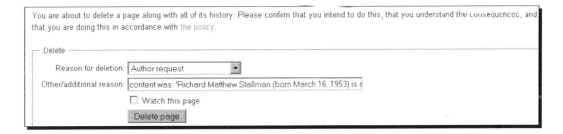

4. Click on **Delete page**.

Recovering Deleted Pages

Once you click on Delete page you can still recover the page by visiting the **Deletion log**. From here, you can select a page that has been deleted and restore it.

What just happened?

When logged in as a sysop (or administrator) we can remove a page from the wiki by clicking on the **delete** tab at the top of the page. While this removes the page from the wiki, it can still be recovered as there is a copy that remains in the database.

Formatting pages

We have seen that creating pages in MediaWiki is extremely simple. Now, we want to make the content on these pages a bit more readable, and a bit more exciting. Studies have shown that when people are reading on the web, the text needs to be broken up into different sections, you need to make use of bulleted text, and images go a long way. Luckily, we can do all of this by formatting the text in our wiki content. Formatting content in our wiki is done through wiki syntax, like we saw when we created our link. The syntax can be entered directly into the editing page when we are typing our content, or you can use the edit toolbar. We will cover how to use the edit toolbar shortly.

Wiki syntax

Wiki syntax is a special set of markup characters that is used by MediaWiki for formatting content. As we know, to show our content in a standard web page we use HTML tags for formatting. MediaWiki itself is a web-based site, but it still has its own syntax and markup rules. When a page is rendered, MediaWiki converts its unique markup syntax into the corresponding HTML syntax. So as a user, we don't have to know all the HTML tags to edit our pages. The wiki syntax gives the flexibility to format the content with very easy-to-use steps. The following chart shows the basic difference between some examples of commonly used general text, HTML, and wiki syntax.

General Text	HTML	Wiki syntax
When creating a **wiki** you need to know a few things	When creating a \<strong\> wiki \</strong\> you need to know a few things \<br\>	When creating a '''wiki''' you need to know a few things
◆ How to format text	\<ul\> \<li\> How to format text	*How to format text
◆ How to create bulleted text	\<li\> How to create bulleted text	*How to create bulleted text
◆ How to create links	\<li\> How to create links \</ul\> \<br\>	*How to create links
Click here to learn all of these tricks.	\<a href="learn.html"\>Click here \</a\> to learn all of these tricks.	[[Click here]] to learn all of these tricks.

So you can see, there are some distinct differences between wiki syntax and HTML. Learning how to markup a wiki is not only easy to learn and apply, but as there is less code to type, there is less of a chance that you will make a mistake. The whole process is made to be user friendly.

The edit toolbar

In most content management systems, you can markup the content on your site with a **What You See Is What You Get (WYSIWYG)** editor. The purpose of these tools is to allow someone who doesn't know HTML to edit and format web content using a toolbar. As the person writes their content, they can simply click the different buttons on the toolbar and see their content change right before their eyes. What you see in your editor is exactly how it will show up on someone's browser. Think about Nvu, Adobe Dreamweaver, and Microsoft's Expression Web Designer. These are extremely powerful WYSIWYG editing tools for building websites.

MediaWiki, as an extremely user friendly editor, does not have a WYSIWYG editing tool. It may look similar to the tools that most content management systems provide, and it has an extensive toolbar, but you are not able to see the formatted text as it would appear in your browser. This is why I stressed previewing your pages before saving them, earlier!

We have already seen MediaWiki's editor quite a few times but we haven't done anything with the edit toolbar just yet. The following table explains what each button does and displays the corresponding wiki syntax:

Button	Function	Wiki syntax
B	Emphasizes text with boldface.	'''text'''
I	Emphasizes text with italics.	''text''
Ab	Creates a wikilink (internal link).	[[text]]
	Links to another web page.	[www.sitename.com]
A	Formats the text as a Heading 2.	==text==
	Adds an image to the page if the image has been uploaded to the site.	[[Image:picture.jpg]]
	Adds previously uploaded media, such as audio or video, to the page.	[[Media:file.ogg]]

Button	Function	Wiki syntax
$\sqrt{n}$	Inserts a mathematical formula into the page.	$formula$
W	Marks the text to be ignored by MediaWiki when rendering the page, making it non-wiki text. For more on the <nowiki> tag see the following section dedicated to it.	<nowiki> text </nowiki>
(signature)	Inserts your signature into the page to show that you contributed to the page. Your signature consists of your username (or IP address if you are not logged in) and a timestamp.	--~~~~
—	Adds a horizontal line to your page.	----

Don't be fooled into thinking that this is the extent of formatting options available to you in MediaWiki. These represent some of the most commonly used syntax available to you. Not only is there a long list of available syntax to markup your content with wikitext, but you can combine formatting, and even make use of some HTML which we will see shortly. We will cover a bit more about this in Chapter 5, *Advanced Formatting*, but for now, let's play around with the syntax available to us via the edit toolbar.

Time for action – editing text with the edit toolbar

The editing toolbar is used for quick format changes and gives you some of the most commonly used wikitext to work with. We are going to create a dummy page in the following exercise. Right after you have finished, feel free to delete this page to keep your wiki looking professional.

1. Create a new page in your wiki. I would suggest using the URL method since we will be deleting the page anyways. Name the page "Sample".

2. Click on **create** to open the editing page.

3. In the textbox, type **Sample of Heading 2**. Highlight this text and then click on the Heading 2(**A**) button on the edit toolbar.

4. Hit return to add an extra line break and type **bold**. Highlight this and click on the Bold(**B**) button.

5. On the next line, type **italics**. After highlighting this, click on the Italics(*I*) button.

6. Now type the word **both**. After you highlight this text, click on the Bold (**B**)button. Highlight it again and click on the Italics(*I*) button.

7. Now hit return again to add another line break. On this line, type the words **link to something**. Highlight and click on the **Create link button**.

8. Hit return to add the additional line break and add your signature by clicking on the **Signature button**. Your Editing page should look like the following screenshot:

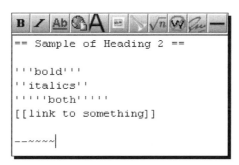

9. Since we know what the page will look like, click on **Save page**. Your page should look almost exactly like the following screenshot. The only difference should be your signature.

Once you are satisfied with the results, go ahead and delete this page.

What just happened?

Using the edit toolbar provided by MediaWiki, we were able to format the content of our page and add a signature at the bottom. We also learned something valuable. Unless we hit enter for a carriage return, MediaWiki does not place the text on a new line even though in the editor, the text is listed vertically. If we wish to add a line break, we need to hit the *Enter* key. This takes the place of the <br> tag in HTML.

The nowiki tag

You may have been left scratching your heads back there when we were talking about the edit toolbars button. After all, why would an author want to tell MediaWiki to ignore all of the content between the `<nowiki>` and `</nowiki>` tags?

If you were paying attention to the last activity, you probably can think of one reason right off the bat why we would want MediaWiki to avoid parsing our content. Go back and look at the previous two screenshots to see if you can figure it out. Don't worry, I'll wait.

Did you see it? If you answered *quotation marks*, then you get the extra credit question right! If you are writing an article for your wiki and it includes a quote, say, "*The Internet is a telephone system that's gotten uppity*", Clifford Stoll, what would we get when we click on the **Show preview** button? We're going to get: *The Internet is a telephone system that's gotten uppity,* Clifford Stoll. Why, because the " " tells MediaWiki to convert the text in between to italics.

Think that is bad, what about a wiki dedicated to teaching wikitext? Or one that exists for web designers? All of the tags that would be used to teach the audience different things would wind up turning a simple page into a nightmare.

As we have seen, the `<nowiki>` tags take care of this. Now, if we type the following into our page:

```
<nowiki>
One of the main differences between wikitext and HTML is how links are
created.

In wikitext, you simply need to enter your link between two brackets
like so [http://www.packtpub.com].

HTML, on the other hand requires a rather long tag. The same link
would be typed as such:
<a href="http://www.packtpub.com">Packt Pub</a>.
</nowiki>
```

So, if now we can click **Show preview** and everything should turn out all right.

Nowiki

One of the main differences between wikitext and HTML is how links are created. In wikitext, you simply need to enter your link between two brackets like so [http://www.packtpub.com]. HTML, on the other hand requires a rather long tag. The same link would be typed as such: <a href="http://www.packtpub.com">Packt Pub</a>.

Pretty cool, huh? You can also use the `<pre>` tag of HTML to ignore both wikitext and HTML tags in your article as well. Unlike the `<nowiki>` tag, `<pre>` does not reformat the text so new lines and spaces will not be removed. The next section will cover some additional HTML tags that MediaWiki will allow you to use.

Formatting with HTML

Formatting text with HTML has become quite popular. It is not uncommon to see e-mails, newsletters, and other documents that have HTML tags inserted into them for formatting purposes. MediaWiki is no exception. While most formatting is done with wikitext, you are permitted to use a limited number of HTML tags for marking up a document in the editing section of a page.

These are the HTML tags supported by MediaWiki:

<b>	<h2>	<s>
<big>	<h3>	<small>
<blockquote>	<h4>	<strike>
 	<h5>	<strong>
<caption>	<h6>	<sub>
<center>	<hr>	<sup>
<cite>	<i>	<table>
<code>	<li>	<td>
<dd>	<ol>	<th>
<div>	<p>	<tr>
<dl>	<pre>	<tt>
<dt>	<rb>	<u>
<em>	<rp>	<ul>
<font>	<rt>	<var>
<h1>	<ruby>	<!-- ... -->

Any tags outside of this list will be ignored by MediaWiki. For instance, the `<img>` tag is not supported. If you trying to insert a picture into your wiki using the following tag:

```
<img src="picture.png">
```

You would wind up with the following result:

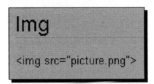

MediaWiki supports certain **nested** tags as well. Nested tags can be placed inside the wikitext to further enhance the formatting. This works especially well with tables and lists. The nested tags that you can use are listed in the following table:

<table>	< blockquote >	<big>
<td>	<ol>	<small>
<th>	<ul>	<sub>
<tr>	<dl>	<sup>
<div>	<font>	

When using HTML, we often want to customize our tags using different options. For instance, we may want to specify a color or our text, or we may want to align our text a certain way. This is done through **attributes**. And yes, MediaWiki allows for certain attributes:

<title>	<align>	<lang>	<dir>
<width>	<height>	<bgcolor>	<clear>
<noshade>	<cite>	<size>	<face>
<color>	<type>	<start>	<value>
<frame>	<rules>	<cellspacing>	<cellpadding>
<valign>	<char>	<charoff>	<colgroup>
<col>	<span>	<abbr>	<axis>
<headers>	<scope>	<rowspan>	<colspan>
<id>	<class>	<name>	<style>
<compact>	<summary>	<border>	

Have a go hero

So far we have created a couple of basic pages for our wiki. That's all well and good, but now that we have seen how we can format our content using wikitext and HTML tags, it's time for you to step up to the plate.

Before moving on to the next section, create a few pages that use the different types of formatting we discussed. Make your fonts bold, or italics, or both. Add some quotes to make use of the `<nowiki>` tag. Scatter some HTML tags and attributes around.

Make sure to keep your design clean by not overusing all of the tags in one article, instead, spread them out over a few pages using different tags in each. When you are done, we can move forward.

Links

There are really no dead ends on the Internet. Likewise, your wiki should have no dead ends. In order for it to be a success, you need to build relationships between your content. These relationships are built through links.

Think about Wikipedia for a moment. How many times have you landed on a page only to find yourself wanting more, and satisfying that want by clicking on a link to take you to another page, and then another. If you are like me, there are plenty of times you have wound up reading about a topic that is entirely different from the original page you were searching for.

To give your visitors the opportunity to extend their search, or even get lost in a world of information, we are going to spend some time teaching you how to create links in your content. We have seen how easy it is to create links using the edit toolbar. Using it, we can create **internal links** and **external links**. While using the toolbar is one way to create a link, knowing the correct syntax will make writing articles go by much faster. After all, isn't it a tad bit easier to type two brackets around a word than it is to highlight the word, move the mouse to the button, click the button, and then move the cursor back to the text so you can start typing again?

The following lessons should be applied to the articles you write from here on out, but don't forget to go back and update the pages you have already created with what you have learned.

Internal links

As we have covered internal links earlier in this chapter, I am going to introduce you to a concept that MediaWiki employs called **self linking**. A self link is when a page contains a link to itself. When this happens, the link that is created appears in bold text and the link is not clickable. For example, say we are on the Main Page and we create a list of links to important pages in our wiki. It just so happens that the Main Page is considered as an important page, so it is included. The following screenshot shows what happens to the link:

Main Page

Welcome to FLOSS Pro Populo

FLOSS Pro Populo is a wiki designed to provide information about Free/Libre/Open Source Software.

While we encourage participation from people of all skill levels, FLOSS Pro Populo is designed for the average computer user who is just starting to explore the world of Free or Open Source software and all it has to offer.

Some of our important pages are:

Main Page

Current events

Recent changes

Creating self links is something that you may not come across too often. After all, if you are on the Main Page, odds are you won't be intentionally creating a link to the Main Page on the page.

More often, you will come across **indirect self linking**. A indirect self link often occurs through two instances; the first is when you set up a redirect and the second is when you make use of a navigation template.

An example of a redirect is when you are on page A and you want to create a link to page B, which is a related article. After a while, page B grows to take the place of page A so you redirect page A to page B. The link to page B now becomes a self link and appears in bold face. If the redirect is permanent, you can always edit the page to remove the link if you like.

In the case of a navigation template, you may create a series of links that will appear on five different pages, A, B, C, D, and E. When you visit anyone of these pages, the collection of links will appear. However, if you are on page E, the link to page E will be a self link and thus, appears in boldface. The links to all other pages will be normal. Should you click on the link to go to page A, the self link will now appear for page A and page E's link will be a normal link. It may sound a bit confusing but when we discuss templates later on in this book, it will be much clearer.

Interwiki links

Interwiki links allow us to create links to other sites on the Internet. This gives users the option to avoid pasting in entire URLs (as we would need to do for regular web pages) and instead use shorthand by adding a prefix to another wiki. For example, `[[wikipedia:interWiki]]` links to the wikipedia:interWiki article on the English Wikipedia. For each project we can specify an **interwiki map**, which is a list of target projects with their prefixes. Interwiki links are created by administrators. As wiki projects are not listed like domain names, it is the responsibility of the site owner or project creator to define the wiki map to its server. We will learn more about how to create interwiki mapping later on in this book. Without a mapping the interwiki feature will not work. The best feature about interwiki linking is that these target projects are not restricted to MediaWiki. They don't even need to be a wiki!

Interwiki links can be quite useful if you are linking to large, existing wikis such as Wikipedia. However, they can be just as useful if you have multiple in-house wikis as well. Let's say the company you work for has created a wiki for the IT department, the marketing department, and the human resources department. By setting up interwiki mapping, you can link between your wikis in shorthand rather than having to create an external link.

A site's own namespace prefix cannot be reused as prefix code for an external site/project. However, the prefix used for a target site/project may be the same as the prefix for a project namespace within that project. As a result, to link to a page in the target namespace, just use the same prefix twice. Suppose our IT wiki has a namespace called policies and our human resources wiki also has a namespace of policies. To link our namespace to the policies namespace of the IT site from the human resources site, we need to need to write the link as `[[policies:policies:new policy]]`.

External links

External links are used to take your visitors to another site on the web. We have seen how this can be done with the button on the edit toolbar, but an external link can also be created by enclosing the address of the site you wish to link to between single brackets, `[ ]`.For example, if we were to link to Packt Publishing's homepage, we would write `[http://www.packtpub.com]`. Let's try our hand at creating some external links:

Time for action – creating external links

We are not going to use the edit toolbar for this task. Instead, we are going old school by hand coding our links into our new page.

1. Create a new page in your wiki. It can be whatever you like, just make sure it is something that would contain external links. For demonstration purposes, we will create a list of must have software so there will be multiple links on this page.

2. When you get to the place where you want to insert a link, type it between single brackets. The code used for my site would look like this:

    ```
    [http://www.gimp.com]
    ```

    ```
    [http://www.firefox.com]
    ```

    ```
    [http://www.openoffice.org]
    ```

    ```
    [http://www.videolan.org]
    ```

3. Notice the use of double spaces here. This is because we want a vertical list, not a horizontal one.

4. Once you are done writing, click on **Show preview**. If you created a list, it should look something like this:

    > The following list contains the software that any FLOSS user can't do without:
    >
    > [1] 🗗
    > [2] 🗗
    > [3] 🗗
    > [4] 🗗

Before you go back over the instructions to see what you did wrong, relax a moment. Everything is fine. When you create an external link, they will show up as numbers on the finished page. We will learn how to change this when we get to the next section of this chapter.

For now, you can introduce the link with some text. For example, if we want to link to OpenOffice.org, we can type the following:
Get OpenOffice.org [http://www.openoffice.org]

What just happened?

Using wikitext, we learned how to create an external link to another site. We saw that when we create an external link, it shows up as a number. In the next section we will learn how to change this, but for the time being, we added some text before the link to let our visitors know where the link would take them.

External links are not limited to only Hypertext Transfer Protocol (HTTP). Other protocols supported are:

- HTTPS
- FTP
- Gopher
- NEWS
- mailto
- IRC

Fixing your external links

The truth is, people are used to clicking on a link that contains words, not a number. The manner in which MediaWiki displays external links could be confusing to your visitors. As we are building our wiki to make things easier for our visitors, we need to change this.

There are actually two ways to go about changing this. The first is to add a label after your link that looks like this:

```
[[actual_link  link_label]]
```

So if we were to change our link for OpenOffice.org we would type:

```
[http://www.openoffice.org| OpenOffice.org]
```

Our page will show **OpenOffice.org** as the link instead of a number as shown in the following screenshot:

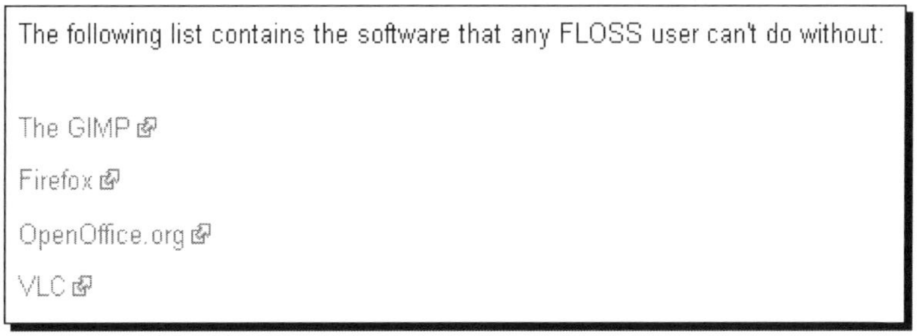

The following list contains the software that any FLOSS user can't do without:

The GIMP

Firefox

OpenOffice.org

VLC

The second way to display our external links in a more user friendly format is to simply type the URL into the text. That's right, if we type `http://www.openoffice.org` directly into the page without the brackets, it will create a more friendly list that looks like the following screenshot:

> The following is a list of must have software:
>
> http://www.gimp.com 🔗
>
> http://www.firefox.com 🔗
>
> http://www.openoffice.org 🔗
>
> http://www.videolan.org 🔗

While this manner of changing the way your external links look works, it's not as descriptive as the first method. For instance, if you don't know that `http://www.videolan.org` will take you to the VLC media player, it could still be confusing to your visitors.

Have a go hero

Now that we know how to make our external links more user friendly, go back and change any links that still show up as a number.

Summary

In this chapter, we covered quite a bit of material that focused on the heart of our wiki, the content. We learned that we write articles for our wiki and these articles are contained in the pages that we create. We also learned how to go about making our content more attractive to the reader through different formatting techniques. Even though this chapter contained a great deal of information, specifically we covered:

The different ways we can create a new page

- How to write content for our pages
- How to delete a page
- How we can use the edit toolbar to format our content
- How we can format our content using wikitext and HTML
- How to create links to other pages and sites

Now that we've learned about creating content, we are ready to tackle the challenge of using advanced formatting techniques to enhance the quality of our wiki's appearance. In the next chapter, we will be doing just that.

5
Advanced Formatting

We learned in Chapter 1 that wikis have been around for some time now. As we have progressed through the book, we have seen how wikis are a great way to share content in a true social media setting. However, this is not the days of WikiWikiWeb! Nowadays a site's audience expects structured, colorful content rich with images, video, and audio. That's what we are going to give them.

Some of what we are going to cover includes:

- How to create anchor links
- How to organize content into lists
- Organizing content into tables
- Using mathematical formulas
- Using magic words to format your wiki

Let's roll up our sleeves and get to work.

Anchor links

One of the most useful features of MediaWiki is the ability to create anchor links on a page. **Anchor links**, also called **anchors**, allow us to link from the current page to another section of the same page. Confusing? Let's see if this clears it up for you. Suppose we are on a page where we have lots of subsections and there is a link to each subsection in the table of contents. When we click on the link for the subsection, the page automatically scrolls down to that section. Most often we see these links in the **Table of Contents** of a page, as seen in in the following screenshot:

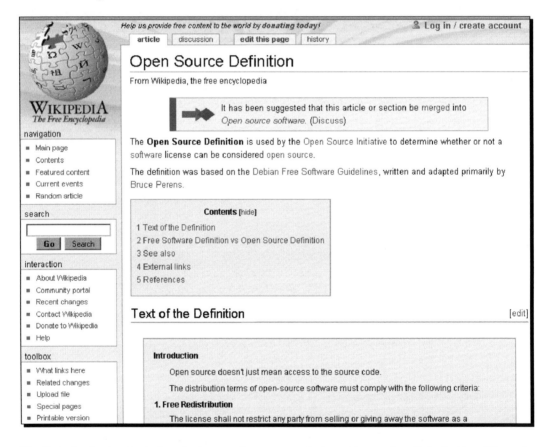

The links in the **Contents** box in the previous screenshot are the anchor links to the different subsections of the page. By clicking on any one of these links, you will be taken to that portion of the content. This is great if you only need to read a small section of a long article.

So let's create some anchors on a page in our wiki.

Time for action – creating anchor links

In MediaWiki, HTML headers or wiki's sections and subsections automatically become HTML anchors that can be linked to as MediaWiki will create a table of contents for articles using these tags. Also, `id` attributes of HTML tags in the wiki can be used as anchors. Items such as `<div id="section1">The first section of our page </div>` can be anchored no matter where this text exists in the page. In order to create anchors on a page, we need to have a page with some content on it. Once this page is opened for editing we can begin.

1. Locate the portions of the page and add the section, subsection, or sub-subsection wikitext to the header. For a section use ==section== , for a subsection use ===subsection===, and a sub-subsection would be ====sub-subsection====. Substitute your wiki's header text for the words between the =.

2. Now that you have an appropriate number of content that has been sectioned off, we can begin creating anchor links. On the page, find where you would like the anchor links to show up and type: `[[#section name| Section name]]`. The words `section name` in this example should be substituted with the various sections, subsections, or sub-subsections on your page.

 Creating an anchor to sections, subsections, or sub-subsections does not require a change in the syntax. MediaWiki does not differentiate among them when creating anchor links.

3. Once you have created all the anchors for your page, click on the **Show preview** button to see if the page came out as expected.

4. When you are satisfied with your edits, click on the **Save page** button to publish the page to your wiki.

Once you are finished, your page should look something similar to the following screenshot:

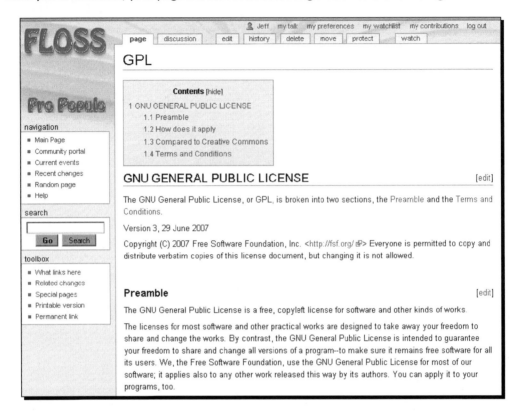

What just happened?

Using the appropriate wikitext, we edited a page to contain various section headings. Once we had all of our sections and subsections marked up appropriately, we used another piece of wikitext to create anchor tags to these sections so our visitors can jump directly to the area of the page that they are looking for.

By creating these sections, we also did two things. The first is that we added an **[edit]** link to each section/subsection of our page that can be found to the right of the heading. This allows our visitors to open only that section for editing so they don't have to wade through the entire page's content. The other by-product of creating sections is that if we have three or more sections and/or subsections, MediaWiki creates a table of contents for us at the top of the page.

Additionally, we added the pipe (|) to the wikitext. This is done because `[[#anchor name]]` is the actual wikitext that creates an anchor. However, when this is used without the |, the result on your page is **#Anchor name**. As we don't want the # sign to precede our text, we use the | and add the text we want to appear after it.

To create an anchor to the section of another page, you can use the wikitext `[[page name#anchor name| anchor name]]`.

Have a go hero

Now that you know how to create anchors, go back to your other pages and make sure that if they need to be broken into sections, subsections, and/or sub-subsections, you do so. Then, go ahead and create anchor links where it is appropriate. Remember, if you are linking between pages, you can create an anchor to the section of another page as well.

Lists

When writing for the web, it is advisable to break up your content. Studies show that breaking your articles up into sections, like we just learned how to do, makes it much easier for visitors to read. The same is true for lists.

When someone reads a web page, they actually scan the content more than they engross themselves in it like they would a printed document. Lists help the reader absorb much more of the content than if they were just reading a series of paragraphs on your page.

A web page can display the following types of lists:

◆ Unordered lists
◆ Ordered lists
◆ Definition lists

You can use any one of these lists in MediaWiki as well by providing the appropriate HTML or wikitext.

 You can read more about making your pages easier to read from any one of the following sites: `http://www.w3.org/TR/WCAG-TECHS/ G153.html`, `http://www.useit.com/alertbox/9710a. html`, and `http://gd4.tuwien.ac.at/languages/html/ webstyle/site/chunk.html`.

Unordered lists

An **unordered list** is a list that is not preceded by numbers or letters. Instead, each item in the list is offset by a bullet, usually a circle or square. In the *Lists* section, we used an unordered list to explain the three types of lists we will be talking about in this chapter.

Time for action – creating an unordered list

Creating an unordered list in your wiki is really easy. Use the asterisk (*) sign at the beginning of each line for creating a list element. The number of asterisks you add before the line will indicate the level of the list element in the unordered list. For example, two asterisks (**) will indicate a second-level list element. Three asterisks (***) will indicate a third-level list element, and so on.

If you wish to start another list on your page, put a line break (an empty line) at the end of the first list and then start another list with a top level asterisk (*).

1. Create a new page in your wiki that will involve a list.

2. On your page, type your content. When you are ready to add your list, hit *Enter* to add a line break.

3. Start your list with an asterisk. Add additional lines to the list with two or three asterisks, depending on the level.

   Your lists should look something like this on the editing page:

```
*Office suites
*Multimedia tools
*Security software
*Web browsers
*And many others

*Essential Software
**Office Suites
***OpenOffice.org
***AbiWord
**Multimedia
***GIMP
***Juice
***Audacity
**Tools
***Filezilla
***PeaZip
```

```
***X-Chat 2
**Web
***Firefox
***NVU


*Cool Software to Have
**General
***Celestia
***Blender
**Security
***ClamWin
***WireShark
```

4. Once you have entered your lists, click on **Show preview** to make sure that the lists appear the way you want. If everything looks good, then click on **Save page**.

After you have saved your page, your lists should look similar to the following screenshot:

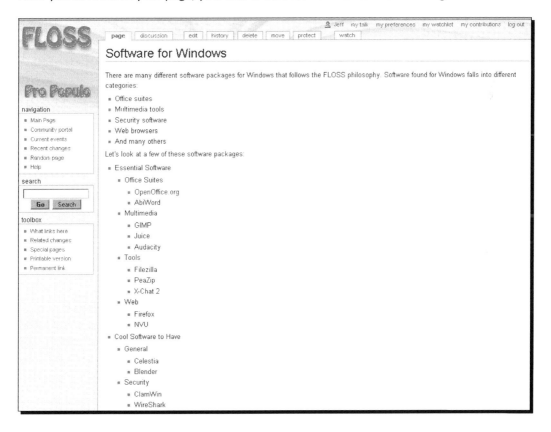

What just happened?

Using wikitext, we were able to create an unordered list to help break up a page on our wiki. Additionally, we were able to create a multi-level unordered list by adding additional asterisks before each line. The asterisks being the syntax used to create the list.

We can make use of the `<ul>` and `<li>` tags that creates a list in HTML if we choose. However, if you are familiar with HTML, then you know that each `<ul>` tag needs to be closed with a `</ul>` tag and the syntax can look messy on the page and while it is good practice to close the `<li>` tag with `</li>` even if it is not necessary. Consider the following code:

```
<ul>
<li>Office suites</li>
<li>Multimedia tools</li>
<li>Security software</li>
<li>Web browsers</li>
<li>And many others</li>
</ul>
```

Using the wiki syntax, we are able to create a list in a simple manner that is easy to read if someone else needs to edit the page.

Ordered lists

Ordered lists are used when we want to have a 1, 2, 3, and so on in front of each line on the list. These are usually used to designate steps or levels of importance. Creating ordered lists on our page is just as easy as it was to create an unordered list.

Time for action – creating an ordered list

When creating an ordered list, we will use the hash (#) sign for each list element. Similar to an unordered list, we can create a second-level list using two hashes (##) and a third-level list using three hashes (###).

If we need to create multiple lists, we would need to insert an empty line between them as we did with the unordered lists.

1. Open a new page in your wiki where you will be creating an ordered list.

2. Begin typing your content. When you are ready to begin your ordered list, enter a hash before each line. Your list should look like this:

```
#Windows
#Mac
#GNU-Linux
#Unix
```

3. Start typing a multi-level list using multiple hash signs at each line. On the editing page, your list should look like this:

```
#Windows
##Office suites
###OpenOffice.org
###AbiWord
##Web software
###NVU
###Firefox

#Mac
##Office suites
###OpenOffice.org
###AbiWord
###Bean
##Web software
###Firefox
###NVU
###Smultron
```

4. When you have finished with your content, click on **Show preview**. If everything appears the way you want it to, click on **Save page**.

After saving your page, it should look similar to the following screenshot:

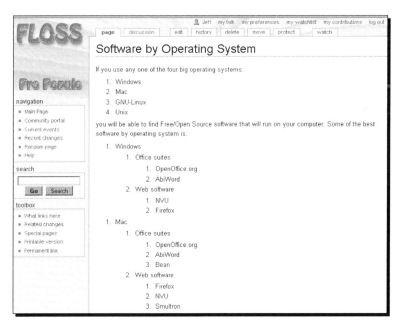

What just happened?

Instead of creating a list that is separated by bullets, we used the hash sign (#) to create an ordered list that includes successive numbers before each list element. We also learned that by using multiple hash signs before a list element, we can create a multi-level ordered list.

Using HTML for ordered lists

When creating a basic ordered list like we did in the previous example, we would want to avoid using HTML tags for the same reasons we avoided them with our unordered list. There is quite a bit more typing that needs to be done, and someone who is unfamiliar with HTML may have a hard time editing the page.

One instance where we may want to use HTML syntax with an ordered list is when we wish to create a list where we use sequential letters instead of the default sequential numbers. Let's use the multi-level list we created in the last example.

```
#Windows
##Office suites
###OpenOffice.org
###AbiWord
##Web software
###NVU
###Firefox

#Mac
##Office suites
###OpenOffice.org
###AbiWord
###Bean
##Web software
###Firefox
###NVU
###Smultron
```

Instead of the above code let's try something a bit different. Let us take out the 1 and 2 next to Windows and Mac and use a capital A and B instead. To do this, we need to define a `type` attribute for the top-level `<ol>` tags. By setting the `type=A`, we are able to change from a number to a capital letter.

```
<ol type=A>
<li>Windows
  <ol><li>Office suites
     <ol><li>OpenOffice.org
         <li>AbiWord
     </ol>
      <li>Web software
```

```
            <ol><li>NVU
                <li>Firefox
            </ol>
          </ol>
    <li>Mac
      <ol><li>Office suites
        <ol><li>OpenOffice.org
            <li>AbiWord
            <li>Bean
        </ol>
          <li>Web software
            <ol><li>Firefox
                <li>NVU
                <li>Smultron
            </ol>
        </ol>
    </ol>
```

What we see as the output on the page is shown in the following screenshot:

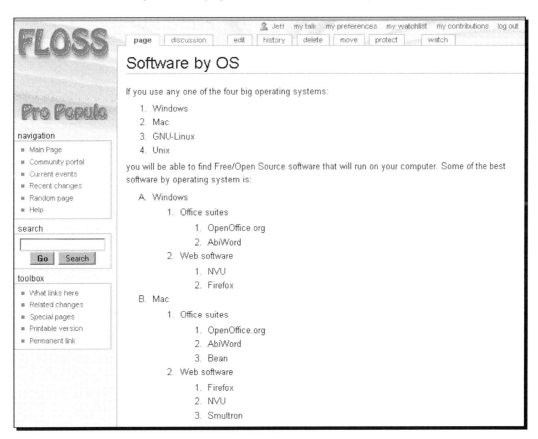

To set an attribute for an ordered list, we using the following:

- The number "1" for sequential decimal numbers: 1, 2, 3, 4, 5, and so on
- Lowercase letter "a" for lowercase alphabetic letters: a, b, c, d, e, and so on
- Uppercase letter "A" for uppercase alphabetic letters: A, B, C, D, E, and so on
- Lowercase letter "i" for lowercase Roman numerals: i, ii, iii, iv, v, and so on
- Uppercase letter "I" for uppercase Roman numerals: I, II, III, IV, V, and so on

Have a go hero

Using HTML, create some ordered lists and set the attributes to something other than the sequential number sequence. You can use any text editor to create an HTML file. Just be sure to save it with the .html or .htm extension. After you have saved the file, you can preview it in any browser to see how it looks.

Definition lists

Definition lists are great for creating glossary-type listings for your wiki. As the name suggests, a definition list creates a list of terms with the corresponding definitions. These types of lists are not formatted like the unordered and ordered lists we just worked with. Instead, they are typically displayed with the terms on the left side of the pages, and the definition on the right or directly below it.

Time for action – creating a definition list

Wiki introduces people to free and open source software, so we need to have a glossary for all the newcomers (we don't want to scare them away by calling them newbies). When creating a definition list, the wiki syntax must follow certain rules:

- Each definition term should start on a new line
- To indicate a definition term, a semicolon (;) is used at the beginning of the line
- To indicate the definition, a colon (:) is used at the beginning of the definition text

So let's get started with our glossary.

1. Open a new page in our wiki where we will create the glossary.

2. Enter the list of words, and make sure you include a semicolon before each.

3. Follow each word with its definition. Make sure to place a colon before you begin to type the definition.

Each word should appear in a format similar to the following example:

```
;copyleft
:Term used for the copyright agreement and license statement
created by Richard Stallman for software developed under the GNU
project.  Software under this license allows you to receive and
use the source code of the software to which the license applies.
Additionally, you are permitted to redistribute the licensed
software and to make derivative works provided that the source
code of the derivative is also made available under
similar conditions.
```

4. To begin your next glossary term, hit *Enter* to go to a new line.

5. Continue the process until all of your terms have been entered into your glossary. When you are done, click on **Show preview** to view the page. Click on **Save page** when you are satisfied.

If you followed along with the instructions, you should have a page that looks something like the the following screenshot:

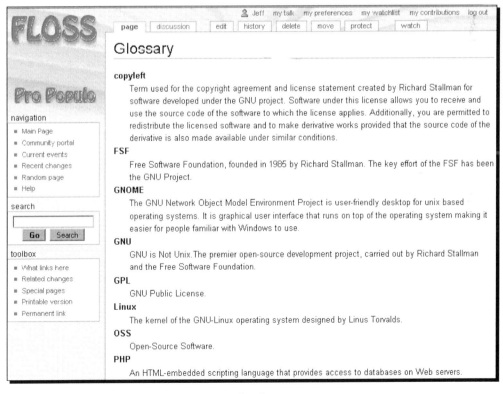

When we created our unordered and ordered lists, we could easily separate them by an empty line space. With a definition list, we are required to use the HTML tag `<br>` if we need to create a break between two or more lists.

What Just happened?

Using the wiki syntax of a semicolon and colon, we were able to build a definition list that displays a glossary of terms on our wiki.

Unlike the other two types of lists, ordered and unordered, the definition list uses no sequential numbers or letters, and does not offset the terms with a bullet. Instead, the term is displayed in a bold face font and the definition appears below the term.

Have a go hero

As I said earlier, lists are a great way to break up a page so that your visitors can scan an article for information without having to read paragraphs of content on their computer screen. As you have just mastered the three ways in which you can insert a list into your wiki, I issue you this challenge—use a mixture of unordered, ordered, and definition lists on the same page. If you are really feeling like a hero, try changing the attributes on your ordered list to include something other than the default sequential numbers!

Using tables

When it comes to building websites, developers have come to think of tables as a bad word. Instead of using tables to layout a web page, most developers opt for **Cascading Style Sheets (CSS)** to define positions and the layout of a page.

When we talk about tables as they pertain to our wiki, we are not talking about the layout of the site. Instead, we are using tables only to organize and display content to our viewers. In this instance, the use of tables is encouraged.

Table syntax

To create a table in MediaWiki, we need to use curly braces and a vertical line like {| |}. {| is used to open the table and |} to close the table. All the content will be between these two tags. This is also known as **wiki-pipe** syntax.

Note: Both opening and closing table syntax must reside on a separate line. No other tags, apart from attributes of the tables, may exist in those two lines or else the table will not be rendered properly.

There are some important rules we need to follow in regards to table syntax. They are stated as follows:

- To start a table row, enter a line and a dash (|-) after the opening tag. There is no closing symbol for indicating the end of a row. We have to start a new row to add the next line of text or symbols.

- To start a column, put a line (|) followed by data or content after the row syntax. If we want to put more than one column of data in a single line, then we have to use (||) instead of (|). The default syntax will have one line (|).

- Each row must have same number of cells as the other rows so that the number of columns in the table is kept constant. This rule can have an exception if the table cells span multiple rows or columns. If we have any blank cell, we must put a non-breaking space ( ) in it so that the cell is displayed. If this rule is broken, the table will not be displayed properly.

Time for action – creating a table

In the previous section, we created some lists to separate software according to the operating system. This information may be better displayed in a table, don't you think? Let's use the syntax we just learned to change this page so that it makes use of a table. For this example, I am actually going to create a new page to display the content. The reason for this is because if you wish to visit the example site at a later date, I want to make sure all of the examples are there for you to see.

1. Our table is going to have four columns: #, Windows, Mac, and GNU-Linux. Under each column, we will have three different rows. When we add the header column with the others, it will bring our total number of cells to 16. In your wiki, open a new page to display your table on.

2. In the editing section, start your table off with the correct syntax, {|.

3. Before you enter your first column, place the wiki-pipe |, before it. Do this for each additional column header until you are finished.

4. When you have finished the column headers, tell MediaWiki to start a new row with the proper syntax, |-.

   So far, your table should be written like this:

   ```
   {|
   |Windows
   |Mac
   |GNU-Linux
   |-
   ```

5. Now that the column headers have been created, we will enter the rest of the content. Make sure to include the wiki-pipe before the content of each cell.

6. As you complete each row, use the wiki-pipe with a dash to indicate a new row, |-.

7. When you finish entering in the content for each cell, close out your table with the |} syntax.

   Using our example, our table will look like this when written in wiki-text:

   ```
   {|
   |#
   |Windows
   |Mac
   |GNU-Linux
   |-
   |1
   |OpenOffice.org
   |AbiWord
   |Emacs
   |-
   |2
   |ClamWin
   |Skim
   |Celestia
   |-
   |3
   |Audacity
   |Freemind
   |Firefox
   |}
   ```

8. Click on **Show preview**. Do not save the page yet.

When we preview the page, we should see something similar to the following screenshot:

Well, that's definitely a table, but it's rather drab. As we are trying to create a site that people actually want to visit, let's dress this table up a bit to make it more readable. We are going to add a caption using the plus sign (+), and then we are going to alter the column and row headers using an exclamation point (!) and double exclamation points (!!).

9. Go back to the editing section of your page. Add a new line underneath the opening {|. The new line will have a |+ in front of it. Following the example, our new line will be entered as such: |+Best FLOSS Applications by OS.

10. Remove the lines that contain the header content (#, Windows, Mac, and GNU-Linux).

11. Under the line containing the caption, type the following:

```
!# !! Windows !! Mac !! GNU-Linux.
```

12. Replace the wiki-pipe before each number in the table with an exclamation point. This single exclamation point will make each number stand out as well.

Now, our syntax should look like the following. Note the changes that appears in bold:

```
{|
|+Best FLOSS Applications by OS
!# !! Windows !! Mac !! GNU-Linux
|-
!1
|OpenOffice.org
|AbiWord
|Emacs
```

```
|-
!2
|ClamWin
|Skim
|Celestia
|-
!3
|Audacity
|Freemind
|Firefox
|}
```

13. Now, go ahead and click on **Show preview**. If you like what you see, click on **Save page**.

When we save the page, our table will be a bit more readable. It should look something similar to the following screenshot:

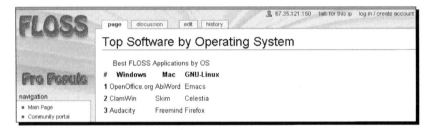

What just happened

Using wikitext, we were able to organize our content into a table. As the original table was too plain, we dressed up the content a bit using the plus(+) sign to give our table a caption, and exclamation points to distinguish our header row and column from the rest of the table. What we did in this exercise is build a foundation for creating tables that we are going to build upon in the following exercises.

Styling your table

When we added the caption and formatted the headers on our table, we made it look a bit better but let's face it, it still looks like an old dial-up served page from the early 1990's. Lucky for us, we can give this table a bit more of a modern look.

As we have seen, wiki syntax supports many HTML parameters which are also known as attributes. As we are about to see, one of the most important attributes that it supports is the style attribute. We will use this extensively as we format our table and cells. We have seen which HTML tags are supported earlier in the book. When using HTML parameters, we need to keep the following things in mind:

- To add parameters to a table, we can use the `style` parameter to define properties related to the table.

- To add parameters to a cell, we can add a parameter list after the line symbol | and close the parameter list using another line symbol |. We then put the value of the cell after that. The syntax will look like this: | Parameter | value.

- We can directly put HTML tags such as `<font>`, `<I>`, and so on, inside the cell.

- When we add parameters to a table, we must keep a space between the parameter list and the table opening syntax.

Some of the style parameters we can define in MediaWiki are: `color`, `width`, `height`, `cell spacing`, `cell padding`, `font color`, `font size`, `alignment`, and so on. We are going to use some of these to make our table really stand out on the page.

Time for action – formatting our table

In this example, we'll go back to the table we have been working with and using CSS apply some `style` attributes to it. Using these, we will define the background and foreground colors, and the height and width of the table. We will also go ahead and apply cell padding and change the spacing of our cells.

1. Open up the table we have been working on and click the **edit** tab.

2. Edit the first line (where the table opening syntax of {| is) to read:
   `{| style="background:#cccc99;color:black;width:80%;" border="1" cellpadding="5" cellspacing="0" align="center"`

3. Change lines 4 and 14 to read |- style="background:white; color:black".

4. Change line 9 to read |- style="background:#f0f0f0; color:black".

   Your complete table syntax should now look like this on the editing page:

```
{| style="background:#cccc99;color:black;width:80%;" border="1"
cellpadding="5" cellspacing="0" align="center"
|+Best FLOSS Applications by OS
!# !! Windows !! Mac !! GNU-Linux
|- style="background:white; color:black"
!1
|OpenOffice.org
|AbiWord
|Emacs
|- style="background:#f0f0f0; color:black"
!2
|ClamWin
```

```
|Skim
|Celestia
|- style="background:white; color:black"
!3
|Audacity
|Freemind
|Firefox
|}
```

5. Click on **Show preview**.

When you preview your page, you should see something like this:

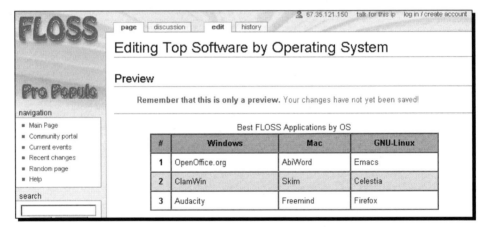

Now that table looks good! You can play around with the colors if you like. Once you have found a scheme you are happy with, save your page and we can move on!

What just happened

Using HTML parameters, mainly the `style` attribute, we were able to take our plain table and make it much more aesthetically pleasing. We were able to change the color of the background, the table width, the cell padding, the border, the cell spacing, and the alignment. More importantly, we were able to make our wiki look much more professional to our visitors.

Nested tables

When you visit Wikipedia, you may notice that their Main Page has different sections such as **Today's featured article**, **In the news**, and **Today's featured picture**. But how do they split the page up like that? The answer is **nested tables**.

As the name implies, a nested table is a table inside of another table. The table actually resides in the cell of another table. If we look back at the Wikipedia Main Page, we can view the source code that creates this by clicking on the **view source** tab at the top. While it looks rather complicated, we will see just how easy it is to make our Main Page look just like this.

Time for action – creating a nested table

Before we go ahead and write the syntax to create a nested table on our Main Page, we need to determine what it is we want to break our page up into. Wikipedia uses things such as news and featured articles. For the example we are using in this book, we are going to use Featured Software, FLOSS News, and Top Downloads.

 Remember, we disabled the ability for guests to edit the Main Page earlier. In order to perform this exercise, you need to be logged into your wiki as an administrator.

1. Open the Main Page of your wiki for editing.

2. First, we are going to create the main table for the page. In our Main Page, enter the following syntax. You may substitute the content to better fit your wiki.

```
{| style="background:#ccccc99;color:black;width:100%;" border="0"
cellpadding="5" cellspacing="2" align="center"
|-
| style="width:50%;background:#f5fffa; border:1px solid #cef2e0;
color:black;align:center;vertical-align:top" |
{| style="color:black;width:99%;background-color:#cef2e0 font-
weight:bold;border:1px solid #a3bfb1;" border="0" cellpadding="5"
cellspacing="2" align="center"
|-
| '''Featured Software'''
|}
;Firefox
:Firefox is a web browser created by Mozilla. As of July
2009,Firefox had 22.47% of the recorded usage share of web
browsers, making it the second most popular browser in terms
of current use worldwide, after Microsoft's Internet Explorer.
This is one of the most widely known FLOSS applications. You can
download Firefox from http://www.getfirefox.com.
;OpenOffice.org
:OpenOffice.org is a fully featured office suite that is
comparable to Microsoft Office. OpenOffice.org contains a word
processor, presentation software, a database, a spreadsheet
program, and a graphics program. There is no charge for
```

```
OpenOffice.org and the software can be downloaded from
http://www.openoffice.org
| style="width:50%;background:#f5faff; border:1px solid #cedff2;
color:black;align:center;vertical-align:top" |
{| style="color:black;width:99%;background-color:#cedff2;
font-weight:bold;border:1px solid #a3b0bf;" border="0"
cellpadding="5" cellspacing="2" align="center"
|-
| '''FLOSS News'''
|}
* Adobe is rolling out an open source media framework for Flash.
* Security researchers warn of exploits in XML.
* Open source backers take up lobbying.
* Free Software Foundation targets Amazon's DRM.
|-
{| colspan=2 align=center style="width:100%;background:#faf5
ff; border:1px solid #afa3bf;color:black;align:center;vertical-
align:top"
|
{| style="color:black;width:99%;background-color:#ddcef2 font-
weight:bold;border:1px solid #afa3bf;" border="0" cellpadding="5"
cellspacing="2" align="center"
|-
| '''Top Downloads'''
|}
{| style="color:black;width:99%;background-color:#faf5ff;;
border:0px solid #afa3bf;" border="0" cellpadding="5"
cellspacing="2" align="left"
|-
| rowspan=2 | Insert logo here
| Ubuntu GNU-Linux Operating System. Find Ubuntu here:
http://www.ubuntu.com
|-
| '''Previous Downloads'''
|}
|}
```

3. Click on **Save page**. The content area of your Main Page should look something like the following screenshot:

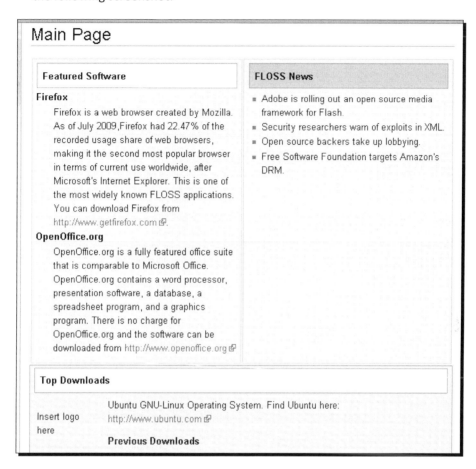

What just happened?

Nothing would be better to read right now than a *What just happened?* section. If you are an accomplished web developer, you probably can see exactly what we just did. For those who are scratching their head right now, let's explain this section piece by piece here.

Creating the main table

The first part of our syntax:

```
{| style="background:#cccc99;color:black;width:100%;" border="0"
cellpadding="5" cellspacing="2" align="center"
|-
```

creates the main table. We will nest the other tables (our FLOSS News, Featured Software, and Top downloads) into this.

The Featured Software table

As we move down the syntax, we come to our first table.

```
| style="width:50%;background:#f5fffa; border:1px solid #cef2e0; color
:black;align:center;vertical-align:top" |
{| style="color:black;width:99%;background-color:#cef2e0 font-
weight:bold;border:1px solid #a3bfb1;" border="0" cellpadding="5"
cellspacing="2" align="center"
|-
| '''Featured Software'''
|}
```

We see a width set to 50%. This sets up the split that will occur in our main table. As we move down, we see another table starting with line 3. The width here is set to 99% so that we can leave some margin space between our the content in this table and the content in the other cells in this table.

This means that our nested table, Featured Software, will take up almost half of the main table. We also set the color and alignment. As we approach the last few lines, we give the table a title, Featured Software, that is aligned to the center. In this table, we used a definition list to provide some content for our visitors. After the two featured applications, we see:

```
| style="width:50%;background:#f5faff; border:1px solid #cedff2; color
:black;align:center;vertical-align:top" |
```

This sets up the second half of our nested table, FLOSS News.

You may have noticed that the Featured Software table is created before the main table is closed with a |}. This is because all of the other tables need to exist in here. The lines that read | style="width:50% are actually part of the main table, not the nested tables.

FLOSS News

The second nested table, FLOSS News comes in at:

```
{| style="color:black;width:99%;background-color:#cedff2; font-
weight:bold;border:1px solid #a3b0bf;" border="0" cellpadding="5"
cellspacing="2" align="center"
|-
| '''FLOSS News'''
|}
```

Like Featured Software, FLOSS News takes up almost half the main table width.

For this table's content, we went with an unordered list of news stories related to free and open source software. The content is followed by the section of the main table where our third nested table will be housed:

```
|-
{| colspan=2 align=center style="width:100%;background:#faf5ff;
border:1px solid #afa3bf;color:black;align:center;vertical-align:top"
|
```

Top Downloads

Top Downloads actually splits into two sections as well:

```
{| style="color:black;width:99%;background-color:#ddcef2 font-
weight:bold;border:1px solid #afa3bf;" border="0" cellpadding-"5"
cellspacing="2" align="center"
|-
| '''Top Downloads'''
|}
{| style="color:black;width:99%;background-color:#faf5ff;;
border:0px solid #afa3bf;" border="0" cellpadding="5" cellspacing="2"
align="left"
|-
| rowspan=2 | Insert logo here
| Ubuntu GNU-Linux Operating System. Find Ubuntu here: http://www.
ubuntu.com
|-
| '''Previous Downloads'''
|}
|}
```

We first see the Top Downloads table, and then we nest another table in here so that we can add both a picture (to be uploaded later) and the text. The picture, you can see, takes up two rows set by the rowspan attribute.

Do you see the last two lines of the syntax? Both contain a |} to close out the Top Downloads table and the page's main table.

Whew! That was pretty intense, but we really accomplished quite a bit with tables. We learned how to create tables, format them to look appealing, and how to use them to format our page. Okay, so we did use them to modify the layout of the page a bit, but we had good reason to. We wanted to break our Main page up to display three different content sections and make it look better for our visitors. If we were creating a wiki for work, we may want to break the main page up into sections for policies, work related news, and important documents. There are actually no limits to what you can include in these nested tables if you are creative about it.

Also, don't feel limited to nesting only three tables. Try four, or six, or twelve! Be aware that adding nested table can slow down the loading time of older browsers.

Pop quiz – tables

Yep, time to test out what we learned about tables! Let's see how you stack up with these questions:

1. We can define HTML attributes to format our tables.

    a. True

    b. False

2. A table that has four columns and eight rows, including a header row, has how many cells?

    a. 12

    b. 24

    c. 32

    d. 64

3. When we place a table inside of another table, it is called a:

    a. Nested table

    b. Embedded table

    c. Inserted table

    d. Nomenclature table

4. The `font color` attribute cannot be used to format a table in MediaWiki.

   a. True
   b. False

Mathematical formulas

Maybe you are creating a wiki for your company's human resources department and you come across an extremely tough formula for figuring out a retirement package. Or better yet, maybe you are developing a wiki to share the next greatest computer algorithm with the world. These examples may be on completely different ends of the spectrum, but they show us one thing, we never know when we are going to need to insert a mathematical formula into our wiki. Lucky for us, MediaWiki gives the ability to insert formulas into our articles.

MediaWiki uses a subset of **TeX markup** for mathematical formulas. The formulas are shown in a graphical format using PNG files when they are displayed in a wiki. In order to create mathematical markup with TeX we have to insert the syntax for the symbol between the `<math>` and `</math>` tags. Extra spaces and line gaps will be ignored inside the tag.

Unfortunately, the `<math>` tag does not work by default in MediaWiki. We will have to go into our `LocalSettings.php` file and enable this. If you are going to be using `<math>` tags rather frequently, I would suggest you enable TeX. Another reason you may wish to enable TeX is because it allows you to use geometric shapes, arrows, Greek typeface, and other really interesting images on your wiki.

An alternative to the TeX markup and the `<math>` tags is plain old HTML. You can display many of the same mathematical markups with HTML, however, they do not look as good and TeX is semantically superior when it comes to mathematical markups. Also, HTML does not have the extensive library of symbols that TeX offers.

If you are using a hosted web server, you may not be able to use TeX. Not only do you have to enable Tex, but you have to make sure that it is installed on your wiki's server and then you have to define the path to it in your `LocalSettings.php` file as well. Check with your hosting provider to see if they will install TeX for you—you may be surprised as many will do this for you if you get the right person on the support line. They will also be able to help you define the path in your `LocalSettings.php` file as well.

Time for action – enabling TeX

Let's go ahead and enable TeX on our wiki. You will need to have access to your `LocalSettings.php` file to do this, so make sure that you have cPanel or your FTP program for this exercise. We have made changes to this file before so you shouldn't be worried about this at all.

1. Using either cPanel or your FTP program, open up the backend to your site.

2. Navigate to your `public_html` folder and expand it.

3. Open your `LocalSettings.php` file for editing.

4. Find the line that reads `$wgUseTeX = false;`.

5. Change the word `false` to `true`.

6. Save your changes.

What just happened?

By going into the filesystem of our website, we located the `LocalSettings.php` file and made the necessary change to enable TeX markups on our wiki. Now, we can go ahead and use the `<math>` tag to insert mathematical symbols. We also learned that even if we enable this, we still have to have our hosting provider install TeX and provide us with the path, so we can define this also in our `LocalSettings.php file` where it reads `$wgUseTeX = false;`

Magic words

Magic words are a few reserved words that are used for special purposes in MediaWiki. They are used to create special types of formatting. We can use magic words to show table of contents, display the current date and time, and so on. Programmers sometimes refer to these as **reserved words**. Magic words are divided between **behavior switches** and **variables**. Behavior switches control the behavior and/or layout of the page. They are often used to specify desired omissions and inclusions in the content. For instance, if we wanted to remove the table of contents from a particular page, we could put the magic word _NOTOC_ on our page and the table of contents will be removed for us. Likewise, we can force a table of contents to appear with the _FORCETOC_ or _TOC_ magic words. Magic words that are behavior switches are shown in the following table:

Magic word	Explanation
__NOTOC__	Hides the table of contents (TOC).
__FORCETOC__	Forces the table of content to appear at its normal position (above the first header).
__TOC__	Places a table of contents at the word's current position (overriding __NOTOC__). If this is used multiple times, the table of contents will appear at the first word's position.
__NOEDITSECTION__	Hides the section edit links beside headings.
__NEWSECTIONLINK__	Adds a link beside the **edit** tab for adding a new section on a non-talk page.
__NONEWSECTIONLINK__	Removes the link beside the "edit" tab on pages in talk namespaces.
__NOGALLERY__	Used on a category page and replaces thumbnails in the category view with normal links.
__HIDDENCAT__	Used on a category page and hides the category from the lists of categories in its members and parent categories (there is an option in the user preferences to show them).
__NOCONTENTCONVERT__ or __NOCC__	This tells wikis with language variants not to perform any content language conversion (character and phase) in article display; for example, only show Chinese (zh) instead of variants like zh_cn, zh_tw, zh_sg, or zh_hk.
__NOTITLECONVERT__ or __NOTC__	On wikis with language variants it tells them not to perform language conversion on the title (all other content is converted).
__INDEX__	Tells search engines to index the page (overrides $wgArticleRobotPolicies, but not robots.txt).
__NOINDEX__	Tells search engines not to index the page.
__STATICREDIRECT__	On redirect pages, doesn't allow MediaWiki to automatically update the link when someone moves a page and checks "Update any redirects that point to the original title".

Variables are those magic words which provide specific information about a page, wiki, or the date/time. Variables are used between {{ and }} tags and they are called variables because they are always changing.

The list of variable magic words is quite extensive and can be found at `http://www.mediawiki.org/wiki/Help:Magic_words#Variables`.

Time for action – inserting a magic word

Some interesting magic words to use are the number of pages and local timestamp variables. We are going to go ahead and place these two magic words on our Main Page.

1. Open your Main Page for editing.

2. At the bottom of the page, type the following:

   `Number of pages in this wiki: {{NUMBEROFPAGES}}.`

3. Drop down two lines and type: `{{LOCALTIMESTAMP}}.`

4. Click on **Save page**.

The bottom of your Main Page should now have something similar to the following screenshot:

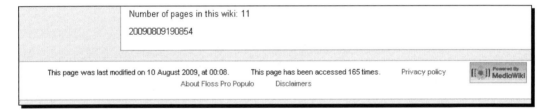

What just happened?

By inserting magic words into our wiki, we were able to display information to our visitors. The screenshot shows us that we have 11 pages in our wiki at this time. Below that, we see that the current server time is August 9, 2009, 8:08:54pm EST displayed as **20090809190854**. This will be continuously updated, thanks to the variable magic words we used. Using magic words, we can also alter the behavior of a page, or the wiki itself.

We can also make use of some other magic words that allow us to track a page's revisions or even the number of page views. These can be especially helpful when you are creating a wiki for a collaboration project and you need to make sure you have the latest revision.

Change the Timestamp

You can use other magic words to display a timestamp in different formats. For example, {{CURRENTMONTHABBREV}} {{CURRENTDAY}} {{CURRENTYEAR}} will display something like: **Dec 20 2009**, depending on the current date.

Summary

In this chapter we learned about lists, tables, and other formatting techniques that we can use to not only make our wiki look better, but also to better manage and display our content. We have also seen how easy it is to use wiki syntax to create attractive and sophisticated designs. In the process we are starting to accumulate quite a bit of content. Now, it is time for us to organize our content before we lose track of what we have created so far. So, let's move on to the next chapter where we will learn all about organizing and managing our content.

6
Putting the Media in MediaWiki

Over the years, broadband technologies and developments in web-based technologies have turned the web into a multimedia warehouse. It is uncommon nowadays to find a site that does not include images, videos, or audio to help relay information to its visitors.

MediaWiki allows you to do the same with your wiki. You can create image galleries to show off pictures of a corporate event, an audio file can playback an important speech for a wiki that provides information, and video can be used to demonstrate techniques on a wiki developed for e-learning.

In this chapter, we are going to learn how to harness all that multimedia has to offer to our wiki. Specifically we will cover:

- How to upload images
- How to create an image gallery
- How to embed audio files
- How to embed video files

So let's open up our wiki and get started.

File uploading

Before we can do anything with multimedia files, we have to first cover uploading files. If you are familiar with sites such as Wikipedia, you may have seen the **Upload file** link in the **toolbox** as shown in the following screenshot:

As your wiki should be open at this point, take a look at the **toolbox** section of your Main Page. If you have installed MediaWiki according to the directions in this book, our wiki will not have this option yet because we have not enabled our site for file uploading. Let's go ahead and take care of that right now.

The **Upload file** link will show up in the toolbox of any page on your wiki once it is enabled, not just the Main Page. By default, you will only be able to upload files if you are logged in as a registered user.

Time for action – enabling file uploads

In order to enable file uploads, we will have to edit the `LocalSettings.php` file again. You will need to use a file manager, such as cPanel or your FTP program to modify this file.

1. Open up the tool you will be using to modify your `LocalSettings.php` file and navigate to it. Remember, it is usually found in the `public_html` folder.

2. Open the `LocalSettings.php` file for editing.

3. Locate the line that reads `$wgEnableUploads = false;`.

4. Change the word `false` to read `true` as shown in the following screenshot:

```
## To enable image uploads, make sure the 'images' directory
## is writable, then set this to true:
$wgEnableUploads       = true;
$wgUseImageMagick = true;
$wgImageMagickConvertCommand = "/usr/bin/convert";
```

5. Save the changes to this file.

Now that your `LocalSettings.php` file has been changed, let's take a look at the wiki again. Go back to the Main Page of your wiki and click on the refresh button of your browser. When you see your **toolbox**, you will now have the **Upload file** link.

 Using your FTP program, or your file manager, you can check to see if the file permissions for your `Images` folder is set to Read, Write, and Edit for User, Group, and World (777). If not, change the permissions to this, otherwise you won't be able to upload anything to your wiki. If you have problems setting the permissions for this folder, or any other folder, consult your web hosting provider. For an excellent tutorial on changing file permissions on a GNU/lomuix server, visit `http://catcode.com/teachmod/`.

What just happened?

In order to continue on with the exercises, we needed to first enable file uploads on our site. By once again editing the `LocalSettings.php` file, we have taken the necessary steps to do this. Now, our visitors can upload files (images, audio, video, and so on) to our wiki. These files will be stored in the wiki's database and can be used in the various pages of our site.

Uploading images

Images will probably be the most commonly used type of multimedia on your wiki. By default, MediaWiki only allows for certain image files to be uploaded to a site. These files are: JPEG or JPG (Joint Photographic Experts Group), PNG (Portable Network Graphics), and GIF (Graphics Interchange Format). Other common file formats, such as TIFF (Tagged Image File Format) and BMP (Bitmap), require modifications to the configuration file which we will cover later.

MediaWiki also limits the size of the file you can upload to 8 MB. This too can be changed, however you have to keep in mind that if you are using a web hosting provider, your storage space is limited. Allowing larger files will use up that space more quickly. Also, larger files require greater bandwidth usage when they are displayed. With hosting providers, if you exceed your maximum bandwidth for a period of time your site may not be displayed until the account is reset (usually every month), or you may be charged extra for exceeding your limit. You also need to remember that larger files take longer to load on your page. If a page is loaded with multiple large image files, visitors may become frustrated by having to wait to view the content they are looking for and choose another site. The point being, increasing the size limit may seem like the cool thing to do for your visitors, but weigh the ramifications before doing so.

Time for action – uploading an image

First, make sure you have an image that fits the guidelines (the right format and file size). Keep in mind, in this exercise, we are only uploading an image file. We will learn how to insert the image file into a page on our wiki in the next exercise.

When you have your image, we are ready to go

If you are following along but don't have the type of media files needed for these exercises, go to Wikimedia Commons, http://commons.wikimedia.org/wiki/Main_Page, to find media files that fall under licensing options that you can freely use on your site. Many of the files used in this book can be found here as well.

1. From the **toolbox**, click on the **Upload file** link. You will see a page as shown in the following screenshot:

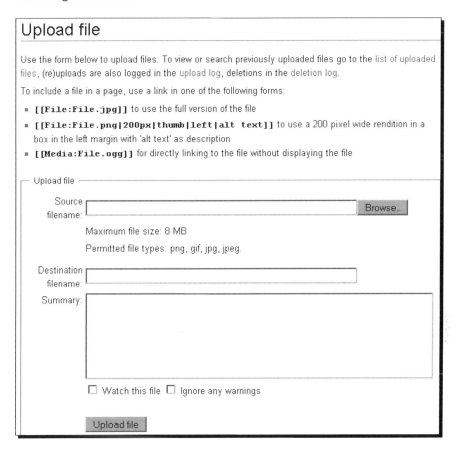

2. Click on the **Browse...** button to locate your file.

3. When you have found the right file, select it.

4. When you select the file for uploading, the **Destination filename** will be populated using the original filename for the image. If you wish to change this, do so by modifying the text in the **Destination filename** box.

5. Add a summary of the image in the **Summary** textbox. This step is optional, but can be helpful later on when trying to find different images.

6. Click on the **Upload file** button.

Once you have uploaded the file, you will be taken to the file's information page as shown in the following screenshot:

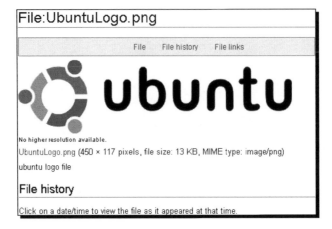

What just happened?

Using the Upload file feature we just enabled, we were able to upload an image to our wiki's database. This file can then be used on any page in our wiki, and can even be downloaded by the wiki's visitors.

We can view a list of uploaded files by navigating to a special page named **File list**. From the toolbox, click on the **Special pages** link. Now, scroll down to the section titled **Media reports and uploads**. Then, click on **File list** and you will be brought to a page that lists the files that have been uploaded to your wiki along with information about the files as shown in the following screenshot:

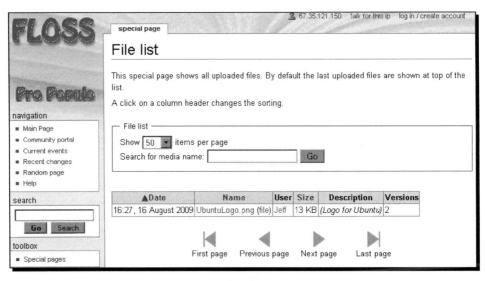

Existing file names

Before uploading files, you should always use the **File list** page to see if a similar image has been uploaded already (hence the need for the summary), or if there is already a file with the same name you intend to save your new file as in the **Destination filename** textbox. By entering a file name in the **Search for media name box** and clicking on **Go**, you can search for a file with a name similar to the one you wish to upload. You can sort the different files on this page by clicking the column header for **Date**, **Name**, and **Size**. Once you have selected a column to sort by, you can choose either **ascending** or **descending** by clicking on the arrow next to the sort field.

If you do upload a file and try to save it as the same name as an existing file, you will be alerted to this with the **Upload warning** page.

The Upload warning page will tell you that:

A file with this name exists already, please check Image:imagefilename.extension if you are not sure if you want to change it.

You then have the option to **Save file** which ignores the warning and saves the file anyway, or to **Re-upload** and return to the upload form to make the appropriate changes. Remember, authors usually watch their pages so they will be alerted to changes to the images. This fact combined with being a good administrator means that if something is uploaded inappropriately in place of an existing image you will most likely catch an instance where someone overwrites an image file. As you can always revert to the original file using the **history** tab, you shouldn't worry too much about this.

Inserting an image onto a page

Now that we have uploaded a file, we need to get it onto one of our pages. Using the example wiki we are building in the exercises, we will go back to the Main Page to do just that.

When you look at the Main Page of FLOSS Pro Populo, you may remember we created nested tables in the last chapter. In the bottom table, we included a section called **Top Downloads** where we highlighted Ubuntu. When we created this table, we had not yet learned how to upload and embed an image into our page so we included the text, **Insert logo here**. Now, we are ready to fix that.

Time for action – uploading an image onto a page

Well, we have our image uploaded and a page ready to be graphically enhanced, so let's get to it.

1. Open up the page where we want to insert our image and click on the **edit** tab.

2. Find the location where you wish the image to be placed and type the code: `[[Image:imagename.extension]]`. For example, we are going to insert the Ubuntu logo on our Main Page. The file name is `UbutnuLogo.png` so we will type: `[[Image:UbuntuLogo.png]]`.

3. Once your image has been placed, click on **Show preview**. Don't click on **Save page** just yet.

When we insert the image, we may not yet be satisfied with the end result.

The image looks nice, but the size is a bit disproportionate and I think it could use a caption so that in case someone can't view the image, they will be able to read a description of it. So let's add the caption and make the image a thumbnail instead of the full-sized graphic:

4. Go back to the `Image` line on your page. Change it to:
`[[Image:filename.extension |thumb|Your caption here]]`

For the example site, it will read:
`[[Image:UbuntuLogo.png|thumb|The Ubuntu logo]]`

5. Click on **Show preview**.

6. If you like the changes, you can click on **Save page**.

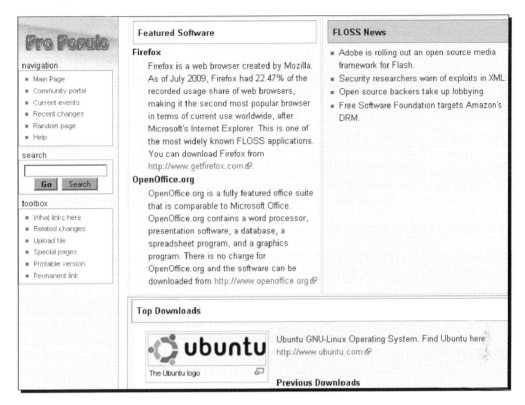

What just happened?

With a bit of wikitext, we were able to take the image that we uploaded in the previous exercise and insert it into the Main Page of our wiki. At first, the image was too large for the screen so we used a pipe (|) followed by the word `thumb` to display the image as a thumbnail. We also added a caption by using another pipe followed by the caption for our image. This gave us a clean-looking page with some graphics.

As we didn't have to make any changes to our graphic, we also learned that the thumbnail is automatically created for us by MediaWiki. If we were to click on the thumbnail image, we would be taken to the image's page where we could view, and download, the full-sized image.

If you receive an error that reads: **Error creating thumbnail: Unable to run external programs in safe mode,** it is because the line in our `LocalSettings.php` file `$wgUseImageMagick = true;` is set to `true`. By changing the value to `false`, the error will stop as MediaWiki will use its built-in resizing functions rather than the third-party ImageMagick software.

Have a go hero

We have seen that adding attribute values offset by pipes in the wikitext allows us to use a thumbnail and add a caption. You can do other things as well. Try to center your image by using `|center` placed after the image name, or make the thumbnail image 100px with `|100px` inserted after the `|thumb`. Use the Internet to find some other attributes you can add to your images as well. W3 Schools, `http://www.w3schools.com`, is a great place to start.

Creating an image gallery

If you have used content management systems in the past, one component or extension you almost always find yourself looking for is one that displays multiple images in a gallery format. With MediaWiki, this feature is built-in so there is nothing more we need to install or activate.

Galleries in MediaWiki are built using the `<gallery>` tag. When used on a page, it creates four columns of thumbnails for us. This is great for any scenario where we need to display multiple images at once.

Time for action – creating a gallery

Obviously, we need multiple images if we are going to create a gallery. While some wiki's may not find a need for an image gallery, it doesn't hurt to learn how to do this. If you find yourself short on images to use for this exercise, try finding some at Wikimedia Commons. Before you create a gallery, go ahead and save some images to your computer and upload them to your wiki.

1. Open a new page on your wiki where you will create your gallery.

2. In the editing box, begin with the gallery tag `<gallery>`. Once you have typed this, hit *Enter* to drop to a new line.

3. On the next line, type `Image:filename.extension`. Do not include the double brackets when using the `<gallery>` tag.

4. Hit *Enter* and type the syntax for the second image on the next line, repeating until you have entered all of your images for the gallery onto the page.

 You can add captions to your images or even a link by using a pipe. For example, your image named `sample1.jpg` with a caption would be entered as: `Image:sample1.jpg |Our first image`. To insert a link, you would type: `Image:sample1.jpg|[[Link|Caption]]`.

5. Once you have added all of your image files, hit *Enter* and type the closing tag, `</gallery>` on the last line.

6. Click on **Show preview**. If you are satisfied, click on **Save page**.

Your syntax should look like this when complete:

```
<gallery>
Image:image1.jpg
Image:image2.jpg
Image:image3.jpg
...
Image:image20.jpg
</gallery>
```

Obviously, you would substitute your file names for the images in the example. Your MediaWiki gallery should look similar to the following screenshot:

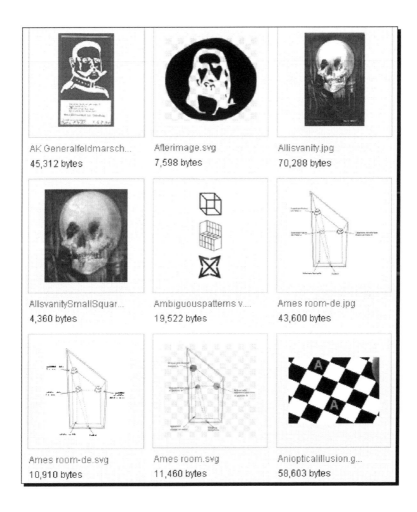

AK Generalfeldmarsch...	Afterimage.svg	Allisvanity.jpg
45,312 bytes	7,598 bytes	70,288 bytes
AllsvanitySmallSquar...	Ambiguouspatterns v...	Ames room-de.jpg
4,360 bytes	19,522 bytes	43,600 bytes
Ames room-de.svg	Ames room.svg	Aniopticalillusion.g...
10,910 bytes	11,460 bytes	58,603 bytes

What just happened?

By using the `gallery` tag, we were able to create a gallery of images to be displayed in our wiki. We also were able to use the pipe(|) to give our images a caption as well as a link to a page related to the picture.

Video files

With the advent of Adobe Flash (formerly Macromedia Flash), the Internet has been rich with video. Flash is a program that allows you to create web-ready video and animations that you can host on your website with ease. Flash movies are saved in a special file format with the extension `.swf`.

While Flash can be a great way to entertain your visitors, it can also provide you with an excellent medium for teaching and training. While many people follow written directions to learn something new, there are many others who like to see something being done firsthand. This is where including Flash videos on your wiki can be a tremendous addition. Sites that use MediaWiki as an e-learning platform make use of embedded video files all the time. Even corporate sites often relate information to customers and employees by using animated videos.

 Adobe Flash is a commercial software product. If you are looking for something to create Flash videos for your wiki that doesn't have the same price tag, check out `http://osflash.org` for some open source options.

Unfortunately, Flash files cannot be embedded into your wiki through the default installation. In order to allow our wiki to display `.swf` files, we have to install an extension. **Extensions** are pieces of PHP code that give a wiki extended functionality. They allow the administrator to expand their site to the needs of the visitors. These tools are usually not installed by default because they may not be used by every wiki, so it keeps the need for server resources low. Wiki administrators can instead choose to install the extensions they wish to use on their site.

Time for action – installing the Flash extension

Before we can begin embedding Flash files, we have to install the extension. This extension can be found at `http://www.mediawiki.org/wiki/Extension:Flash`. After we download and install the extension, we will need to make some changes to our `LocalSettings.php` file again so that the extension works properly.

1. Open your browser and point it to the URL for the Flash extension:
   `http://www.mediawiki.org/wiki/Extension:Flash`.

2. Download the file from the link provided on the page. This link can be found at the right-hand side of the page in the box next to the table of contents as shown in the following screenshot:

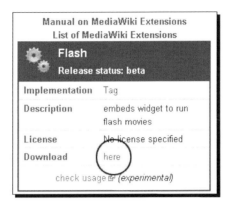

3. You will be taken to the download page. With this extension, you actually have to create the `.php` file yourself. On the download page, you will need to select all of the code on the page starting with `<?php` all the way to the end.

4. Once you have selected all of the code, copy your selection.

5. Open up your favorite text editor (Notepad, Emacs, and so on) and paste the code you just copied.

6. Save the file as `Flash.php` on your local computer. If you are using Notepad, make sure you change the *Save as file type* to *All files*.

7. Using your file manager, or FTP program, upload `Flash.php` to the `extensions` folder on your server. This can be found under the www folder in the root directory.

   Now you have uploaded your extension to your server. Before we move on, we have to modify the `LocalSettings.php` file.

8. Open your `LocalSettings.php` file for editing using your file manager or FTP program.

9. At the bottom of this file add the following:

```
#Flash.php extension for displaying Flash files
require_once("$IP/extensions/Flash.php");
$wgFileExtensions[] = 'swf';
```

10. Save your file.

What just happened?

In this exercise, we copied the PHP code for the Flash extension and pasted it into a text editor. When we saved it as `Flash.php`, we created a small PHP program that will allow us to extend the capabilities of our wiki.

After we created this file, we uploaded it to the `www/extensions` folder on our web server. We then told MediaWiki to allow this extension to run, and to allow us to upload `.swf` files (Flash) by editing the `LocalSettings.php` file. All of this was done to prepare MediaWiki to display flash movies on our site.

 In Appendix A, *The Best Extensions for MediaWiki*, you will be introduced to the MediaWikiPlayer extension that allows you to embed many more types of video and audio into your wiki.

Time for action – uploading a Flash file

The gruelling part is over. Now we need to upload a Flash file to our wiki and display it on a page. The `Flash.php` extension we uploaded enabled a new tag in our wiki, `<flash>`. In addition to this tag, we can add a series of attributes to our page that can manipulate how our movie is displayed. A few of these attributes are shown in the following table:

Attribute	Value	Action
height	px or %	Adjusts the height of the movie
width	px or %	Adjusts the width of the movie
align	center, left, right	Aligns the movie on the page
menu	true/false	Allows a menu to be shown by right-clicking
play	true/false	Automatically play the file or wait at first frame

To add a movie to a page, we need to have a `.swf` file that we want to use. For display purposes, I used a file called `Reticulum Rex` from Creative Commons from `http://mirrors.creativecommons.org/reticulum_rex/`. This video will explain a new form of licensing content for my visitors. If you don't have a Flash file, you can use it for this exercise as well.

1. Using the **Upload file** link in the tool box, upload your `.swf` file. Make sure that it is less than 8 MB.

2. Open a new page for editing.

3. On the new page, locate where you want the video to be displayed. You can embed the file anywhere you wish, even between text on the page. On our example site, the video will be the only content on the page.

4. In the place you are going to embed your video, type the following:

```
<flash>file=flashfile.swf</flash>
```

Substitute your filename for `flashfile.swf`.

5. If you wish to add attributes, separate them with a pipe (|). For example,
`<flash>file=flashfile.swf|align=center|menu=true</flash>`.

6. Click on **Show preview**. If you are happy with your page, click on **Save page**.

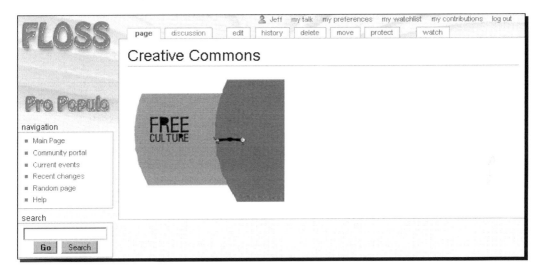

What just happened?

Completing these exercises were a big step in your development as a wiki administrator. Not only did you handle installing your first extension, but you provided a whole new medium for content on your wiki, Flash videos.

By uploading a `.swf` file to your wiki's database, you made it available for your users to display the video on a page. Creating a new page, we used the `<flash>` tag to insert this movie file onto our page to be played for our visitors. Also, we were able to modify how a movie is displayed on the page by learning about some of the different attributes that can be used with the `<flash>` tag.

Audio files

Sound files can be as helpful to your wiki as the video files we just uploaded. Embedding audio into your wiki can provide your visitors access to music, audio books, speeches, class lectures, and anything else you want to deliver in an audio format. In this exercise, we are going to learn how to embed an audio file into our wiki so that our visitors can listen to whatever it is we have to say.

When working with audio files in MediaWiki, the preferred format is **Ogg**. The reason MediaWiki chose this format is simply because it's free and best fits with the general aim of allowing access to all by avoiding proprietary standards such as MP3. Unfortunately, the Ogg format is not as popular in existing sound software, making it important that we install an extension that will play our sound files directly from our wiki.

 You and your visitors can convert existing MP3 files into OGG files with any number of programs available for download on the web. One of the best tools for creating and editing sound files in the Ogg format is Audacity, which can be found here: `http://audacity.sourceforge.net/`.

Time for action – installing the OggHandler extension

Before we get started with uploading sound files and embedding them into our pages, we have to first ready our wiki for this by installing another extension. Unlike the Flash player extension, this time we will be downloading the actual file and uploading it to our server. Once we have the extension in place, we will need to make a few changes to our `LocalSettings.php` file as well to tell our wiki to look for the new extension to handle requests dealing with Ogg files. We also have to allow our visitors to upload Ogg files as well.

1. Download the OggHandler Extension from `http://www.mediawiki.org/wiki/Special:ExtensionDistributor/OggHandler`. You will be asked to select the development version you are working from (we are using 1.15.x) and then click **Continue**.

2. The automatic download should begin. If it does not, click on the link to begin downloading. Make sure to save the file. We do not want to run it on our local computer. The file is named `OggHandler-MW1.15-r48478.tar.gz`.

3. When the download is complete, you will need to transfer the extension to your web server. If you are using an FTP program, create a folder named `OggHandler` in the `extensions` folder located in the `public_html` folder. Extract all of the compressed files and move them to the `OggHandler` folder with the FTP program.

4. If you are using your file manager, such as cPanel, then you do not have to create the `OggHandler` folder. You can upload the file `OggHandler-MW1.15-r48478.tar.gz` directly to the `extensions` folder. Extract the files into this folder and your `OggHandler` folder will be created for you.

5. Navigate back to the `LocalSettings.php` file and open it for editing.

6. Add the lines:

```
#Add other file extensions to upload
$wgFileExtensions = array('png','jpg','jpeg','ogg','doc','xls',
'ppt','mp3','pdf');

#Ogg handler extension
require( "$IP/extensions/OggHandler/OggHandler.php" );
```

7. Save your file.

What just happened?

By downloading and installing the OggHandler extension, we were able provide greater functionality in our wiki that allows us to play audio, and even video, files using the Ogg format. These files can be played directly in our wiki's pages so our visitors do not have to download the files or install any new software to play them back.

We also edited our `LocalSettings.php` file to not only tell our wiki to look for the OggHandler extension, but also to allow our visitors to upload Ogg files as well. We also added a few extra file formats to the permitted file formats such as `doc`, `xls`, `ppt`, and so on. Now, our visitors can upload other files as well and include links to them in any pages they create.

Time for action – embedding Ogg files

As stated earlier, Ogg is not limited to audio files. While it produces a better quality audio file than MP3, it can also be used for video files as well.

Now that our wiki is ready for us to use audio files, we need to learn how to embed them into our pages. Make sure you have at least one Ogg sound file for this exercise. If not, you can find some at Wikimedia Commons: `http://commons.wikimedia.org/wiki/Main_Page`. That is where I found the file `Tremolo_Picking.ogg` that I will be using.

To embed a file that has been uploaded, we will be using the `[[File]]` wikitext.

1. Using the **Upload file** link in the toolbox, upload your Ogg file to your wiki.

2. Open a new page for editing. In this example, I created a page called **Sound Test**.

3. On the page, locate where you wish to place your file and type: [[File:filename.ogg]].

4. Click on **Show preview**.

Your wiki should now show a page similar to the one in the following screenshot:

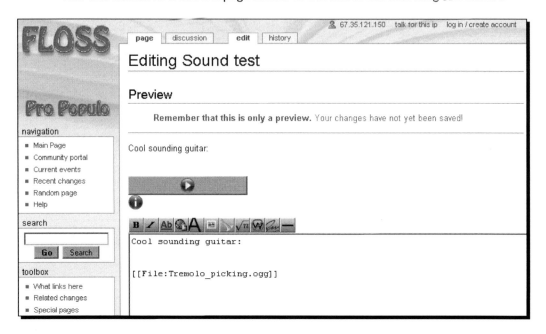

You can test out the sound file by pressing the play button on the page. The icon below the player takes you to the file's page and provides information related to the file, such as who uploaded it, the file size, how long the file takes to play, and so on.

> You can remove the information icon by adding |noicon to the syntax, for example: [[File:Tremolo_Picking.ogg|noicon]].

5. If you are pleased with the page, click on **Save page**.

When you click the play button, you should see the Ogg player as shown in the following image:

The More link

Clicking on **More…** will display a menu that lets you find out more about the file, allows you to download the file, and lets you choose the media player.

What just happened?

Through a series of modifications to our wiki, we have enabled our visitors to upload, and play, Ogg files. These files have the ability to play either audio or video making our wiki a media rich environment.

Pop quiz – multimedia

Before we wrap up this chapter, let's see how much you learned about multimedia files in MediaWiki:

1. The default settings allow for all visitors to upload a file in MediaWiki.

    a. True

    b. False

2. Which column heading cannot be used to sort files from the File list special page?

    a. Name

    b. User

    c. Date

    d. Size

3. You can allow more file extensions to be uploaded by modifying the `$wgFileExtensions = array` line in the `LocalSettings.php` file.

    a. True

    b. False

Summary

In this chapter, we saw how we can use multimedia to enrich our wiki's content. We saw how to upload and embed images into our wiki's pages, giving our visitors images that can be related to our content. We also saw how we can embed Flash movies into our wiki's pages to give our wiki even more ways to teach, train, and entertain our visitors. Finally, we saw how we could add Ogg files to play back both audio and video on our wiki.

Most importantly, we took another step forward in building our administrative skills when it comes to MediaWiki. In this chapter, we learned how to install extensions in our wiki to give it even more functionality. We will deal with more extensions throughout the book and even see some of the most important extensions for our wiki. But first, we need to understand how to organize all of this content we are starting to create. In the next chapter, we will see how to do just that!

7
Organizing Your Wiki's Content

Until now, we have focused mainly on creating content in your wiki. By this point, you should have quite a few pages in your wiki as a result of completing the exercises in this book. As our wiki grows in popularity the amount of content it hosts will continue to grow so it is important to organize the content, so that our wiki looks better to our visitors and editing and reviewing content is much easier for our users. If we think of our wiki as a library, it is easy to see why we need to organize it. After all, if you walk into a library with no system for organizing the books, movies, music, periodicals, and other items, you would find it hard to locate what you are looking for. Likewise, if we have no order in our wiki, then our visitors could find themselves frustrated when trying to find the information they are looking for. If they become too frustrated, they will go elsewhere.

MediaWiki has many built-in features that will not only help us keep our content organized, but make it extremely easy to do this. In this chapter, we will learn how to make use of these tools including:

♦ How we can create namespaces

♦ How to create categories

♦ How to set up a template for our users

♦ Why we would redirect a page

♦ How to move and swap a page

Namespaces

Namespaces are used by MediaWiki to group together pages that have a similar purpose such as help pages, user profiles, or talk pages. This is not to be confused with pages that contain similar content. These pages are grouped by categories which we will discuss later in this chapter. Pages that exist within a namespace in a wiki are noted by the *namespace prefix* that helps to form the title of the page. For example, if we have a page called **Uploading a video file** that exists in the **Help** namespace, it would appear as **Help:Uploading a video file**. Perhaps you want to create a new page for an upcoming marketing project for your company. This would appear as **Project Marketing project**. MediaWiki makes use of 18 built-in namespaces. The odd numbered namespaces represent **talk** namespaces while even numbered ones represent **subject** namespaces.

Numerical index	Namespace	Description
0	Main	This groups together a majority of the site's content. There is no namespace prefix for the mainspace.
1	Talk	The discussion pages attached to the mainspace pages.
2	User	Pages that contain information about users and their history.
3	User talk	Used to leave messages to a user.
4	Project	Used for information related to the operation and development of the wiki. This is also known as the meta namespace.
5	Project talk	Used to discuss project pages.
6	File	Stores metadata for files uploaded to the wiki. This includes images, sound, video, and other files accessed through the Media namespace.
7	File talk	Used to discuss files and media.
8	MediaWiki	Contains system messages and other important content.
9	MediaWiki talk	Discussion pages related to the MediaWiki namespace.
10	Template	Used to hold templates used in the wiki.
11	Template talk	Discussion pages for the various templates used in the wiki.
12	Help	Holds help files, how-to's, and other instructions for users.
13	Help talk	Used to hold discussions related to the help files.
14	Category	Holds information related to the different categories created for the wiki.
15	Category talk	Used to hold discussions regarding the wiki's categories.
-2	Media	Used for direct linking to media files `[[Media:song.ogg]]` rather than the information page.
-1	Special	Groups special pages created by MediaWiki itself.

Talk pages are accessed by clicking on the **discussion** tab at the top of a page.

The last two namespaces, denoted by the negative sign, are used for pages created by MediaWiki. Users cannot create, delete, or edit any pages in these two namespaces without special extensions. The remaining 16 namespaces are all used for user-created content.

The following screenshot shows the **Help** namespace for the Joomla! documentation wiki (`http://docs.joomla.org/Beginners`):

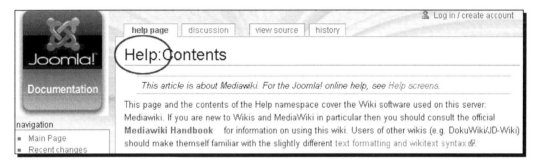

Time for action – creating a page in a namespace

Content that is housed in many of the namespaces is created on the fly. For instance, when you first register as a user, a new page in the **User** namespace is created. When you create a **Help** page, a new page appears in the **Help** namespace. If you add to the discussion page for an article on your wiki, a new talk page is created. For **Main**, **Project**, **Template**, **Help**, and **Category** pages, we can add new pages directly into the namespace.

For example, if our IT department wanted a user manual for a new software package that was just installed, we could create a project page for this. In this instance, we would have to designate the namespace or it would default to a regular article.

1.   Open your wiki in your browser and log in.

2.   In your browser's address bar, type the following:
     `http://www.yoursitename.com/index.php/Project:Project page name`.

     For the example site, I will be entering:
     `http://www.flosspropopulo.com/index.php/Project:`
     `Using our new software`. Hit *Enter*.

3. Your new page should open up and look similar to the following screenshot:

4. Right now, the **project page** tab is red because the page doesn't exist yet. Click on the **edit this page** link to create the page.

5. When you are satisfied with the page, click on **Save page**.

When the page has been saved, it will look similar to the following screenshot:

You may have noticed that while the tab reads **project page**, the namespace is the title of our wiki. In this example, **Floss Pro Populo** appears instead of the word **Project**. As the project page deals with organization of the wiki, it defaults to the wiki's sitename to represent a project taking place within the wiki itself. This can be changed; however, it is something that should be done by more advanced MediaWiki administrators.

What just happened?

Instead of simply creating a new page, we used the URL to create a new page and included it in a specific namespace. In this example, we created a new project page explaining the project that will include creating a user manual for a new software package. We also saw that of the 18 namespaces, we can directly create new pages using this method in only five of them. The other 13 namespaces have their pages created by MediaWiki itself when different actions are taken.

If you try to create a page in a namespace that doesn't exist, it will default to the Main namespace. MediaWiki will not create the new namespace for you.

Pop quiz – namespaces

Namespaces are important because they help keep our pages organized. As an administrator, it is important to know what kind of pages the different namespaces hold so we can find what we are looking for. To make sure that you have a solid grasp of namespaces, let's take a moment to test your knowledge.

1. All namespaces can be edited by the users.

   a. True

   b. False

2. Most pages in the namespaces are created by MediaWiki when the user does something. Which of the following namespaces does not allow a user to create a page?

   a. **Help**

   b. **File**

   c. **Special**

   d. **User**

3. According to the example above, which URL will correctly create a new page in the **Category** namespace?

   a. **Category:New page**

   b. `http://www.wikiname.com/Category:New page`

   c. `http://www.wikiname.com/index.php/Category:New page`

Creating a custom namespace

There may come a time when you feel the need to create a new namespace for your wiki. For instance, let's say that you are using MediaWiki to create a site dedicated to a user manual. In this manual, you may want to include tutorials for new users. You have the option of creating a namespace called tutorials to organize these pages where the purpose is to teach new users. A good example of this is Joomla!'s documentation site where they too have a namespace called tutorials.

Time for action – creating a new namespace

Creating a new namespace is extremely easy and requires us to go into the `LocalSettings.php` file and enter a few lines. That's it! As we have edited this file many times, this should be an easy task for us by now.

1. Open the `LocalSettings.php` file for editing.

2. Scroll down to the last line of the file and type:

   ```
   #Custom namespaces
   $wgExtraNamespaces[100] = "namespace";
   $wgExtraNamespaces[101] = "namespace_talk";
   ```

3. Substitute `namespace` for the name of your new namespace. In the example wiki, I used `Tutorials` and `Tutorials_talk` for the custom namespaces.

4. Save the changes to your `LocalSettings.php` file.

Now, you can create a new page in your newly-created namespace using the URL method in the previous exercise.

What just happened?

As we wanted to organize some pages into a namespace called **Tutorials**, we needed to create a custom namespace. We did this by adding a few lines to the `LocalSettings.php` file, one to create the namespace itself, and another to create the associated talk page.

We also indentified each custom namespace with a numerical index. For custom namespaces, MediaWiki requires us to begin with the number 100. The namespace **Tutorials** was given the numerical index of `100` and its associated talk namespace, **Tutorials_talk**, was given `101` as talk pages use odd numbers for this.

Categories

While namespaces help us to organize a page by the purpose it serves in the wiki, we need to be able to organize the actual content as well. This is where categories come into play. Categories allow us to take content pages that are related and group them together. Unlike namespaces, which can only be created by those with access to the `LocalSettings.php` file, categories can be created by the wiki's users.

Time for action – creating a category

There are two ways to create a category. The first method involves using the URL and the second makes use of adding wikitext to an existing page. Once the category is created, we can add more pages to this category. As we create the category pages, you will notice that the categories, and subcategories, follow the **Unicode order**.

 Unicode characters are:
!"#$%&'()*+,./0123456789:;<=>?@ABCDEFGHIJKLMNOPQRSTUVWXYZ[\]^_'abcd efghijklmnopqrstuvwxyz{|}~

The first method we will use to create a category involves using the URL the same way we did to create a new page in the **Project** namespace earlier in this chapter. In this example, we will be creating a category called **Office Suites** in the FLOSS wiki.

1. Open your wiki in your browser and log in.

2. Enter the URL `http://www.wikiname.com/index.php/Category:Category name`. You would substitute wiki name with the URL for your wiki and Category name with the name of your new category. For the example, I enter `http://www.flosspropopulo.com/index.php/Category:Office Suites`. Hit *Enter* when you are done. The following screenshot shows how the category page looks so far:

3. As the category page is not yet created, you have two options. First, you can click on the **create** tab to create an empty category page. The second option is to click the **edit this page** link. Follow along with the second option and click the **edit this page** link.

4. Enter some content that explains the category page.

5. Click on **Show preview** to see how your category page looks. If you are happy with how it reads, click on **Save page**.

What just happened?

Using the URL method to create a new page, we added a category to our wiki. Once the category page was created, you probably noticed that at the bottom there is a note telling you that **This category currently contains no pages or media**. This is because while we created a new category, we haven't added any pages or files to the category yet. In the next exercise, you will learn how to add pages to your categories.

Adding a page to a category

Some of you may remember that I said there is more than one way to create a category page. Don't worry, I haven't forgotten. We are going to learn the second way when we learn how to add a page to a category.

Time for action – add a page to a category

To add a page to a category, we only need to add a small amount of wikitext to the bottom of the page: `[[Category:Category name]]`. That's all it takes. Now, if the category name is for a category that has not yet been created, then MediaWIki will create it for you. So there you go, the second method for creating a new category! So let's add a page to our **Office Suites** category in the example.

1. Create a new page. For the example wiki, we will create a new page called **OpenOffice.org**.

2. Enter the content for your page.

3. At the bottom of the page, type the wikitext to add it to a category. For the example, we will enter `[[Category:Office Suites]]` at the bottom of the page.

That will add the page to our **Office Suites** category, but what if I want to add this page to another category? After all, **OpenOffice.org** is available for Windows, Mac, and GNU-Linux, so shouldn't it be in these categories as well? Let's take care of that right now.

4. Beneath the first category enter the syntax for each additional category. Our example will look like this when we add the other categories:

```
[[Category:Office Suites]]
[[Category:Windows software]]
[[Category:Mac software]]
[[Category:GNU-Linux software]]
```

 In this code example, I left the Office Suites category for effect. You would not need to type it in twice in your wiki.

5. Click on **Show preview**. If everything is as you want it to look, click on **Save page**. Your new page will look like the following screenshot. Note the categories list at the bottom of the page.

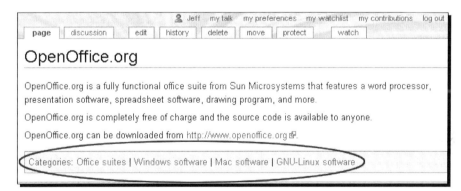

What just happened?

As we created a category page in the previous exercise, we needed to add a page to it. To do so, we added a bit of wikitext to the bottom of a new page to put the page into the category. As the page we created could easily fit in other categories, we added additional `Category` tags to our page for the other categories. As these categories did not yet exist in our wiki, MediaWiki created them for us. Our category page for **Office Suites** now looks similar to the following screenshot:

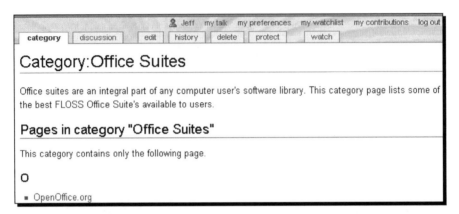

Have a go hero

Categories provide automatic indexes that are useful as tables of contents. The category tag lists the page on the appropriate category page automatically, and also provides a link at the bottom of the page to the category page. Go ahead and add categories to the pages you have created for your own wiki to better organize the content that you have already created.

To further organize your content, add categories to your category pages to create subcategories. No special syntax is needed, just use the category tag `[[Category:Category name]]`!

Finding categories

You can view the category list on your wiki by clicking on the **Special pages** link in the **toolbox**. In the **Lists of pages** section, you will find the **Categories** link. Click on this to view all the categories created in your wiki.

Page templates

Often times, we may have content that we need to include on several pages. For instance, we may want to include a legal disclaimer to certain pages. Or maybe we want to include a header or footer to all pages that fall into a specific category. Basically, if we have content that we want to include on more than one page, we can use a **template**. Creating a template means we don't have to type the same disclaimer, or header, or footer every time we want to put it onto a page. Instead, we only have to create the template, and include the template tag wherever we want the content to be displayed. If this reason is not enough to make use of templates, consider this—if we want to change some of the content in let's say, the disclaimer, we only need to change the template and all the pages will be updated. If we weren't using a template, we would have to find each page where the disclaimer content was entered and make the necessary changes to keep it consistent. Using templates is just smart management.

Time for action – creating a template

We are going to use the URL method to create a new template. When we do this, we will create an empty page where we can create the template. Once it is saved, it can be added to any page we choose with the template tag `{{templatename}}`. Of course, the name we save our template as will be substituted for `templatename`.

For our sample wiki, we will create a template that adds a thank you to the user for supporting free and open source software. A link to both the **Free Software Foundation** and the **Open Source Initiative** will be included as well. This template can then be added to the bottom of each page that describes software.

1. Open your web browser. In the address bar, type `http://www.wikiname.com/index.php/Template:nameofyourtemplate`. For the example wiki, we will enter `http://www.flosspropopulo.com/index.php/Template:Thank you`. Hit *Enter*.

2. After you hit the *Enter* key, you will be taken to the new **Template** page. Click on **edit this page** to create and write the content for your template. For the sample wiki, we use:

    ```
    ----
    Thank you for supporting free and open source software. You can
    learn more about these projects from http://www.fsf.org and
    http://www.opensource.org.
    ```

3. Click on **Show preview** to see your new template. If you are satisfied, click on **Save page**.

4. Open an existing page in your wiki. At the bottom of the page, type {{templatename}} substituting your template for `templatename`. In the example, we will be opening the **OpenOffice.org** page and typing {{Thank you}} at the bottom

.5. Click on **Save page**.

What just happened?

While creating a new template, we created a footer that can be added to any page simply by using the template tag in a page. This tag {{templatename}} is what placed the content below the horizontal rule in the previous screenshot. Anytime we include the tag for this template, {{Thank you}}, this piece of content will appear.

Templates with parameters

While the last use of the template tag can really benefit us when we are creating our pages, there is another manner in which we can use templates in our wiki. Do you remember when we created a new namespace called **Tutorials**? Let's say that we want users to create tutorials for us on our site. Now, if we have 20 different users contributing tutorials, I will bet that there will be 20 different layouts for our tutorial pages. To help keep things more consistent, we can add parameters to our template so that it acts like a **subroutine** would in a program. Each page where we use this template would have the same parameters; however, the values for each would change. This keeps the pages in the tutorial namespace consistent.

 A **subroutine** is a section of code in a program that executes a task that is one part of the larger program as a whole.

Time for action – using parameters in a template

While this may seem a bit difficult at first, after you complete the exercise you will see how simple it really is. If you have programming experience, the concepts of this should be second nature to you.

In our example, we will make the parameters boldface by enclosing them with ' ' '. However this is not necessary. What is necessary is for us to enclose the value of the parameter in triple brackets {{{ and }}}. For example:

```
'''parameter'''||{{{value}}}
```

Notice that the parameter is separated from the value by two pipes (||).

1. Create a new template page using the URL method. For the example wiki, we will create a template called **Tutorial** by typing
    `http://www.flosspropopulo.com/index.php/Template:Tutorial.`

2. Now, we need to create our template. We use the {| to open the syntax and |} to close it.

3. Use some of the formatting techniques we have learned throughout the book. For an example, we will use:
    ```
    {|style="width:80%; " border=0"
    |-
    |width=30%|
    |width=70%|
    |-
    |  colspan="2" align="center"|'''{{{TutorialName}}}'''
    |-
    |'''Introduction'''||{{{intro}}}
    |-
    |'''Prerequisites'''||{{{prereq}}}
    |-
    |'''Steps'''||{{{steps}}}
    |-
    |'''Summary'''||{{{summary}}}
    |}
    ```

4. This can serve as a guide for you as well. Simply change the parameters and the values to something that better reflects your wiki.

5. Make sure the syntax is correct by clicking on **Show preview**. If everything looks like the following screenshot, you can click on **Save page**. If anything is off, double check your syntax and make the necessary corrections.

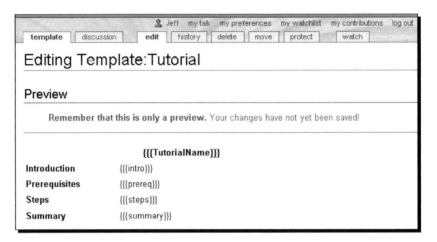

Now that we have created the template let's put it to use. We will need to pass values on to our parameters on this page.

6. Open a new page for editing.

7. Open the template with double brackets {{. Using the example, we would type {{Tutorial |. Make sure to end this line with a pipe. Hit *Enter* to drop to the next line.

8. Now we will pass values on to the parameters. Type your first parameter followed by an equal sign (=) and the value. For example, TutorialName = Installing MediaWiki|. Hit *Enter* and give your next parameter a value. Continue with this until all parameters have a value.

9. Close the page with double brackets, }}.

10. Click on **Show preview** to see if everything is good. If you like what you see, click on **Save page**.

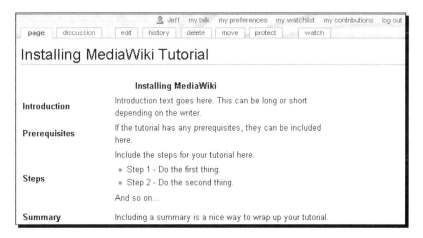

What just happened?

Using the **Template** namespace, we were able to assign parameters to our template. Now, we can apply this template to any page that we want to have a consistent look. Once we declare this template on a new page, we need to pass values on to the parameters. If you don't pass a value to a parameter, it will display the wikitext for the missing parameter. For example, if we fail to include an introduction using the sample tutorial, the page will display {{{intro}}} where the Introduction would be. The pages will now have the same layout, however the content will change. Using this technique, we created a template called **Tutorial** for the sample wiki and applied it to a new page. We also saw that we can apply many of the formatting techniques we have learned so far to our template to give it a more unique look and to separate items on the page.

Have a go hero

Templates are a great way to give your wiki a consistent look. Go ahead and create some templates that you can apply to pages in your wiki. For starters, create a disclaimer or some other type of footer that you will use on certain pages and apply this template to your wiki. Once you have been able to master this, go ahead and create a template that makes use of parameters unique to your wiki.

If you are interested in learning more about parameters used with templates, search the Internet for **Named** and **Numbered** parameters. You can visit the MediaWiki page http://meta.wikimedia.org/wiki/Help:Template#Parameters that specifically addresses parameter use in a template.

Page redirection

If you have spent any significant time surfing the web, you must have surely come across an instance when you follow a link but are **redirected** to another page. Generally, this happens for one of the two reasons, either because the content you are looking for has been moved to a different page, or because the page you are on has a similar URL to the page where the content is housed. The latter happens frequently when someone has multiple domains all pointing to one website. For instance, www.mysite.com hosts the website but www.mysite.org and www.mysite.net redirect to www.mysite.com so that visitors can view the content.

Both instances would be ideal scenarios where we would redirect a page in our wiki as well. Take for instance our page **OpenOffice.org** from the example. Perhaps someone wrote an article on **Star Office** years ago. When the name was changed to **OpenOffice.org**, we could redirect the **Star Office** page to the newly-created **OpenOffice.org** page. The second instance from above could be used because generally, people refer to **OpenOffice.org** as simply **Open Office**. We could then create a page called **Open Office** and redirect it to the **OpenOffice.org** page. Both are accomplished by adding the wikitext: #REDIRECT [[Article name]] to the beginning of the edit box. It is important to note that when redirecting an article that contains content, the content does not move to the new page.

You can create a new page with the redirect tag as well.

Time for action – redirecting a page

As we are hoping that many different users contribute to the example wiki, the odds of someone coming along and creating a page named **Open Office** is likely. As we already have a page named **OpenOffice.org**, we would rather add to the existing article than create a new one. Let's go ahead and set up a page redirect to avoid the confusion of two articles on the same topic.

1. Create a new page. In the example, we will create one called **Open Office**.

2. Enter the redirect tag and enclose the page you are redirecting to in double brackets. In the example wiki, we would use:
   ```
   #REDIRECT [[OpenOffice.org]]
   ```

3. Click on **Save page**.

You can see that after you save the page, it creates a nice little redirect message for you and a link to the correct page. If you click on the link, **Open Office**, in this case, you will be taken to the **OpenOffice.org** page. If you enter **Open Office** in the **search** box and click **Go**, you will be taken to the **OpenOffice.org** page, but notified that this is a redirect as seen in the following screenshot:

What just happened?

To further organize our wiki, we used a page redirect to send visitors who search for **Open Office** to the correct page, **OpenOffice.org**. This can be especially useful when we need to send users from duplicate pages created on our wiki, or if we want to be proactive and create pages with similar names and redirect them to the content-filled page. For instance, an internal corporate wiki may have a page titled **Human Resources Manual**. A proactive administrator may create a page titled **HR Manual** and redirect it to the **Human Resources Manual** page.

Editing a redirected page

You can still edit a redirected page by clicking on the text after **Redirected from** in the previous screenshot. Simply follow the link to the redirect page and click on the **edit** tab.

Moving a page

If your wiki is as successful as we hope it is, there will come a time when you will need to move a page. Maybe you created a page and then realized that the title is wrong. Or, perhaps, the original article has grown and the current page name no longer seems appropriate for the content. In MediaWiki, we would fix either of these situations by *moving* the incorrect page to a correct one. Actually, the terms *move* and *rename* are used interchangeably in MediaWiki. When you move a page, the history is moved with the content and a redirect is created from the original page to the one you moved to. This is so that any links to the original page will remain intact, simply redirecting the visitor to the page where you moved everything to.

Time for action – moving a page

Moving a page is very easy to do. When we go to a page, we see the **move** tab. This is what we will use to handle this operation.

Do you remember when we created a page called **Top Software by Operating System** in our example? Looking over that page, we may decide that a better title for this page would be **Top 3 Applications by Operating System**. Let's go ahead and move our original page to this new one because it better describes the content.

1. Open the page that you wish to move. In this exercise, we are opening **Top Software by Operating System** in the sample wiki. Make sure you are logged in.

2. Click on the **move** tab at the top of the wiki.

3. In the **To new title**: box, enter the new page name. For our example, we will use **Top 3 Applications by Operating System**.

4. You have the option to enter a reason here as well.

5. Click the **Move page** button.

After you have completed these steps, you will see something similar to the following screenshot:

If you need to undo this move, simply move the new page back to the original page. You then have the option of deleting the new page. For example, move **Top 3 Applications by Operating System** back to **Top Software by Operating System** and then delete **Top 3 Applications by Operating System**.

 Pages that are in the Image or **Category** namespace cannot be moved. An image can be uploaded again but a category needs to be manually changed so that all category tags that link to the category have been edited. Protected pages cannot be moved by users, only administrators can move these pages.

What just happened?

In the previous exercise, we learned how to move a page using the **move** tab on the given page. When we move a page, we are actually renaming the page. When we rename a page using the **move** tab, we also rename the history page and create a redirect to the new page from the old one.

While we do not discuss subpages in great detail in this book, these pages can also be moved, or renamed, using this technique.

Swapping pages

There may come a time where you need to make some pretty complicated moves. For example, a user creates a page on the example wiki called **Installing MediaWiki** while another user creates a tutorial named **The Installation of MediaWiki**. The title **Installing MediaWiki** fits the tutorial much better than does **The Installation of MediaWiki**. We can't rename the tutorial to the better name because it already exists as a page. Sounds like a bit of a dilemma for the administrator right? Lucky for the administrator, he or she can swap pages to fix this little situation.

Time for action – a more creative way to move a page

Swapping pages is nothing more than a bit of creative moving of the pages, so, you would use the steps laid out in the last exercise here. We will use three different pages here; page 1 is our page titled **Installing MediaWiki**, page 2 is our page titled **The Installation of MediaWiki**, and page 3 is our newly-created page which we will call **Temp**.

1. Create a new page. This page will be a temporary placeholder so you can name it something like **Temp**.

2. Move the first page, in our example this will be **Installing MediaWiki**, to the **Temp** page, page 3.

3. Delete page 1, **Installing MediaWiki**.

4. Move page 2, **The Installation of MediaWiki**, and rename it **Installing MediaWiki**. This is allowed as we deleted the old version of page 1.

5. Delete page 2.

6. Move page 3, **Temp**, to page 2, renaming it **The Installation of MediaWiki**.

7. Delete page 3.

When you are done, the tutorial should now be named **Installing MediaWiki** and the page describing the installation process will be named **The Installation of MediaWiki**. **Temp** should be deleted completely.

What just happened?

Being presented with the problem of renaming a page when a page already exists as our desired name, we used a bit of creativity to resolve our issue. Making use of the move feature in MediaWiki, we were able to swap our pages around so that the pages were named according to our wishes. As our wiki grows, we may find that we have to swap pages on a frequent basis as our users may inappropriately name pages or create pages using a name that a different page should actually be using.

Summary

As our site grows, we need to be proactive as the wiki administrator and make sure that our content is well organized so that visitors can easily find what they are looking for. In this chapter, we learned how to organize our content by creating namespaces that allow us to group pages with similar purposes together, and we learned how to use categories to group pages with similar content together. We also looked at creating templates to add the same content to a variety of pages, like we would do with a disclaimer. We also took the template feature to another level by adding parameters to it. When we did this, we created a layout so that similar pages can use this template to recreate the layout.

Finally, we learned about redirecting, moving, and swapping pages around so that we can ensure, when a visitor comes to our site, they find the information they are looking for because the page titles will match up with page's content.

As we pointed out, our wiki is growing, so it is time we focus on what we can do as the administrator of our wiki to not only provide quality content to our visitors, but also make sure that our wiki continues to run smoothly. In our next chapter, we will look at some best practices for a wiki administrator including security and dealing with a multi-user environment.

8

The MediaWiki Administrator

In the last chapter, we touched on some of the basic concepts of what it takes to manage our wiki as the administrator. While we focused mainly on content and pages, we should know that it takes much more than content management to effectively run a site.

In this chapter, we are going to start focusing on some of the administrative functions available in MediaWiki. To really get the most out of this you will need some knowledge about PHP for modifying files. It will be great if you have a working knowledge about PHP for changing some of these settings. However, if you are panicked at the thought of having to write code, don't worry; as we go through examples, you will be able to pick up few basics of PHP. So here we go. Don't forget, you have been working with the LocalSettings.php *file of the* config *folder throughout the course of this book so far and we haven't broken anything yet!*

In this chapter, we are going to focus specifically on:

- ◆ The different user types
- ◆ Access and permissions
- ◆ Changing the allowed file types for upload
- ◆ MediaWiki security

Some of what we will cover is information that will help make your job as the wiki administrator, or sysop, much easier. While these exercises will be helpful, there are others included in this chapter that are considered essential steps to take. Most of these will be in the section regarding securing your wiki. As you read this chapter, and take part in the exercises, you will be notified as to which parts are essential to the security, and functionality, of your wiki.

So, if you are ready, let's dive in and get started!

 Any administrator should know some basic things about the system they are managing. These are the file structure of their system, the user permissions, and the critical configuration files. We have seen much of this already, but these things will be reinforced throughout this chapter as well.

User types in MediaWiki

In MediaWiki, the administrator can assign rights and privileges to the different users by making them members of a group. Each group is assigned certain rights by default, but the sysop, as well as the bureaucrat—who we will learn about shortly—can make changes to the rights that each group has. For instance, if a wiki was created as an HR manual, the administrator may not want all users to be able to create and/or edit pages. After all, not many companies would be too keen on an employee being able to change the dress code from business casual to pyjamas on Fridays!

The administrator can also create new groups should they choose. This could help out the sysop in the example above. Perhaps he or she wants to allow employees to discuss certain policies but not create pages or edit pages that contain corporate policies. While the administrator may know the wiki, they may not know the terminology used in the HR department. In this instance, they can create a new group called let's say, **Department Authors.** Now, they can take away edit and create privileges from the **General Users** group, and grant these privileges to the **Department Authors** group. Each department can assign users to this group who will be responsible for creating wiki pages and editing content.

To get a better understanding of the groups in MediaWiki, let's take a look at the ones that are created by default when we installed the software.

Sysop group

Members of this group are the most common privileged users in MediaWiki. A user marked as "sysop" can delete and undelete pages, protect and unprotect pages, block and unblock IPs, issue read-only SQL queries to the database, and so on. A sysop is also known as the administrator or admin in some wiki sites such as Wikipedia.

Bureaucrat group

No, this group doesn't create red tape. This is a higher-level access type than sysop. A bureaucrat can turn any user into a sysop. The first account you created is automatically put into this group.

Bot group

This is a registered **bot account**. If edits are made by a member of this account, then they will not appear by default in the Recent changes list. This is intended for mass imports of data without flooding human edits from view.

Additional groups

There are three additional groups that are known in MediaWiki. These are:

The Developer group

This group was used to give members "siteadmin" rights. The group is deprecated by default, as well as the right so the group no longer exists in MediaWiki installations.

Autoconfirmed

Members of the autoconfirmed group are registered accounts at least as old as $wgAutoConfirmAge and having at least as many edits as $wgAutoConfirmCount. This group is used for administrators who may want to give additional privileges to users who have been members of the wiki for a certain amount of time, or who have helped edit or create a certain number of pages. The following screenshot represents the autoconfirmed group privileges for the MediaWiki site:

Emailconfirmed

This group may be used should the administrator decide to grant additional privileges to members who have a confirmed e-mail address. This, along with the autoconfirmed group, is often used to help prevent spammers and vandals from having access to certain privileges on the wiki.

User group

General user accounts or registered users are created from the registration option in the wiki site. They can in general create new pages, read articles, and edit them.

The all users group

The all users group is designated in MediaWiki by an asterisk (*). This group is implicit for all visitors to the wiki. If the administrator chooses to make a change to this group in the wiki, they may do so by editing the code found here, which we will see in the upcoming exercise. This may be good for a wiki where we don't want visitors to edit any content. We can also block unregistered users or visitors from reading content as well. What's nice about MediaWiki is that it does not follow the concept of least-common privilege. This means that if you have an account with higher-level privileges, you will not lose them if the all users group changes its privileges. Think of this more of a way to control visitors than any other group.

Group	Permissions
Sysop	By default, members of this group have all the necessary permissions to delete and restore pages, block and unblock users, and so on.
Bureaucrat	By default, users in this group can change the rights of other users.
Bot	Members of this group can run automated scripts or bots.
Developer	This is an additional group not enabled by default. Members of this group have the rights to lock and unlock the database.
Autoconfirmed	If this group in enabled, the sysop must set the parameters that determine promotion to this group either after a certain number of days or a certain number of edits.
Emailconfirmed	If this group in enabled, users are promoted here when they have confirmed their e-mail address. This group was discontinued as of version 1.13.
User	User who has registered with the wiki.
*	All users, including anonymous visitors to the wiki.

Pop quiz – user groups

Let's see how much you learned about the different types of user groups in MediaWiki:

1. Which user group is not enabled by default?

    a. Sysop

    b. Developer

    c. User

    d. Bureaucrat

2. Which user group was discontinued as of version 1.13?

    a. Autoconfirmed

    b. Bot

    c. Emailconfirmed

    d. Siteadmin

3. Anyone who has registered with the wiki will be placed in the User group.

    a. True

    b. False

4. By default all users need to confirm their e-mail address when registering with a wiki.

    a. True

    b. False

Changing permissions

We have already seen a few scenarios where we may wish to limit privileges to certain users, or grant additional permission to others. In order to edit the permissions settings, we need to first move them from the `DefaultSettings.php` file to the `LocalSettings.php` file. Once they are in place, we can begin to make changes.

Changing the DefaultSettings.php file

You can make changes to the `DefaultSettings.php` file; however, when you upgrade MediaWiki, these changes will be overwritten. This could be extremely dangerous if you are trying to protect access, or editing, of certain content. By making the changes in the `LocalSettings.php` file, the changes will remain intact when you upgrade.

Time for action – editing group permissions

When editing group permissions, we need to be very careful that we are assigning the right privileges to the right users. Also, if we are restricting privileges, we need to be certain that we are editing the correct lines so we don't lock ourselves out as the administrator. While it is a stretch, I know of quite a few people who have locked themselves out of different systems they were in charge of.

1. Using your FTP program or your file manager, navigate to the `Default Settings.php` file. The path is usually, `/public_html/includes/ DefaultSettings.php`.

2. Open the file for editing. Once it is open, locate the line that reads `$wgGroupPermissions = array();`. This is the first line of the code we will need to copy and can be found around line 1180.

3. Copy the lines of code from `$wgGroupPermissions = array();` to `$wgActiveUserDays = 30;`. This will equal approximately 242 lines of code, depending on which version of MediaWiki you are working with.

4. Close the `DefaultSettings.php` file and do not save any of the changes to this file. You should only have copied lines of code, nothing else.

5. Open the `LocalSettings.php` file for editing from the root of your MediaWiki installation, just as you have before.

6. Scroll to the bottom of the file and paste the code you copied over from the `DefaultSettings.php` file.

7. Paste the copied code into the `LocalSettings.php` file.

8. Save the changes to your `LocalSettings.php` file, but do not close it just yet.

    Now, our file is ready to be edited. Let's continue on and restrict the visitor account so they cannot edit, or create, new pages on our wiki.

9. In our `LocalSettings.php` file, locate the line that reads `$wgGroupPermissions['*']['edit'] = true;`, and the one that reads `$wgGroupPermissions['*']['createpage'] = true;`.

10. Change the word `true` in each line to `false`.

11. Save your changes.

Now, when a visitor opens a page on your wiki, they will see the following screenshot:

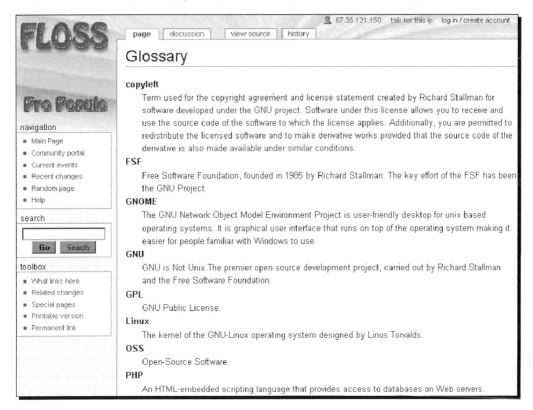

Notice in the previous screenshot, there is no **edit** tab. This is because we took away the ability of our visitors to edit any pages in our wiki. Likewise, when they search for a page that doesn't exist, they will not be presented with the option to create the page. Their ability to create a page in any other method is restricted as well.

What just happened?

By moving the selected code from the `DefaultSettings.php` file to the `LocalSetting.php` file, we are able to edit the code so that even when we update our MediaWiki software, our changes will remain intact. The selected code that we copied was the array called `$wgGroupPermissions`. This array defines the privileges for the various groups in our wiki. Each line, such as `$wgGroupPermissions['*']['createpage'] = true;` is broken down into, the array: `$wgGroupPermissions`, the group: `['*']`, the permission: `['createpage']`, and the parameter: `= true;`. By simply changing the parameter to `false`, we take away that permission.

But what about giving a group extra privileges? Don't worry, we will cover that when we learn how to create a new group.

Have a go hero

You may have noticed that the `DefaultSettings.php` and the `LocalSettings.php` have quite a bit of information in them. To be a better administrator, it is important that you understand what these files do. As a bit of a challenge, go into each of these files and copy all of the text to a text editor or word processor. Print them out and dissect the different lines of code to see if you can understand what is going on in these two files. Even if you are a novice when it comes to PHP, you may be surprised at how straightforward the code is.

Creating groups

There may come a time when you need to create a new group. The example we used earlier about the need to create a special group so that assigned individuals can create departmental pages is ideal, so let's use that here.

Time for action – creating a new group

Creating a new group is just as easy as it was to block users from doing certain things in our wiki. In this example, we are going to create a group called **DepartmentAuthors**. We will give this group the ability to create pages and edit pages.

1. Open your `LocalSettings.php` file for editing.

2. Locate the lines that grant permission to those in the **Users** group to create pages and edit pages. They are:

   ```
   $wgGroupPermissions['user']['edit'] = true;
   $wgGroupPermissions['user']['createpage'] = true;
   ```

3. Change the parameter in each line from `true` to `false`.

4. Right above the section of code that reads:

   ```
   // Implicit group for accounts that pass $wgAutoConfirmAge
   ```

   Enter the following code:

   ```
   //Group for DepartmentAuthors
   $wgGroupPermissions['DepartmentAuthors']['edit'] = true;
   $wgGroupPermissions['DepartmentAuthors']['createpage'] = true;
   ```

5. Save your settings.

6. Open your wiki and log in as the sysop.

7. Navigate to **Special pages | User group rights**. The URL for the sample we are building would be `http://www.flosspropopulo.com/index.php/Special:ListGroupRights`.

When you open the **User group rights** page, you will see the following screenshot:

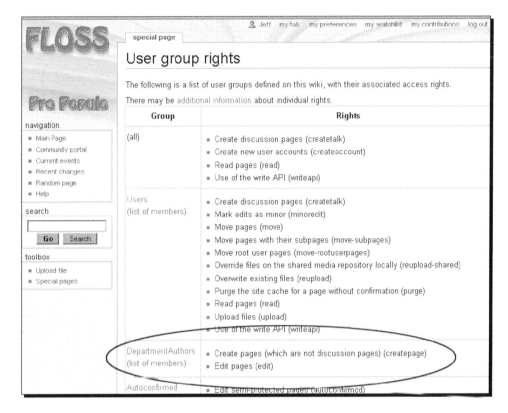

Now, our new group, **DepartmentAuthors**, is an option. You can also see the permissions that each group has. Notice that **Users** and **all** no longer have the ability to create pages or edit.

Adding users to a group

We have created this new group called **DepartmentAuthors** but we don't have anyone in this group yet. Let's go ahead and populate this group with some of our more trusted users.

Time for action – adding users to a group

Well, we have protected our wiki's content from being edited by certain people. In this example, we don't want just any employee to be able to change a manual so we created a new group and gave this group the privileges needed to create and edit content. Currently, the sysop is the only person who can create and edit the content on the site. As we are busy as the administrator, we better get some people in this group so they can start getting us some content! We are going to start by creating a new user called **Author** and then move them into the **DepartmentAuthors** group.

1. Open your wiki and click on the **log in/create account** link in the upper right corner of the screen.

2. As we are going to create a new user, click on **Create an account**.

3. Fill out the **Create account** screen giving your user a **Username** of Author and then a **Password** and **Real name**.

4. Click on **Create account**.

5. When you create the new account, you are automatically logged in to the wiki. As this account is a general account, we need to log out, and then log back in as our sysop (bureaucrat).

6. When you are logged back in with your bureaucrat account, click on **Special pages | User rights management**. Alternately, you can access this page using the URL `http://www.flosspropopulo.com/index.php/Special:` `UserRights`. Either way, you will be taken to a page where you see:

7. Where it asks you to **Enter a username**, type in **Author** and then click **Edit user groups**. The page will change to look similar to the following screenshot:

8. Place a check mark in **DepartmentAuthors** and click on **Save user groups**.

The **User rights log** will update immediately showing you that the change was successful. If you wish, you can go back to the **User list** and see that the **Author** is now part of the **DeparmentAuthors** group:

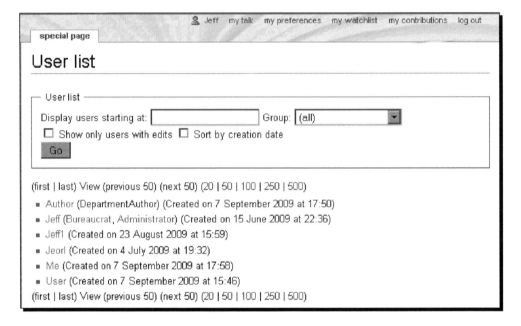

What just happened?

Adding a few lines of code to the `LocalSettings.php` file was all it took to create a new group. We simply named the group to the array and assigned permissions to this group. Once we had our new group created, we were able to add users to it.

Most importantly, these last few exercises should have reinforced the fact that even if you are not an experienced PHP coder, you can still successfully change the lines of code to effectively manage your wiki as long as you take the necessary cautions when doing so.

By playing around with the different permissions in MediaWiki, we can do some pretty amazing things. If there is just a single sysop and we take away the create new page option from the users, then the wiki becomes a blog. Cool, huh? We can use the wiki as a blog by just resetting few variables. Can we turn a wiki site to a forum? The answer is yes. Just turn on the new page creation option and turn off the edit option. Users can then create new pages (similar to a forum post), and can leave comments on talk pages (equivalent to forum reply). This way we can set different configuration options according to our needs.

File uploads

We know that MediaWiki allows us to upload files as we have done this already. The developers of MediaWiki were extremely restrictive in what type of files the system allows users to upload though. While this was done to help inexperienced wiki administrators, it is something that can be rather restrictive, especially if we want to collaborate via our wiki. By modifying our configuration, we can change the file types our users are allowed to upload. As we trust our users, we are going to allow them to upload `.pdf`, `.docx`, `.pptx`, and `.xlsx` files to the wiki.

Time for action – editing the allowed file types for uploading

The allowed file type list is available under `DefaultSettings.php` file. In order to change this configuration, we have to copy the following line from `DefaultSettings.php` and paste it into the `LocalSettings.php` file. Once we have done this, we can add our file extensions and get our users going.

1. Open the `DefaultSettings.php` file for editing.

2. Around line 1899, you will find the line `$wgFileExtensions = array ( 'png', 'gif', 'jpg', 'jpeg' );`. This defines which type of files our wiki will accept on upload. Copy this line of code.

3. Open your `LocalSettings.php` file for editing.

4. Type the line `#File extensions` at the bottom of the file. This comment will let you know that the following line(s) define the file extensions allowed. Hit the *Enter* key.

5. On the next line, paste the line you copied from the `DefaultSettings.php` file.

6. Add the extensions, `.pdf`, `.docx`, `.pptx`, and `.xlsx` to the file so that it now reads: `$wgFileExtensions = array( 'png', 'gif', 'jpg', 'jpeg', '.pdf', '.docx', '.pptx', '.xlsx' );`.

7. Save your changes.

What just happened?

As we are such nice administrators, we decided to allow our users to upload more file types than the default allows. We copied over the array `$wgFileExtensions` from the `DefaultSettings.php` file to the `LocalSetting.php` file so we could add the extensions. We did not make any changes to the `DefaultSettings.php` file because when we have to update MediaWiki, the changes made will be overwritten. By adding this line to the `LocalSettings.php` file, we can safely update later without having to worry about our configurations.

MediaWiki security

Security in cyberspace is a large concern nowadays. Malicious hackers have seen how lucrative it is to take advantage of poorly configured websites and exploit them to stealing credit card, personal, and confidential information. While wikis generally do not house much financial or personal information, they can be a place where confidential information is stored. What's worse is that the collaborative and social nature of a wiki makes it a prime target for vandalism.

As running a wiki should be a great experience, we are going to learn some basic steps on how you can provide better security for your wiki. Unfortunately, web application security is a highly specialized field that cannot be taught in the course of this book. What you will learn is a good foundation for how to secure your wiki. I strongly encourage you to read more about web application security. If this is a topic that you feel you need to learn more about, visit `http://www.owasp.org`. Not only do they have a great deal of information, tools, and tutorials, but they have a live site that you can download and learn just how malicious hackers attack sites with step-by-step guides and hands-on exercises. Guess what, they used MediaWiki to build their entire site!

Time for action – stopping bad behavior

One of the biggest concerns for a wiki administrator is that a spam bot will start editing pages on his or her wiki, loading them with spam.

We have seen earlier in the book that certain developers create add-ons for MediaWiki called **extensions**. These extensions greatly increase what we can do with MediaWiki. One important extension deals specifically with MediaWiki security—Bad Behavior. This extension helps prevent spammers by blocking spam bots, preventing e-mail scraping, and helping prevent against vandalism. We are going to install this extension to help secure our site.

1. Download the Bad Behavior extension from `http://www.bad-behavior.ioerror.us/download/`. Make sure to save the file where you can locate it.

2. Move the contents of the file `bad-behavior.2.x.xx.zip` to the MediaWiki `extensions` folder on your server. You can do this using your FTP program (using ASCII mode), where you would have to unzip the file first, and then move them to the folder. You can also upload the zipped file to your server using your file manager and unzip it into the `extensions` folder.

If you are using your FTP program to move the files to your server, you do not have to upload the files: `bad-behavior-lifetype.php`, `bad-behavior-wordpress.php`, or `bad-behavior-wordpress-admin.php`. If you upload the compressed file and unzip it on your server, you can delete these files.

3. Open your `LocalSettings.php` file for editing.

4. Add the lines to the file:
```
//Bad Behavior
include_once( 'includes/DatabaseFunctions.php' );
include( './extensions/bad-behavior/bad-behavior-mediawiki.php' );
```

5. Save your changes.

What just happened?

Installing the extension, Bad Behavior, we helped to protect our site from one of the most common attacks that are launched against wikis, spam. Using this extension, we are making an effort to block spam bots from editing pages in our wiki.

Have a go hero

Bad Behavior 2 is an extended version of the Bad Behavior extension that creates a special page **Special:Bad Behavior** that logs Bad Behavior activity. If you are feeling up to it, go to `http://www.umasswiki.com/wiki/UMassWiki:Bad_Behavior_2_Extended` (another great example of MediaWiki in action!) and follow the instructions for installing the files for Bad Behavior 2.

Bad Behavior 2 actually can behave badly on some systems. If you install these files and proceed to your wiki only to find a host of error messages instead of all your hard work, try two things. First, in the line you add to your `LocalSettings.php` file, `include ( 'extensions/Bad-Behavior/bb2ext.php' );`, making sure that you change `Bad-Behavior` to `bad-behavior` as this is case-sensitive.

If this doesn't work, don't fret. Simply remove the line: `include( 'extensions/Bad-Behavior/bb2ext.php' );` from your `LocalSettings.php` file and your wiki will be fine, however you will lose the functionality of the Bad Behavior extension.

Time for action – checking up on logins

Any seasoned administrator will tell you that the log files are a goldmine of information. When it comes to security, it is the first thing that is looked at when there is a potential breach. As the administrator of a wiki, there will be times when you will need to view log files, and most likely, you will be viewing the user logs.

This next extension makes it easy for the MediaWiki sysop to view these log files. UserLoginLog adds login information to the special page called **Logs**. Now, you can review records for login attempts and see the IP address of the person who logged in, or attempted to log in.

1. Open your browser and point it to `http://www.organicdesign.co.nz/Extension:UserLoginLog.php`. On this page, you will see the following code:

```php
<?php
# Extension:User login log
# - Licenced under LGPL (http://www.gnu.org/copyleft/lesser.html)
# - Author: [http://www.organicdesign.co.nz/nad User:Nad]

if (!defined('MEDIAWIKI')) die('Not an entry point.');

define('USER_LOGIN_LOG_VERSION','1.0.0, 2007-07-30');

$wgServerUser = 1; # User ID to use for logging if no user exists

$wgExtensionFunctions[] = 'wfSetupUserLoginLog';
$wgExtensionCredits['other'][] = array(
        'name'          => 'UserLoginLog',
        'author'        => '[http://www.organicdesign.co.nz/nad
                            User:Nad]',
        'description' => 'Creates a new MediaWiki log for user
                            logins and logout events',
        'url'           => 'http://www.mediawiki.org/wiki/
                            Extension:UserLoginLog',
        'version'       => USER_LOGIN_LOG_VERSION
        );

# Add a new log type
$wgLogTypes[]                        = 'userlogin';
$wgLogNames   ['userlogin']         = 'userloginlogpage';
$wgLogHeaders ['userlogin']         = 'userloginlogpagetext';
$wgLogActions ['userlogin/success'] = 'userlogin-success';
```

```
$wgLogActions['userlogin/error']    = 'userlogin-error';
$wgLogActions['userlogin/logout']   = 'userlogin-logout';

# Add hooks to the login/logout events
$wgHooks['UserLoginForm'][]         = 'wfUserLoginLogError';
$wgHooks['UserLoginComplete'][]     = 'wfUserLoginLogSuccess';
$wgHooks['UserLogout'][]            = 'wfUserLoginLogout';
$wgHooks['UserLogoutComplete'][]    = 'wfUserLoginLogoutComplete';

function wfUserLoginLogSuccess(&$user) {
        $log = new LogPage('userlogin',false);
        $log->addEntry('success',$user->getUserPage(),wfGetIP());
        return true;
        }

function wfUserLoginLogError(&$tmpl) {
        global $wgUser,$wgServerUser;
        if ($tmpl->data['message'] && $tmpl->data['messagetype'] ==
           'error') {
             $log = new LogPage('userlogin',false);
             $tmp = $wgUser->mId;
             if ($tmp == 0) $wgUser->mId = $wgServerUser;
               $log->addEntry('error',$wgUser->getUserPage(),
               $tmpl->data['message'],array(wfGetIP()));
               $wgUser->mId = $tmp;
             }
        return true;
        }

# Create a copy of the current user for logging after logout
function wfUserLoginLogout(&$user) {
        global $wgUserBeforeLogout;
        $wgUserBeforeLogout = User::newFromId($user->getID());
        return true;
        }

function wfUserLoginLogoutComplete(&$user) {
        global $wgUser,$wgUserBeforeLogout;
        $tmp = $wgUser->mId;
        $wgUser->mId = $wgUserBeforeLogout->getId();
        $log = new LogPage('userlogin',false);
```

```
        $log->addEntry('logout',$wgUserBeforeLogout->getUserPage(),
                    $user->getName());
        $wgUser->mId = $tmp;
        return true;
        }


function wfSetupUserLoginLog() {
        global $wgLanguageCode,$wgMessageCache;
        if ($wgLanguageCode == 'en') {
            $wgMessageCache->addMessages(array(
                'userloginlogpage'    => "User login log",
                'userloginlogpagetext' => "This is a log of
                    events associated with users logging in
                    or out of the wiki",
                'userlogin-success'   => "Login completed
                                        successfully",
                'userlogin-error'     => "Login failure from
                                        $2",
                'userlogin-logout'    => "Logout completed
                                        successfully",
                'userloginlogentry'   => ""
                ));
            }


        }
```

2. Copy the code in its entirety.

3. Open a text editor, such as Emacs or Notepad. Paste the code into the text editor.

4. Save the file as `UserLoginLog.php`. If you are using Notepad, make sure to select **All files (*.*)** as the type.

5. Upload this file to the `extensions` folder of your wiki.

6. Open your `LocalSettings.php` file for editing.

7. Add the lines:
```
//User Login Log
include("$IP/extensions/UserLoginLog.php");
// User ID for UserLoginLog extension
$wgServerUser = 101;
```

8. Save your edits.

Open your wiki and log in as the sysop. When you are successfully logged in, go to **SpecialPages | Recent changes and logs** and find the **Logs** page. Click on this link and you will see that it recorded your successful login as shown in the following screenshot:

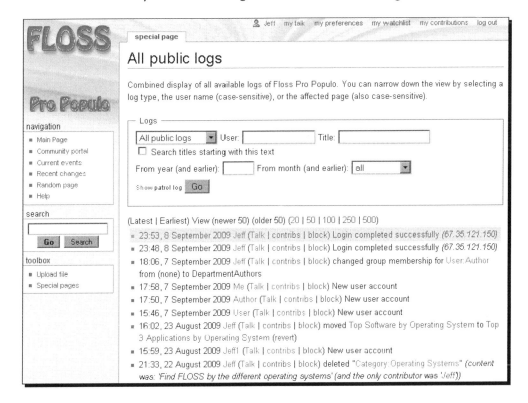

If you are wondering why there are two successive logins with the Jeff account above, that is because I tested it twice!

What just happened?

By adding the UserLoginLog extension, we enhanced the functionality of our MediaWiki's **Logs** page to include login attempts. Now, we can track when people logged in to our wiki and what IP address they used should we ever need to research an act of vandalism or a security breach.

Have a go hero

As previously stated, log files can be an administrator's best friend when it comes to troubleshooting or security. Read up on the different log files that MediaWiki offers to you and take some time to look through them. The more comfortable you are with the log files, the easier your job will be when your wiki rivals Wikipedia in content!

Best practices

As the administrator, you have to perform some checks on regular basis. It is better if you make a checklist of all the required actions and go through them at least once a week (or more frequently if required). Following are the checks that you must perform:

Stay up-to-date

It is always important to stay up-to-date regarding the installed software. We are not installing a final product. We have to remember that frequently we have a version release for MediaWiki. Each version contains a release note. Go through the release note and see if any vulnerability has been fixed. Even if it does not contain any security update, it is always better to update the server software. It is not just MediaWiki that needs to be updated—we have to update PHP, MySQL, and other installed software in our web server as well. In order to get messages from MediaWiki about updates and news, you can subscribe to the following site for e-mail notifications: `http://mail.wikipedia.org/mailman/listinfo/mediawiki-announce`.

PHP recommendations

If you are using a shared host, then you might not have access to the PHP setup file. However, if you are running a dedicated server or your local server at home or in your office, you can set up the PHP configuration file yourself. If you do not have access to the PHP setup file, talk to your hosting provider about what steps they have taken to secure your site. They may have already taken these steps, or may be willing to do this for you. The filename is `php.ini`. It is located under `c:\windows\php.ini` on Windows, and under `/etc/php.ini` in a Linux environment. Here are some recommendations:

- **Disable** `register_globals`: Many PHP security attacks are based on injection of global variable values, and so, making sure it's off can plug many potential vulnerabilities. MediaWiki should be safe even if this is on; turning this off is a precaution against the possibility of unknown vulnerabilities.

- **Unless you require it specifically, disable** `allow_url_fopen`: Remote PHP code execution vulnerabilities may depend on being able to inject a URL into `include()` or `require()`. If you don't require the use of remote file loading, turning this off can prevent attacks of this kind on vulnerable code.

- **Disable** `session.use_trans_sid`: If this is on, session IDs may be added to URLs sometimes if cookies aren't doing their thing. This can leak login session data to third-party sites through referrer data or cutting and pasting of links. You should always turn this off if it's on.

MySQL recommendations

In general, you should keep access to your MySQL database to a minimum. If it will only be used from the single machine it's running on, consider disabling networking support. If it will be used over a network with a limited number of client machines, consider setting the IP firewall rules to accept access to TCP port 3306 for MySQL only from those machines or only from your local subnet, and reject all accesses from the larger Internet. This can help prevent accidentally opening access to your server due to some unknown flaw in MySQL, a mistakenly set overbroad GRANT, or a leaked password.

If you create a new MySQL user for MediaWiki through MediaWiki's installer, somewhat liberal access is granted to it to ensure that it will work from a second server as well as a local one. You might consider manually narrowing this or establishing the user account yourself with custom permissions for just the places you need.

Summary

In this chapter, we saw that there is more to running a MediaWiki site than writing good content. As our wiki grows and we add users, we will have to decide what we will allow our users to do on the wiki. We learned that through proper management of the user groups, we can take away privileges and provide users with extra privileges.

By default, MediaWiki is rather restrictive in what type of files it allows us to upload. However, to be a truly collaborative site, we may need to make changes that give our users a bit more of an option. We learned that we can control the type of files we allow our users to upload to our wiki if we have enough trust in our user base.

Finally, we approached the subject of security. We were able to install two extensions that will help keep our wiki more secure and we learned of some best practices we need to follow as an administrator.

In the next chapter, we are going to tackle how we can manage a multi-user environment. With the knowledge we gained so far, this should be a breeze.

9
Multi-user Environment

Throughout the course of this book we have emphasized how well MediaWiki performs as a collaborative tool. In the previous chapter, The MediaWiki Administrator, we were introduced to how we can restrict users from adding or editing content. We have even seen specific examples of how organizations use MediaWiki as the platform to deliver content with no option for editing or creating. Even though these options exist, in its truest form, a wiki is a collaborative environment. This means we may have multiple users accessing the system and participating in building the wiki. The count might be more than few thousands for a given moment if the site is popular. With any platform that caters to a diverse group of people, issues are bound to arise. Contributors may make mistakes in their articles, there may be conflicts over changes made to a page, and many other issues can arise when dealing with people.

Working in a multi-user environment definitely has its advantages, but as a wiki administrator, it is important to keep in mind that not all users have good intentions. As the system is open, anyone—including malicious users with bad intentions—can partake in any activity on the site. An open system can face a lot of user-related problems. The first major problem is that anyone can edit or add contents. This can be dangerous if the added content is not legal or if it is copyrighted. As the user can avoid being tracked, the site has to take the responsibility for such acts. Another major attack can be on the content itself—people with bad intentions can change content without any reason or present false information. Vandalism is also a common occurrence on such sites, and the concerns regarding false information have plagued even the most well-respected of sites—Wikipedia.

In this chapter, we will take a detailed look at these issues and learn how we can address them.

This chapter will be broken into three sections: User Accounts, Administration, and Community. Under these three sections, we will look specifically at:

◆   How the user can change their profile

◆   How the user can change editing preferences

◆   How the administrator can monitor content

◆   How to block users

◆   How to revert to an original page

◆   Setting up and using talk pages

◆   Resolving editing conflicts

Let's take a look at how we can manage a wiki where there will be multiple users so we can make it a community where people are encouraged to visit.

Users

We have seen in previous chapters how to create user accounts. In the previous chapter, we learned how we can restrict what the users can do on our wiki. While preventing guests from creating articles and making edits takes away from the spirit of the wiki, it is sometimes a necessity. Requiring users to be registered is known as **privileged access**. If the site is protected by privileged access, then it is obvious that the site will be more secure than an open system. Most of the privileged access is provided by having user accounts with different levels of **access type**. A username separates one identity from those of other people. There are many advantages of user accounts and privileges; some of them are as follows:

◆   The system can be set such that adding, editing, and deleting content may be performed only by registered users who are logged in to the system.

◆   Users can set their preferences such as skins, time zones, file format, and so on.

◆   User can be identified by a name rather than the IP address of the user's machine. So even if a single user accesses from multiple machines, he or she will be identified by his or her username rather than IP addresses.

◆   Usernames are easier to remember than IP addresses.

◆   Users can have their personal profile pages based on their user account names, and this helps others to learn about them.

- User accounts give more flexibility when accessing content. Sometimes an administrator may block an IP address in order to stop malicious users from vandalizing a site. However, if the IP address is shared between multiple users, then it is not very wise to block it as this would stop more than one person from accessing the site. However, if we block a user account instead, then other users from the same IP address can still access the system.

- Users can create their own preferences for articles and monitor different topics, and even get notified about certain changes to the site.

You can see from this list that not only do user accounts help make our wiki more secure and manageable, but they give the user more options as well. In the following exercises, we will look at how the user can benefit from having a registered account.

Preferences

When it comes to how an individual user sees and uses your wiki, quite a bit can be changed from the user's **Preferences** page. Clicking on the **my preferences** link users can alter their preferences in any one of the following tabs:

- **User profile**
- **Skin**
- **Math**
- **Files**
- **Date and time**
- **Editing**
- **Recent changes**
- **Watchlist**
- **Search**
- **Misc**

With changes in the version of the software, the preferences can change too. However, these are the common preferences that you will find upon clicking **my preferences** on the top navigation panel once you are logged in.

User profile

The **User profile** details the user's personal information. The profile can be accessed when a user first creates an account because once they click on the **Create account** button, they are taken to a page confirming their account as shown in the following screenshot:

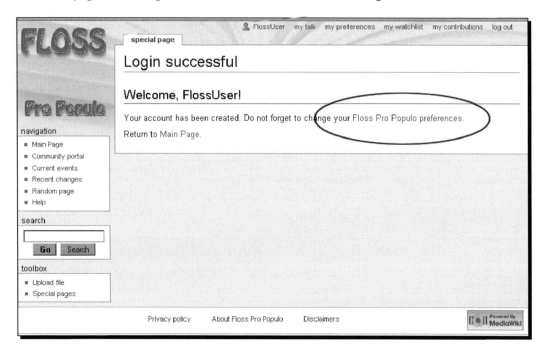

By clicking on the link shown in the previous screenshot, the user is taken immediately to their **Preferences** page. However, if the user needs to make changes to their profile at a later date, they have to go through a different route.

Time for action – changing the user profile

In this exercise, we are going to update our user profile to include our real name and e-mail address so we can receive notifications when certain things are done to pages that we are watching or have created. We are also going to learn how to change the signature for our profile so that when we use the syntax to insert our signature on a page, it will appear differently than our username which is the default.

1. Open your wiki and sign in as the user whose profile you need to change.

2. When you are at the **Main page**, click on the **my preferences** tab at the top of the screen:

3. After clicking on the tab, you will be taken to the **Preferences** page. This page is broken down into three sections, **User profile**, **Change password**, and **E-mail**.

4. If you have not done so, you can enter your **Real name** and **E-mail** address to your profile. These are optional fields, however, you have to provide an e-mail address if you want notification on changes made to pages and your user talk page, or even on simple or minor edits (such as spelling change, missed words, and so on) made on your created or watch page.

5. In the **Signature** box, define what you want your signature to be when you enter ~~~ or ~~~~ in an article. Using ~~~ will display only the signature while using ~~~~ will display the signature and timestamp. For example purposes, we will enter **Jeff as Floss User** in the textbox. For your user account, enter whatever you wish. If you leave this blank, your user name will appear when you add the signature syntax in the wiki.

Treat signature as wikitext

If **Treat signature as wikitext** (without automatic link) is unchecked, then:

- The software enters [[User:Name| in front of your nickname text, and]] after it.

- Any characters in your nickname that would otherwise constitute wiki markup and HTML markup are escaped as HTML character entities. A nickname of]] | [[User talk:Name|Talk will thus produce a signature of]] | [[User talk:Name|Talk, which is probably not what you want.

If **Treat signature as wikitext** (without automatic link) is checked, then:
- Nothing is added to the text that you specify. What you specify is what is used between the two dashes and the timestamp.

- Wiki markup and HTML markup are not escaped, allowing you to include links, font tags, images, and templates in your signature.

6. Make any changes to the **E-mail** section. For the example, we added a check to **E-mail me when a page on my watchlist is changed**.

7. When your changes have been made, click on **Save**. If you provided an e-mail address, you will be notified that the confirmation will be sent to this address. The following screenshot shows the changes we made:

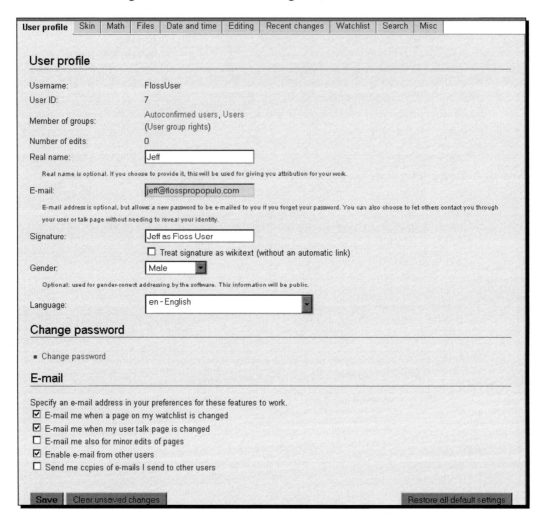

After saving, you may have to bypass your browser's cache to see the changes.

- **Mozilla / Firefox / Safari**: Hold down *Shift* while clicking **Reload**, or press *Ctrl+Shift+R* (*Cmd+Shift+R* on Apple Mac).
- **IE**: Hold *Ctrl* while clicking **Refresh**, or press *Ctrl+F5*.
- **Konqueror**: Simply click the **Reload** button, or press *F5*.
- **Opera**: Completely clear their cache in **Tools | Preferences**.

What just happened?

After creating a user account, we went into the **Preferences** page using the **my preferences** link, to update our **User profile** and tell MediaWiki how and when to notify us when using our e-mail address. After completing this exercise, we can begin to see how the users can control what they can do with MediaWiki. Also, we were able to see where we can change our password should we need to do that at a later date.

You can also change your **Gender** and the preferred **Language** on this page. Should you make any changes that you later regret, simply click on the **Restore all default settings** button.

Skins

A MediaWiki skin is the style in which a page is displayed. Different stylesheets are used to define the different skins so it's not the body of the page that changes, but rather the HTML code. The default skin used is the MonoBook skin. This is what we have been viewing in our wiki site all this time. From the **Preferences** section, you can click the **Skin** tab to show all the skins available for your wiki. You can preview the skins by clicking the **Preview** link just beside each skin's name. When you install MediaWiki, there are eight skins that are installed by default:

- **Chick**
- **Classic**
- **Cologne Blue**
- **Modern**
- **MonoBook**
- **MySkin**
- **Nostalgia**
- **Simple**

Time for action – changing the skin

Changing the skin is extremely easy to do. Before you go ahead and make a change, preview each of the skins to see which one you prefer. When you click on the **Preview** link, a new window will open displaying your **Main page** using the selected skin. Don't worry, no changes have been made yet! Once you find a skin you like, follow these steps to make the change permanent:

1. If you have not done so, open your wiki and log in.

2. Navigate to the skins page by clicking the **my preferences** link and then the **Skins** tab.

3. Select the radio button for the skin you would like to use. For the example, we will be using **Cologne Blue**.

4. Click on **Save**.

If you are following along, you should see your **Preferences** page with the new skin applied as shown in the following screenshot:

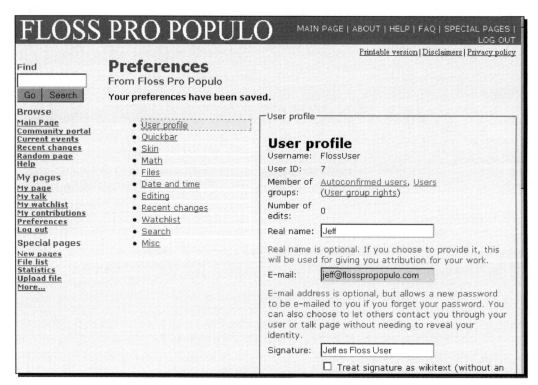

What just happened?

With a quick click of the mouse, we were able to change the way our wiki looks. To clarify things, this is the way the wiki will appear to the individual user. Changing the skin will not change how the wiki appears to other visitors.

We will see in Chapter 10, *Advanced Customization*, how we can find new skins for our wiki and even how to go in and change the HTML and CSS for existing skins to make them fit our own design styles.

To prevent users from changing their skins, you can remove the **Skin** tab from the **Preferences** page by setting the `$wgAllowUserSkin` option in `LocalSettings.php` to `false`.

Editing preferences

The **Editing** tab allows the user to change the different options available when editing content on a page. While most of the changes made only require you to use a check box, you also have the option of setting the number of **Rows** and **Columns** in the edit box by changing the default numbers. It is important to note that certain features; **Enable section editing by right clicking on section titles**, **Edit pages on double click**, and **Show edit toolbar** all require JavaScript to be enabled in order for them to work.

Time for action – changing the editing preferences

So far, making changes to the preferences has been relatively easy. Changing the editing preferences is simple as well. In this exercise, we are going to set the editing preferences so that we see a preview on the first edit and we are prompted every time we leave the summary section blank.

1. If you haven't done so, open your wiki and log in.

2. Click on the **my preferences** link. When you are on the **Preferences** page, select the **Editing** tab.

3. In the **Editing** section, locate the line that reads: **Show preview on first edit** and place a check next to it.

4. Locate the line that reads: **Prompt me when entering a blank edit summary** and place a check next to it.

5. Click on **Save**.

Before you click on **Save**, your screen should look similar to the following screenshot:

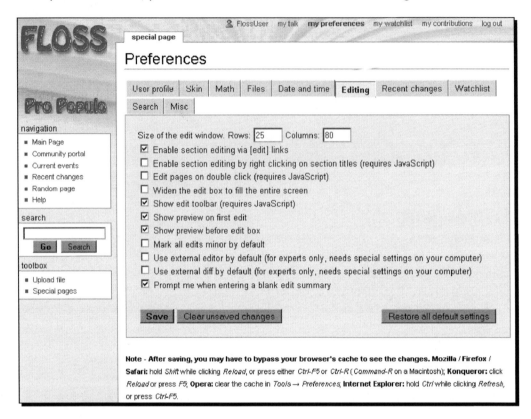

Once you click on the **Save** button, you will be taken back to the main **Preferences** screen and a box will inform you that **Your preferences have been saved**.

What just happened?

When adjusting the preferences for the user, we changed the default editing settings. Now, whenever we edit a page for the first time, we will automatically see a preview of the changes. Also, whenever we leave the editing summary blank, we will be notified as shown in the following screenshot:

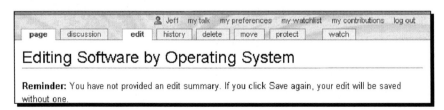

Have a go hero

We have seen how easy it is to change the prefrences of a user. As we have only looked at three of the available tabs, take some time to look through the remaining sections. While you are exploring these, make whatever changes you feel are necessary for your account. Remember, if you change things and need to revert to the default settings, you can always click on the **Restore all default settings** button.

> Restore all default settings

Administration

Users have it easy in the multi-user environment. All they have to do is change the preferences on their account to differentiate themselves from the rest of the group. As a sysop, the management of a multi-user wiki is not so simple.

To make sure your wiki runs smoothly and provides up-to-date, accurate content to your visitors, you have to be on top of things. One of the most difficult tasks is the monitoring of content. As stated before, it is unfortunate that a public wiki is always at risk for vandalism and inaccurate content. Even corporate wikis that only allow certain individuals to create and edit content requires diligence on the part of the sysop. While vandalism is less of a concern, working with multiple authors can present many challenges, especially when it comes to editing pages.

All the exercises we perform in this section of the chapter will all help the sysop maintain the integrity of their wiki's content.

Page history

There will be times when you need to view all of the edits that have taken place on a particular page. Perhaps you have a corporate wiki and someone made a change to a policy that effects an upcoming lawsuit against your company. Your boss may be interested when this took place. Perhaps you have a public wiki and someone came in vandalized a few pages. The page history can help you locate the culprit and block them from access (this is coming up later in this section).

Each page, except **Special pages,** contains a history of all the changes made to that page. This is known as the **page history**, though it is also called **edit history**. It consists of the old versions of the wiki text, as well as a record of the date and time of each edit, the user name or IP address of the user who edited it, and the edit summary they included. This history tool can be used to track changes very easily and is accessed by clicking the **history** tab at the top of the page. Page history is the most suitable option for tracking changes related to the page. We can also revert changes from the history which we will learn later in the *Community* section of this chapter. Having a solid understanding of the way the page history functions will help the sysop in many different ways.

Time for action – viewing the page history

When viewing the page history, you will see that edits are listed from newest to oldest. Also, each edit will take up one line to show the time and date of the edit, the contributor's name (or IP address if they are a guest), the edit summary, and other information helpful to the sysop. In this exercise, we are going to see how we can view this information, but more importantly, how we can use this information.

> **1.** Open your wiki and log in. Open up a document that you have made some changes to.

> **2.** Click on the **history** tab at the top of the page. You will be taken to a page that looks similar the following screenshot. Notice that we have separated this page into three different sections: one area where you can search the page history by year and month, one area where you can determine how many results are displayed, and the list of page edits.

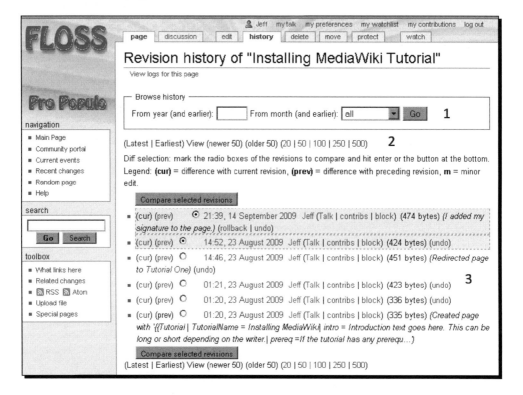

In the list of page edits, you can see that the edit summary is included. For example, in the first line dated **21:39, 14 September 2009** the words **I added my signature to the page** are in parenthesis and italicized, designating them as the edit summary.

3. Looking at the page history section, you will see the words **(cur)** and **(prev)**. These are used to take you to a new page called **diff** page, as seen in the following screenshot. A diff page is a page where the difference between the two versions is shown. The first item on the line, **(cur)**, shows you the current revision that appears below the changes, so you can see how the page is now rendered. On the other hand, **(prev)** takes you to a diff page showing the changes between that edit and the previous version. The later version (the one on the same line as the last you clicked on) appears below the changes; so you can see how the page was rendered. The two columns of radio buttons can be used to select and compare any two versions of the page. As we proceed through this exercise, we will compare the version from **21:39, 14 September 2009** to the one from **01:21, 23 August 2009**.

4. Click the left-column radio button next to the line for **01:21, 23 August 2009**. The right column is then populated with buttons till the row before this line.

5. Click the right-column button next to the line that reads **21:39, 14 September 2009**.

6. Now, click **Compare selected versions**. This takes you to a diff page showing the changes between the two versions. The more recent version (in this case, line **21:39, 14 September 2009**) appears below the changes, so you can see how the page was rendered as shown in the following screenshot:

What just happened?

By clicking on the **history** tab for a page, we are able to see a history of all edits made to that page. We are able to see the date and time each edit took place, and also the user who made the change. If we know that a specific user vandalized pages on our site, we can look through the page history of other pages as well to see if he or she made any edits to them.

We also saw that we can compare the changes between versions of a page as well. By selecting the version we want and clicking on the **Compare selected revisions** button, we are presented with a side-by-side comparison of how the pages are different.

Having this available to us can make our job as the sysop of a multi-user wiki much easier because we can see exactly which users have contributed to a page and when. Of course, how this information is put to use can serve endless possibilities.

Recent changes

By clicking on the **Recent changes** link in the **navigation** box, you are taken to a page that gives you the whole list of changes made in the wiki site, aptly named **Recent changes**. This page is great for sysop because it gives you a listing of newly-added pages, changes and edits, reverted pages with history, differences, and a lot of other options. Using this page, users can monitor and review the work of other users. Regular checks of this page by the wiki administrator means mistakes can be corrected and vandalism can be eliminated more quickly.

You can also create a link to the page as `[[Special:Recentchanges]]`.

Recent changes page looks as shown in the following screenshot:

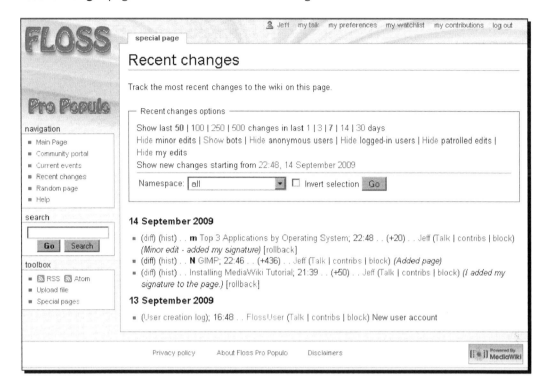

The previous screenshot shows recent changes occurred over two days. Let's look at what what each entry means, from left to right:

♦ The first thing on the list is a **diff** link. This links to the diff page for this edit; it is not available for new pages or for page moves. The entry under **14 September 2009** for **GIMP** is a new page, however the **diff** is not a link.

♦ The **hist** link corresponds to the page history on the edited page; it shows not just this edit but also older and newer ones. For page moves, the **hist** link leads to the history of the new page title.

♦ A bold **m** indicates that the user marked the edit minor. Only logged-in users can mark an edit as minor to avoid abuse. An example of a minor edit is seen in the entry for **Top 3 Applications by Operating Systems** on September 14.

♦ A bold **N** indicates that the page is new. It is possible for a change to possess both the minor and new indicators; this is typically used for new redirects. In the example, the page for **GIMP** created on September 14 is a new page.

♦ A bold **!** indicates that the page is unpatrolled. We will focus on patrolled and unpatrolled edits at the end of this chapter.

- The next link is a link to the current version of the page.

- Next is the time in UTC format. You can change the time to your time zone using the preferences that we have just learned.

- The next link is a link to the user's home page. Note this is not a link to your home page, rather the user who edited or created the page's.

- The next link points to the user's talk page.

- The **contribs** link points to the **User contribution** page listing all of his or her contributions.

 When we do a page move, a link is provided for the old as well as the new title after the **user talk** link in **Recent changes**.

We can also filter our Recent changes list with the options provided in the page. We can hide minor edits from being shown in the Recent changes list. We can also hide patrolled edit and logged-in-user information. We can filter the changed list by namespace. We can also choose the number of edits and days for the Recent changes list.

It is always important and good practice to go through the **Recent changes** page in order to view latest changes made to the site. The topic you are going to add may be found there. Maybe somebody else has just added that; you can reduce redundancy here. You can also view the list to check if any page has been changed..

Pop quiz – Recent changes

Now, it's time to see how much you learned about **Recent changes**.

1. Which designates a new page?

   a. !

   b. N

   c. NEW

   d. m

2. A lowercase m (m) signifies:

   a. a minor edit

   b. a major edit

   c. a malicious user

   d. a moniker

3. Vandalized pages are signified by a:

    a. V

    b. X

    c. !

    d. nothing

4. You can change your timezone from the **Recent changes** page.

    a. True

    b. False

5. The maximum number of changes you can show at one time is:

    a. 25

    b. 100

    c. 250

    d. 500

Watching pages

Even the smallest of wikis can easily grow to hundreds of pages. This being said, it is easy to see how it can become nearly impossible to find all the changes made to your edits, or to pages that you created. MediaWiki has a wonderful feature to address this problem. It is called *watching a page*. You can watch any page you want, even if you didn't create it or edit it in any way.

 If you watch a page, that page will be added to your **watchlist**. When the page has been changed, edited, or added to, you will get an automatic notification from the system based on your preference setting (remember when we added our e-mail address). Also, on your watchlist page, all the pages that have been modified since your last visit will be shown in bold so you can easily identify the changes.

Time for action – watch a page and revert

In this exercise, we are going to watch a page that is very important to us. As the administrator, there will most likely be certain pages you need to keep an eye on. Users too may want to watch certain pages for changes, such as a page that addresses workplace policies in a corporate wiki, or perhaps you follow a wiki like Joomla!'s documentation site. Wouldn't it be nice to know when the documentation has been updated to match their latest version?

1. Open your wiki and log in.

2. Navigate to the page you wish to watch.

3. Click on the **watch** tab at the top of the page. You will now be told that the page you selected has been added to your **watchlist** as seen in the following screenshot:

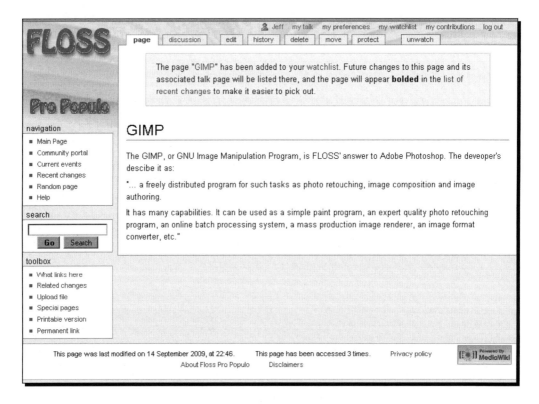

When you visit the page again, there will be an **unwatch** tab instead of **watch**. If you wish to stop watching the page, click this tab and you will no longer be watching the page.

Another way to watch

You can also choose to watch a page when you create or edit it. At the bottom of the page in the editing window, you have the option to **Watch this page**. Simply check this box before you save the page.

What just happened?

Simply clicking on the **watch** tab of a page adds it to our watchlist. Now, we can keep a close eye on any changes made to that page. We may do this because we are the page creator, the wiki administrator, or just an interested reader.

Once we have added pages to our watchlist, we simply click the **my watchlist** link at the top of the screen. When we are taken to our watchlist, it will look similar to the following screenshot:

Revert changes

So, what happens if somebody completely destroys your page? Or if another user edits someone's article, but all the grammar is wrong. Or perhaps you went in to change a bunch of dates on your wiki only to realize later that you entered the wrong year in your edits. Have no fear; MediaWiki can help fix any one of these scenarios. Any time you need to go back to the original content of a page, you can **revert**. When we use the revert function, the page goes back to its original form.

Time for action – reverting to previous content

In our example, it appears that someone has not only changed the text for one of our pages, but someone has vandalized it as well. While one edit may be a legitimate change, as the sysop we don't want this page edited by the public, so we are going to revert to the previous page. In the case of vandalism, we have no other choice than to go back to the clean version of the page. The following screenshot shows the two changes made to the page. Following the screenshot, we will learn how to revert to the original page.

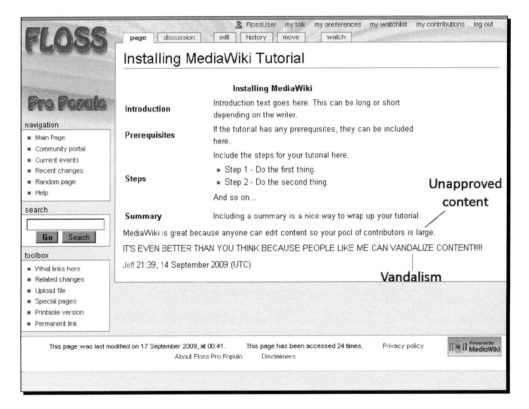

1. Open your wiki and navigate to the page you wish to make changes to.

2. Click on the **history** tab at the top of the page and you will be taken to the page history. Locate the time and date of the revision you wish to revert to.

```
Compare selected revisions

▪ (cur) (prev)    ⊙ 00:41, 17 September 2009  FlossUser (Talk | contribs) (648 bytes) (No
  comments for you!) (undo)
▪ (cur) (prev) ⊙    00:39, 17 September 2009  Jeff (Talk | contribs) (565 bytes) (Added a bit of text
  to the bottom.) (undo)
▪ (cur) (prev) ○    21:39, 14 September 2009  Jeff (Talk | contribs) (474 bytes) (I added my
  signature to the page.) (undo)
▪ (cur) (prev) ○    14:52, 23 August 2009  Jeff (Talk | contribs) (424 bytes) (undo)
▪ (cur) (prev) ○    14:46, 23 August 2009  Jeff (Talk | contribs) (451 bytes) (Redirected page to
  Tutorial One) (undo)
▪ (cur) (prev) ○    01:21, 23 August 2009  Jeff (Talk | contribs) (423 bytes) (undo)
▪ (cur) (prev) ○    01:20, 23 August 2009  Jeff (Talk | contribs) (336 bytes) (undo)
▪ (cur) (prev) ○    01:20, 23 August 2009  Jeff (Talk | contribs) (335 bytes) (Created page with
  '{{Tutorial | TutorialName = Installing MediaWiki| intro = Introduction text goes here. This can be
  long or short depending on the writer.| prereq =If the tutorial has any prerequ...')
```

3. Click on the time and date link. In our example, we selected **21:39, 14 September 2009**.

4. We will now be taken to the page that existed on that date, and at that time.

5. Click on the **edit** tab at the top of the page. You will now be taken to the editing page. As we are reverting, we don't need to make any changes. It is good practice to put something in the edit summary referring to the fact that you reverted to an earlier page.

6. Click on **Save page**. A newline will be added to the page history reflecting the changes you just made as shown in the following screenshot:

```
▪ (cur) (prev)    ⊙ 00:58, 17 September 2009  FlossUser (Talk | contribs) (474 bytes) (Revert)
  (undo)
```

In the case of vandalism, it may be wise to check the contribution history of the user who vandalized the article by clicking on their IP address or user name. Clicking on their IP will often bring you directly to their user contribution page. If you are able to click on their user name, that will bring you to their user page. In the lower-left corner, there is a toolbox with a **User contributions** link. Click on this link. If this user is vandalizing many articles, you may need to take action.

What just happened?

When we noticed that our page had been edited and we did not approve of the changes, we used the page history to revert to an earlier version of the content that met our approval. In our example, we were able to revert from a legitimate change as well as an attack by a vandal. We also learned that when a vandal strikes our wiki, we may want to check their **User contributions** page to see what other articles they may have wreaked havoc on.

More administrative tools

MediaWiki has quite a few more tools that the administrator can use to help monitor a multi-user wiki. While some of these have been mentioned already in the text, such as edit summaries and minor changes, they need further explanation.

Edit summaries

We had a brief discussion about edit summaries in the last exercise when we were reverting to an earlier revision of a page. It is highly recommended that anyone editing a page fills in the **Summary** field because it makes it easier for you and your fellow contributors to understand what has been changed. It is also extremely helpful when going through the history of the page.

The edit summary box can hold one line of 200 characters. If you attempt to enter more than this, only the first 200 characters will be displayed and the rest will be disregarded. In the case of a small addition to an article, it is highly recommended the full text of this addition be copied to the **Summary** field, giving a maximum of information with a minimum of effort. This way, readers of the summary will be unlikely to check the page itself as they already know the extent of the edit. These kinds of summaries allow users to check **Recent changes**, page history, and **User contributions** very efficiently.

In addition to a summary of the change itself, the **Summary** field may also contain an explanation of the change. Note that if the reason for an edit is not clear, it is more likely to be reverted, especially in the case that some text is deleted. To give a longer explanation, use the talk page and make a note about it in the edit summary.

After saving the page, the summary cannot be edited, so try to avoid any errors.

Minor changes

If you look at the previous screenshot, you will see a check box labeled **This is a minor edit**. **Minor edits** have been glossed over in this chapter but now, we will give them a bit more attention.

When editing a page, logged-in users may mark a change to a page as a minor edit. Minor edits deal with changes such as correcting a type, changing the format of the content, or changing the presentation of the content. Minor edits usually do not involve changing the actual content of the page.

By contrast, a major edit makes the article worth reviewing for anyone who watches it closely. Therefore, any change that affects the meaning of an article is not minor, even if it involves one word.

The distinction between major and minor edits is significant because you may decide to ignore minor edits when viewing recent changes. Logged-in users can even set their preferences to not display such edits. No one wants to be fooled into ignoring a significant change to an article simply because it was marked minor, of course. So remember to consider the opinions of other editors when choosing this option.

Users who are not logged into the wiki are not able to mark changes as minor because of the potential for vandalism. The ability to mark changes as minor is another way you can entice your visitors to register.

It is always better to mark the edit as minor if you are doing the following changes:

- ◆ Spelling corrections
- ◆ Simple formatting (capitalization, bold, italics, and so on)
- ◆ Formatting that does not change the meaning of the page (for example, adding horizontal lines or splitting a paragraph into two where such splitting isn't contentious)
- ◆ Obvious factual errors (changing 1873 to 1973, where the event in question clearly took place in 1973)
- ◆ Fixing layout errors

We have to remember the following things when we are marking an edit as minor edit:

- ◆ Any change to the wikitext, even if it does not affect the presentation of the page in HTML (for example, adding a space or a line break), will still be treated as a change according to the database.
- ◆ Marking a major change as a minor one is considered bad manners, especially if the change involves the deletion of some text.

◆ Reverting pages is not likely to be considered minor under most circumstances. When the status of a page is disputed, and particularly if an edit war is brewing, then it's better not to mark any edit as minor. Reverting blatant vandalism is an exception to this rule.

◆ A user's watchlist will only list the most recent change made to a page, even if that edit was minor. Therefore, a minor change will supersede a major one in the watchlist. This is because a user who keeps a watchlist is generally interested in all changes made to a page. If you are uncertain about the changes made to a page, double-check the page history.

◆ If you accidentally mark an edit as minor when it was in fact a major edit, you should make a second "dummy" edit, but make a note in the edit summary that "the previous edit was major". As a trivial edit to be made for this purpose, just opening the edit box and saving (changing nothing) will not work, neither will adding a blank space at the end of a line or a blank line at the end of the page—in these cases the edit is canceled and its summary discarded. However, you can add an extra space between two words, or can even add a line break. These changes are preserved in the wikitext and recorded as a change, although they do not change the rendered page.

◆ It may be worth communicating any disagreement about what is minor via **Talk** or a message to the contributor, being careful to avoid a flame war with other users. There is a gray area here, and many contributors will appreciate feedback on whether they've got it right.

It is also good to remember the following terms since we are using them every now and then:

◆ **Dummy edit**: A dummy edit is a change in wikitext that has little or no effect on the rendered page, but saves a useful dummy edit summary. The dummy edit summary can be used for text messaging, and correcting a previous edit summary such as an accidental marking of a previous edit as "minor". Text messaging via the edit summary is a way of communicating with other editors. Text messages may be seen by dotted IP number editors who don't have a user talk page, or editors who haven't read the subject's talk page, if it exists. A dummy edit should be checked as "minor" by logged-in editors. Consider the following example:

Changing the number of newlines in the edit text, such as putting a newline where no newline exists or adding one more newline to two existing newlines, has no effect on the rendered page. But changing from one newline to two newlines makes a rendered difference as it creates spacing between the contents in Mediawiki and may not be a dummy edit. Adding newlines to the end of the article will not save as a dummy edit.

 Dotted IP number editors are editors who are referred to by their IP address in the dotted decimal notation rather than a username, for example, 192.168.1.230.

◆ **Null edit**: A null edit occurs if a page save is made when the wikitext is not changed, which is useful for refreshing the cache. A null edit will not record an edit, make any entry in the page history in recent changes, and so on. The edit summary is discarded. Consider the following examples:

  ❑ Opening the edit window and saving.

  ❑ Adding newlines only to the end of the article and saving is also a null edit.

Pop quiz – edits

So, are you ready to test what you have learned about edits in MediaWiki? Try the following quiz to see what you have learned so far.

1. How many characters can the edit summary textbox hold?

    a. 200

    b. 400

    c. 600

    d. 1000

2. Major edits always require an edit summary.

    a. True

    b. False

3. Which of the following would not be considered a minor edit?

    a. Changing the date of fall of the Berlin wall from 1998 to 1989

    b. Adding a horizontal rule underneath the page title

    c. Adding a section about Neil Armstrong to a page about lunar landings

    d. Making the words "Berlin wall" appear in italicized font

4. Dummy edits can be used to send text messages to the editors.

    a. True

    b. False

5. When the wikitext changes, you can use a Null edit.

    a. True

    b. False

Your wiki's community

As stated many times throughout the book, a wiki is used best when it is a tool that the community can use. In order for the community to collaborate and use the wiki effectively, we need to make sure that as the sysop, we do our job and allow communication between the users. In this section, we will look at a few tools that MediaWiki has in place to help facilitate communication among the wiki' s users. We will also see how extensions can help make our job as sysops easier, while making the end user's experience richer as well.

Talk pages

The first method of communication among the wiki users should be the **talk pages**. There are two types of talk pages: **standard talk pages** are used to discuss an article, and **user talk pages** are used to communicate with other users or leave them messages. Every page has an associated talk page, except pages in the **Special** namespace. If there is no discussion for a page, the link to its talk page will be red. You can still use this feature, you will just be the first person to do so.

Time for action – starting a conversation on a standard talk page

Let's suppose you come across an article that you would like to see more information on. In the sample that we have created, let's say that a registered visitor wants to see a bit more information for the page titled, **Best software**. The visitor can use the talk page to introduce his or her ideas about the page. Let's see how this can be done.

1. Log in to your wiki and select an article to begin discussing. For our example, we are using the **Best software page**.

2. Click on the **discussion** tab at the top of the page.

3. The talk page will now open. Type whatever you wish to communicate. In the example, we wrote:

    ```
    I would like to see a description of each software package so I
    know what they can do. Does anyone know them well enough to do
    this? ~~~~
    ```

    The four tildes (~) at the end will leave our signature.

4. Click on **Save page**. Your page will now look similar to the following screenshot:

Now the editor of the page, if they are paying attention, can respond to FLOSSuser's request for more information. By opening the discussion page and clicking on the **edit** tab, they can respond. As they would be responding to FLOSSuser's question, they should lead off their discussion with a colon (:) to indent the text like this:

```
:I like that idea. I will be updating this page shortly so that you
and the other visitors will know what each software package is used
for. Are there any other requests? ~~~~
```

Now, FLOSSuser can also make use of the colon (:) when responding, only they would use two colons to indent even further:

```
::Yes, if you have a screenshot for each one I would appreciate that
as well! Thanks. ~~~~
```

The following screenshot shows that the discussion is nicely organized:

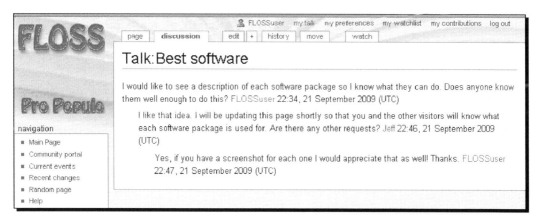

Time for action – starting a conversation on a user talk page

Just as we are able to converse with others through standard talk pages, we can leave messages for others through their user talk page as well. The wikitext formatting is the same; the only real difference comes in how we find a user's page. In this example, FLOSSuser will be leaving a message on Jeff's user talk page.

1. Log in to the wiki.

2. To access a user's talk page, you need to click on their name in their signature (this will be in red, not the standard blue). Open an article that contains their signature and click on the link.

3. If no discussion has been started, you will be brought to the page as shown in the following screenshot:

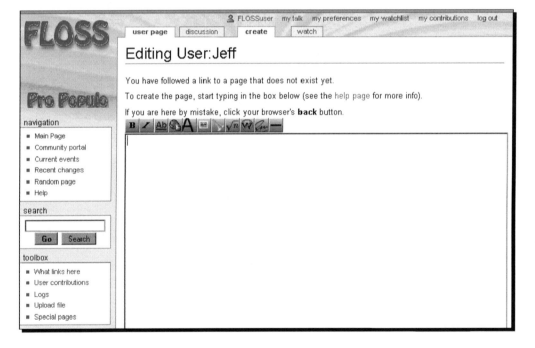

4. This is similar to the newly-created standard talk page in the previous exercise.

5. Add your comments to the user. For our example, we will write:

```
Thank you for making the changes to the Best Software page. I am
a regular contributor to Ubuntu. Do you mind if I create some GNU/
Linux and Ubuntu pages? ~~~~
```

6. Click on **Save page**.

Of course, Jeff can then respond on FLOSSuser's page.

What just happened?

We learned two primary ways of communicating with other members of the community, through standard talk pages where we can discuss things related to a page and through user talk pages where we can interact directly with another user. Talk pages are great because they help develop a sense of community among your visitors. If you, as the administrator, encourage the use of talk pages, you will find that you have to worry about edit wars among users.

Talk page rules

If you look at Wikipedia, they have a page dedicated to how a user should format discussions on the talk pages. I would suggest that you do the same for your wiki.

Conflicts

If you have a large user base, there may be times where one user, let's say Jeff, is editing a page for spelling mistakes. Meanwhile, FLOSSuser is making some heavy content changes to the article. Jeff makes his few changes and saves the page. Meanwhile, FLOSSuser, who has made quite a few significant changes, tries to save but receives the error message indicating an edit conflict as shown in the following screenshot:

Time for action – resolving an edit conflict

When an edit conflict takes place, the edit conflict page is shown with the conflict page source. The first text area shows your wikitext or source. Below that, the differences between the two edits are shown according to the differences or diff option. In the **Differences**, the text you modified is highlighted in yellow while the stored text is highlighted in green. After that, the other **edit** option is shown in an area called **Your text**. If you save your changes using the **Save** button, then the other changes will be gone. So before saving any of the changes, we have to merge both the sources (yes, we have to merge as the process is not automatic).

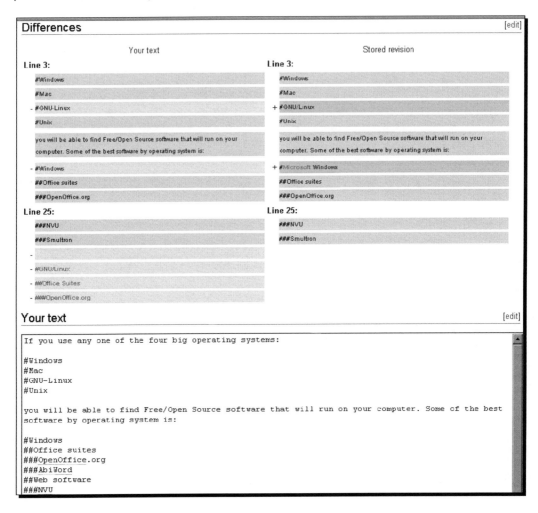

1. Look at the **diff** area to see who made the more complicated changes. In this instance, the user Jeff made some minor changes while FLOSSuser made some significant changes.

2. The user receiving the edit conflict should then merge the two articles together. In this instance, we will copy the text that FLOSSuser created (in the **Your text** area) and paste it into the edit area.

3. Once the content has been moved, FLOSSuser should then make the corrections to the article that Jeff made (shown in the diff area).

4. Click on **Save page**. The changes will now be reflected on the new page as shown in the following screenshot:

If you use any one of the four big operating systems:

1. Windows
2. Mac
3. GNU/Linux
4. Unix

you will be able to find Free/Open Source software that will run on your computer. Some of the best software by operating system is:

1. Microsoft Windows
    1. Office suites
        1. OpenOffice.org
        2. AbiWord
    2. Web software
        1. NVU
        2. Firefox
1. Mac
    1. Office suites
        1. OpenOffice.org
        2. AbiWord
        3. Bean
    2. Web software
        1. Firefox
        2. NVU
        3. Smultron
1. GNU/Linux
    1. Office Suites
        1. OpenOffice.org

What just happened?

Inevitably, two or more people will make changes to a page at the same time. When this happens, the users who save after the first edits have been saved will receive an edit conflict warning. Edit conflicts can be time consuming because the user will have to merge the two edits together using copy and paste. Often times, they should respect the other users edits and go back to include them as well.

In this exercise, we saw what happens when an edit conflict occurs and how to merge the two edits together. This is another reason why the talk pages can be so helpful. If Jeff knew that FLOSSuser was making major changes to the content, he may not have been so anxious to make the minor changes he was responsible for. Of course, in the case where users do not respect one another's edits in resolving a conflict, the sysop may have to revert the page to the state it was in prior to the edits and include what he or she deems appropriate edits.

Discussion extension

There are many extensions that MediaWiki has that can help make the community stronger. Many of these will be discussed in Appendix A, *The Best Extensions*. For now, we are going to concentrate on one extension in particular called **Discussion**.

Time for action – installing the Discussion extension

We saw how the talk pages are a good way to let the community discuss the content on a page, but talk pages are generally geared towards potential edits, correcting the article, or future additions to the page. Let's say you want to allow users to comment on a page or its content. User feedback can be a useful tool in creating good content or for inspiring interesting debates. As a sysop, we probably wouldn't want the reader feedback to be intertwined with the talk page though. Instead, we can install an extension called Discussion to provide a space for user to discuss and debate page content.

1. Download the extension from `http://en.wikicaptions.org/wiki/Extensions:Discussion:Installation`.

2. Upload the compressed `Discussion` file to the `extensions` folder on your server using your file manager or FTP program.

3. Extract the `Discussion` file into the `extensions` folder.

4. On your server, open your `LocalSetttings.php` file and find the value for `$wgDBprefix`. Write down the value. In the example wiki, this is `flossWiki`.

5. Copy the following SQL statement from the URL above to your favorite text editor for editing:

```
CREATE TABLE flossWikidiscussion(
```

```
                discussion_id INT NOT NULL AUTO_INCREMENT, PRIMARY
                KEY(discussion_id),
                page_id INT NOT NULL,
                id TINYTEXT NOT NULL,
                view_group VARCHAR(16),
                post_group VARCHAR(16),
                restricted_post_group VARCHAR(16),
                moderator_group VARCHAR(16),
                max_depth INT,
                counted_depth INT,
                page_size TINYTEXT,
                show_all_page_size INT,
                expanded_depth INT,
                show_all_order INT,
                init_display TINYTEXT,
                time_format INT,
                characters_max INT,
                author_characters_max INT,
                quoting INT,
                preview INT,
                comment_num1 INT DEFAULT 0,
                comment_num2 INT DEFAULT 0
        );
CREATE TABLE flossWikidiscussion_comments(
                comment_id INT NOT NULL AUTO_INCREMENT, PRIMARY
                KEY(comment_id),
                discussion_id INT NOT NULL,
                user_id INT,
                author_name TINYTEXT,
                text TEXT,
                time INT,
                status INT,
                author_status INT,
                parent_id INT,
                depth INT,
                vote INT
        );
CREATE INDEX IDX_discussion_page_id ON
                flossWikidiscussion (page_id);
CREATE INDEX IDX_discussion_page_url ON flossWikidiscussion
                (page_url);
CREATE INDEX IDX_discussion_comments_discussion_id ON
                flossWikidiscussion_comments (discussion_id);
```

6. Change the `flossWiki` to your value for `$wgDBprefix`. For example, your SQL statement will read `yourvaluediscussion` and `yourvaluediscussion_comments`.

7. Copy the edited SQL statement.

8. Open up your database management tool. We have been using **phpMyAdmin**.

9. In **phpMyAdmin**, select the database for your wiki from the upper-left corner of the screen. Once you have selected your wiki's database, a new screen will open as shown in the following screenshot:

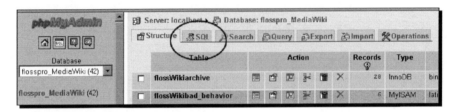

10. Click on the tab marked **SQL**. This will open the SQL screen where you can insert your SQL statement.

11. Paste your edited SQL statement into the available box and click **Go**. This will create two new tables in your database, `yourvaluediscussion` and `yourvaluediscussion_comments`, if you see a message that **Your SQL query has been executed successfully**. If you are not successful, make sure all of your parameters in your SQL statement are correct and that the `$wfDBprefix` value is correct.

12. Close phpMyAdmin and open the `LocalSettings.php` file on your server for editing.

13. Add the following code to the `LocalSettings.php` file:

```
//Discussion Extension
require_once('extensions/Discussion/Discussion.php');
```

If the value for `$wfDBprefix` is empty (null) in your `LocalSettings.php` file you can proceed without adding a prefix in the SQL query. For example, instead of `yourvaluediscussion` and `yourvaluediscussion_comments`, you would change your query to `discussion` and `discussion_comments`.

14. Save your edits.

15. Now open your wiki and log in.

16. Open a page and click on the **edit** tab.

17. Insert the `<discussion />` tab at the bottom of every page you wish to display comments on.

18. When you save the page, you will have the ability to post comments.

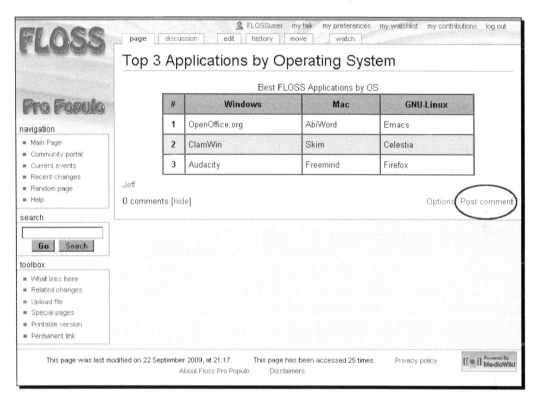

What just happened?

Well, we had to do quite a bit of work, but after we downloaded the extension, created some new tables in our database, and edited our `LocalSettings.php` file, we were able to install a really cool extension called Discussion. As a result, our users can now use the talk pages to discuss edits related to the page, and use the Discussion extension to leave comments or engage in a debate about the content on the page.

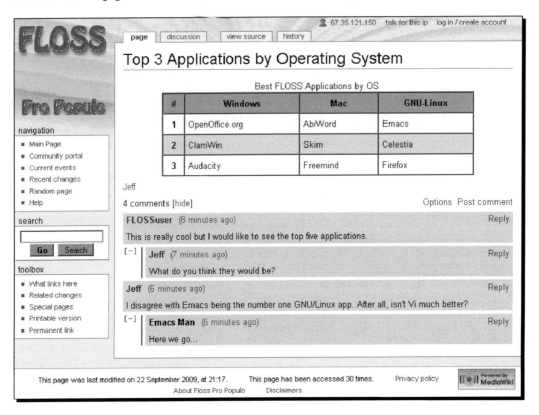

We also saw just how helpful phpMyAdmin can be when it comes to installing extensions on our wiki. Without this tool, we would have to create the database tables ourselves. Unless we know SQL pretty well, this could be a bit of a chore.

> You can add parameters to your `<discussion />` tag as well.
> A complete list of parameters that work with this tag can be found
> here: `http://en.wikicaptions.org/wiki/Extensions`
> `:Discussion:Description`.

Have a go hero

After successfully installing Discussion, we should feel pretty confident in our abilities to install new extensions on our wiki. There are other extensions out there that can help make your wiki more friendly towards a multi-user environment as well. Now that you have accomplished the exercises in this chapter, go ahead and find some more on your own to install. If you need help, refer to Appendix A, *The Best Extensions.*

Summary

We accomplished quite a bit in this chapter. The first part dealt with the users and how they can modify their profiles and change their editing preferences. By clicking on the **my preferences** tab, users are able to change the wiki's appearance by applying different skins or add pages to a watchlist so that any edits can be monitored.

In the second part of this chapter, we were introduced to how the administrators, or sysops, can view a page's history to view previous edits made to the page. If we see an edit that we don't agree with, we learned how we can revert the page to an earlier date to erase these edits. This works especially well should the wiki be a target of vandalism. Finally, we were taken through exercises that helped us build a stronger community for our users. By making use of talk pages, we saw how users are able to communicate directly with one another, or discuss edits and changes related to the page's content. To close out the chapter, we were taken through an exercise where we installed a MediaWiki extension called Discussion. Discussion allows users and visitors to post comments about the content on the page to promote even more interaction among the wiki's visitors.

In our next chapter, we are going to cover advanced customization of our wiki and get into some hacks that can help enhance the functionality of our site. So, what are you waiting for? Turn the page and let's get started!

10
Advanced Customization

Throughout the book, we have seen little ways of turning the default MediaWiki installation into our wiki. We have changed the logo to better reflect our wiki, we have added extensions to increase our wiki's functionality, and we have modified what users can—and cannot—do when visiting our wiki. As we progressed, we have also spent quite a bit of time editing the PHP files in the **backend** *of our wiki and even modifying the database files. If we have participated in the exercises so far, and have taken on some of the hero challenges, then we are more than ready to learn some ways so that we can really customize our wiki.*

In this chapter, we will be dealing with the backend of our wiki quite a bit. The backend consists of the PHP and database files that power our wiki. The changes we will make would be to further customize our wiki so that it not only reflects the look we want, but also to function the way we want. Specifically, we will learn:

- ◆ How to change the skin for the entire wiki
- ◆ Where to find important skin files
- ◆ How to modify the CSS of our wiki
- ◆ How to change the wiki's footer
- ◆ How to modify the navigation box
- ◆ How to move sections around in our wiki
- ◆ Ways to modify users capabilities
- ◆ How to hack our wiki

Once we are done with this chapter, we should have our wiki looking and working the way we want. Of course, we can always go back and make any alterations we choose!

Unfortunately, if you are reading this in black and white you will have to take my word for the color changes made in this chapter, but I assure you, they are there!

Customizing your wiki's appearance

When we talk about customizing your wiki, most people will think about the way the wiki looks. Changing the appearance is also one of the easiest customizations we can make. After all, it was early on in the book that we learned to change the logo from the MediaWiki sunflower to one of our choice. However, by the end of this chapter, you will have learned many other useful ways to make your wiki truly your own.

In this section, we will be dealing with **Cascading Style Sheets (CSS)**. Some prior knowledge of this is required to complete the exercises in the text. If you need to learn more about CSS, check out the tutorials at `www.w3schools.com/css/` or `http://htmldog.com`. You can also search the web for other useful information about CSS.

When it comes to the wiki's appearance, we need to know two things. First, we need to know what it is we can customize. Second, we need to know what are the files that we can customize. To answer the first question, we can change the background color and image, the font color, font type, graphics, buttons, logo, and so on. Basically, anything found in the skin that can be changed. This brings us to our second question. What files allow us to change the appearance? Let's look into that right now.

Time for action – changing the skin

In Chapter 9, *Multi-User Environment*, we learned that a user can change the way the wiki looks when he or she is logged in, by changing the skin. That's all well and good for the individual, but what if we, the sysop, wish to change the skin across the entire wiki for all users? Can we do that? The answer is yes. We can change the skin. And, as we will see, we can later edit the skin as well.

If you want to change the default skin for the site, then you have to modify the `LocalSettings.php` file to reflect this. The newly-changed skin for the site will then be loaded as the default skin for all the site visitors unless they have set a different skin in their preferences. In this case, once users log in, they will see their chosen skin if it is different from the default one. In this exercise, we will be changing the default skin from **Monobook** to **Cologne Blue**.

1. Open the file manager for your wiki. Remember, we use Cpanel for the examples but you can use an FTP program such as FileZilla as well.

2. Open your `LocalSettings.php` file for editing.

3. Find the line that reads: `$wgDefaultSkin = 'monobook';`. This can be found around line 108.

4. Change the word `monobook` to the skin you like. For the example, we will be using Cologne Blue so our editing line will look like this:

   `$wgDefaultSkin = 'cologneblue';`

   It is important that you use lowercase and no spaces between words. This is why Cologne Blue was entered as `cologneblue`.

5. Save your changes.

If we bring up our wiki, and are not logged in, we will see that the appearance of the wiki has changed to reflect our new skin as shown in the following screenshot. If you are still logged in to your wiki from a previous session, you will not notice these changes!

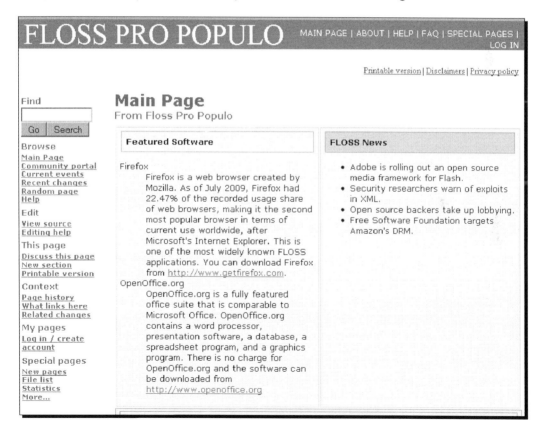

What just happened?

By modifying the $wgDefaultSkin line of the LocalSettings.php file we were able to change the default skin for visitors who are not logged in. This can be quite useful if we want to maintain a consistent look for our wiki. But what happens when our visitors log in and change their skin through **my preferences**? While they can't change the skin for anyone but themselves, it still defeats the purpose of us taking the time to create a consistent look and style to our wiki. If keeping the wiki's skin consistent is important, you will learn how to disable the user's ability to change their skin later on in this chapter.

Making changes to the skin

MediaWiki gives us eight different skins to choose from, but this doesn't quite work for every wiki. After all, for FlossProPopulo, I like the green we used. All the skins provided by the MediaWiki developers use blue. While I think the Cologne Blue skin is nice, I would really like it if it had some green in it.

This is where our knowledge of CSS will be put to use. By going into the skin files, we will be able to change the color scheme to anything we want. Would you prefer the skin be Cologne Pink? Jump right in and change all the instances of blue to shade of pink. Now, we will change the color not only of the skin, but also of the text and background as well.

Before we go any further, we need to learn where these skin files really are. A skin is a PHP class that contains all the necessary functions to generate HTML output for each wiki page that will be shown in our browser. What really happens is that each available skin in MediaWiki is a different class that inherits the Skin class and implements each of the necessary functions to draw the page. In the MediaWiki installation directory, we have a folder named skins. If you browse the folder, you will see a few PHP files, which are the skin files, and a few folders with the same names as the PHP files. These folders contain CSS files for each skin.

The core skin class and other associated classes are inside the includes folder of the MediaWiki installation directory. The names of those classes are:

- Skin.php
- SkinTemplate.php

The SkinTemplate class inherits the Skin class. These are the files responsible for what we see on screen. These classes return different bits of HTML code. However, what is it that holds things together? Which class actually decides the layout of the page on screen? Well, *none* of these classes are used for that! Earlier, we talked about the skins folder. All the skin definitions reside in this folder. The example we have shown in the first image of this chapter used the Cologne Blue skin. So if you open the CologneBlue.php file, you will see many division tags (<div>) have been used to hold the pieces together to show the page's structure. The content returned from skin classes is shown properly using the HTML structure in the appropriate skin file. You must remember that if you want to change the layout, then you have to change the specific skin file in the `skins` folder, not the `Skin.php` file in the `includes` folder.

Time for action – locating and analyzing the CologneBlue.php file

As we want to change the color of the skin to incorporate green, we need to make some changes. In this exercise, we will change the color of what is called the *topbar*. As the example in this chapter makes use of the Cologne Blue skin, this is the one we will be using. Remember, you can apply this to any of the skins available to you.

1. Open your file manager or FTP program so that you can access MediaWiki's files.

2. Navigate to `/public_html/skins/`. You should see a list of folders and files as shown in the following screenshot:

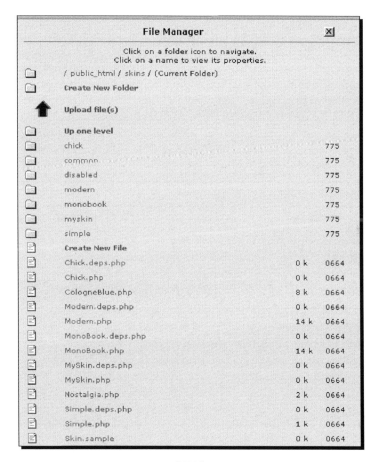

3. As there is no folder for Cologne Blue, open the folder named `common`.

4. Open the file `cologneblue.css` for editing. You can edit the CSS directly in the file manager, or you can download the file and edit it in a CSS editor such as Dreamweaver.

5. Locate the line that reads:

```
td.top {
        background-color: #6688AA; color: white;
        margin-top: 4px; margin-bottom: 4px;
        padding-top: 0; padding-bottom: 0;
        text-transform: uppercase;
        font-family: Verdana, Arial, sans-serif; font-size: 8pt;
}
td.top a {
        font-family: Verdana, Arial, sans-serif;
        background-color: #6688AA; color: white;
        text-decoration: none; font-size: 10pt;
}
```

and change `6688AA` to `04B404` to make the topbar a nice shade of green.

6. Save your changes.

7. Open your wiki. You should now see that the topbar, which was once blue, is green as shown in the following screenshot:

FLOSS PRO POPULO   MAIN PAGE | ABOUT | HELP | FAQ | SPECIAL PAGES | LOG IN

What just happened?

While MediaWiki provides quite a few skins for us to choose from, we will probably want to make changes to the look of our wiki that go deeper than selecting a different skin. To make these changes, we learned that we must go into the CSS file of our skin and modify it. In this instance, we did away with the default blue in the Cologne Blue skin and turned the topbar green to better reflect our wiki. Of course, if green is not your favorite color, you can use any hexadecimal color code you wish. If you haven't memorized the chart of hex color codes, then an online reference can be found at `http://html-color-codes.info`. This is a great reference because you can enter a hex code in to see if it matches a color you are looking for. Also, you can select a color and the site will provide the hex code for you.

Editing CSS

One common thing that web designers like to do is change the background of a web page. Basically, white is considered to be the best choice, but sometimes, a bit more excitement is called for. However, when you change the background color, you often need to change to the text color as well so that they don't clash and we stick to good design principles.

In the following exercises, we will change to the MonoBook skin so you can see what some of the other skin's CSS files look like. In order to see the changes, we need to change the value of `$wgDefaultSkin` in the `LocalSettings.php` back to `monobook`.

Time for action – changing the skin's background

If we are building our wiki for the company we work for, maybe they wish to have a watermark of the company logo as the background for all the wiki pages. Or, perhaps, we are building a wiki for a hobby of ours and the visitors prefer a darker background than the one the default provides. No matter the reason, we can easily go back into the CSS file and with a few modifications, have the background of our choice.

1. Using your file manager or FTP program, open up the backend filesystem for your wiki.

2. Navigate to `\public_html\skins\monobook\`.

 The path may be different according to your hosting provider. If you are having trouble with this, contact your hosting providers help desk to find the appropriate path.

3. Open the `main.css` file for editing.

4. Locate the following lines:

```
body {
        font: x-small sans-serif;
        background: #f9f9f9 url(headbg.jpg) 0 0 no-repeat;
        color: black;
        margin: 0;
        padding: 0;
```

5. Notice that the background is set to `#f9f9f9` which is a very light gray. There is also a reference to `headbg.jpg`. This image file also appears in the background of the MonoBook skin.

6. Change the hex code `#f9f9f9` to `#8CD794`. Then, delete `url(headbg.jpg) 0 0 no-repeat`. Make sure you do not delete the semicolon (;).

7. Save your changes.

Now if you open your wiki, you will notice that the background color has changed and the wavy image is gone as shown in the following screenshot:

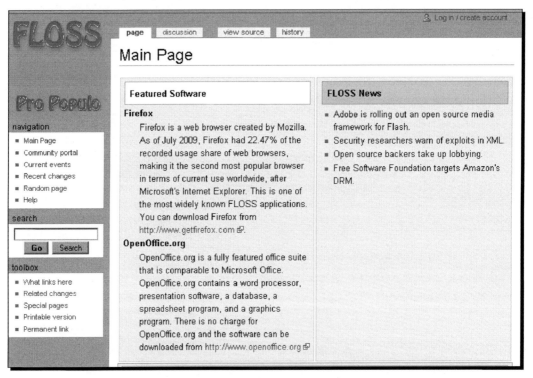

Now that is a bit better, but what if we need to have some sort of image in the background? Let's keep editing this file so we can insert an image as well. Also, I don't like the white boxes that surround the toolbox, search box, and so on. Let's take this a step further and make those boxes transparent so everything shows up with our background color.

8. Reopen the monobook folder found at \public_html\skins\monobook\.

9. Upload your background image to this folder. For our example, we will be using a file called bg-gnu.png. After all, what better image symbolizes FLOSS than a GNU?

10. Open the main.css file for editing.

11. Go back to the body section:

```
body {
        font: x-small sans-serif;
        background: #8CD794;
        color: black;
        margin: 0;
        padding: 0;
```

In the background line, add url(yourfile) 0 0 no repeat. In the example, we will type url(bg-gnu.png) 0 0 no repeat so your body section will look like the following:

```
body {
        font: x-small sans-serif;
        background: #8CD794 url(bg-gnu.png) 0 0 no-repeat ;
        color: black;
        margin: 0;
        padding: 0;
        }
```

12. Now, let's make those white boxes transparent by locating the code reading:

```
.pBody {
        font-size: 95%;
        background-color: white;
        color: black;
        border-collapse: collapse;
        border: 1px solid #aaa;
        padding: 0 .8em .3em .5em;
```

Change the line that reads background-color: white; to background-color: transparent;

13. Make the same change to the background-color lines in the #content section and the #footer section.

14. Save your changes.

If you followed the exercise exactly, your site should look similar to the following screenshot:

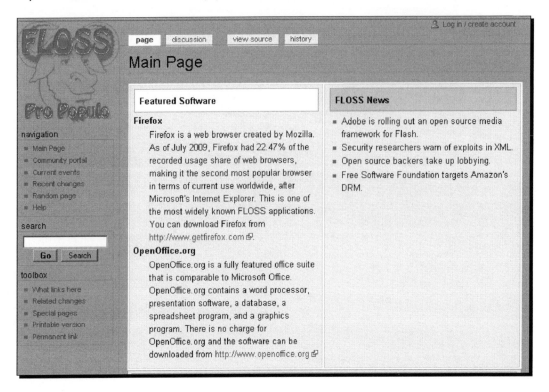

Of course, the image of your choice will be shown rather than the GNU, but you get the idea.

What just happened?

Talk about customization! We just went into the CSS file for our skin and made a bunch of cool modifications. By locating the right class in the CSS file (body) we were able to turn the background for our wiki to a color of our choice. We removed the white background for the .pBody, #content, and #footer classes and made them transparent so our background would show through these as well. Also, we uploaded a graphic file to our monobook folder to place in our background as well.

Background images

If you are planning on using a background image, make sure to lighten it using a program like GIMP or Photoshop. The bg-gnu image used in the example was dropped down to 30% opacity and you can see how well it shows up! The reason you need to lighten the image is that it may be hard to read any text that covers it if you leave it at 100% opacity.

Time for action – changing the color of the text

As we have changed our background color to green, we may have noticed that the default blue text in the navigation box and toolbox don't look so good. That's quite alright because we are going to change that right now.

1. Navigate to `\public_html\skins\monobook\`. (Again, if you are having problems check with your hosting provider for the correct path.)

2. Open the **main.css** file for editing.

3. Locate the following lines of code:

```
a {
    text-decoration: none;
    color: #002bb8;
    background: none;
}
a:visited {
        color: #5a3696;
        }
a:active {
        color: #faa700;
```

These lines define the colors used for the links in the navigation box and tool box, the color used for a visited link, and the color used for an active link. This is what we will be changing.

4. Change #002bb8 to #000000 to change the blue text to black.

5. Change #5a3696 to #E8F715 to change the violet text color to a yellow hue when a link has been visited.

6. Change the #faa700 to #B9292C to change the orange text to a darker red when a link is active.

7. Save your changes.

Now, when you visit your wiki, the colors of your text will be different as shown in the following screenshot:

What just happened?

Again, we edited the `main.css` file to make stylistic changes to the MonoBook skin, giving our wiki a more personal look. This time, we altered the color of the text that appears in our wiki's navigation box and toolbox. We also made changes to the links in these boxes so that they appear in different colors when they have been visited or when they are active.

Have a go hero

Now that you have learned how to manipulate the CSS files for a skin, there are two challenges presented to you.

First, go back into the MonoBook skin and make the necessary changes so that the top links (found in the CSS file under the section commented `/* for top links */`) are transparent and the text follows the color scheme used in the navigation box and toolbox.

The second challenge is to find another skin that you like and apply these exercises to the CSS file it uses. This is your time to play around so really get into making some changes.

Fixing mistakes

Just like we backed up the `LocalSettings.php` file by saving the file as `LocalSettings2.php`, we should do the same for any CSS files we modify. This way, should we forget what the original file was like, we can always revert to it.

Changing the layout

Modifying the way our wiki looks isn't limited to just changing the background color or the color of the text. Within MediaWiki, we have control over the page layout as well. In this section, we are going to cover how to go about customizing the existing layout by making changes to page sections and by moving them around the page. However, before we get into making changes, we have to understand the PHP file associated with the skins.

As stated earlier, when making changes to a skin, we need to look at the PHP file associated with the skin, not the `skin.php` file. For instance, if we wish to make changes to the MonoBook skin, we need to make them in the `MonoBook.php` file.

Let's start by taking a look at the `MonoBook.php` file that can be found in the `skins` directory. This is a large file so we will only look at a small part of it to get an understanding of its structure. The first part of the skin file contains the block of PHP code where the MonoBook skin class is created by extending the existing `SkinTemplate` and `QuickTemplate` classes that define the skin being used. The main function that describes the layout and contents of the skin is the `execute` function under the `MonoBookTemplate` class. The code block is as follows:

```
class MonoBookTemplate extends QuickTemplate
{
  /**
   * Template filter callback for MonoBook skin.
   * Takes an associative array of data set from a SkinTemplate-based
   * class, and a wrapper for MediaWiki's localization database, and
   * outputs a formatted page.
   *
   * @access private
   */
  function execute() {
  // Suppress warnings to prevent notices about missing indexes in
  // $this->data
  wfSuppressWarnings();
  ?>
```

After the above code block, we have an XHTML code section up to the end of the `MonoBook.php` file. The XHTML page template consists of a number of `div` sections. Each `div` is identified by either or both an `id` and `class` attribute in the `<div>` tag. The stylesheet then controls *how* each `div` block is drawn, and *where* on the page it is positioned.

Take a look at the following code snippet of the `MonoBook.php` file:

```
<div class="portlet" id="p-personal">
 <h5><?php $this->msg('personaltools') ?></h5>
 <div class="pBody">
  <ul>
   <?php foreach($this->data['personal_urls'] as $key => $item) { ?>
   <li id="pt-<?php echo htmlspecialchars($key) ?>">
    <a href="<?php echo htmlspecialchars($item['href']) ?>"
     <?php if(!empty($item['class'])) { ?>
      class="<?php echo htmlspecialchars($item['class']) ?>"
     <?php } ?>>
     <?php echo htmlspecialchars($item['text']) ?>
    </a>
   </li>
   <?php } ?>
  </ul>
 </div>
</div>
<div class="portlet" id="p-logo">
 <a style="background-image: url(<?php $this->text('logopath') ?>);"
 <?php ?> href="<?php echo htmlspecialchars($this-> data['nav_urls']
         ['mainpage']['href'])?>"
  <?php title="<?php $this->msg('mainpage') ?>">
 </a>
</div>
```

As you can see, there is a division, `<div>`, with the ID `p-personal` and class `portlet`. These `<div>` tags work as individual blocks and together they build the layout of the page. If you examine the full code section, you will find that many similar `<div>` tags have been used, and corresponding stylesheets have been declared in the folders named according to the skin names. So for the MonoBook skin, we have a folder named `monobook`, and the CSS file that defines the style rules for the page is `main.css`. The `portlet` class that we have seen in the code snippet defines the basic style of the `div` blocks not part of the main content area. Each block is furnished with the style defined for it in the stylesheet that is referred to by the `div` ID or class.

The main page section is a block with the ID `column-content` that contains the block with the ID `content`. The `content` block contains the main content heading with the `firstHeading` class and the `bodyContent` block, which contains a subheading identifying the MediaWiki site name, the `contentSub` block, the actual page contents, and a `visualClear` block. Let's explore a few important identifiers in the `main.css` file for the MonoBook skin.

- `column-content`: It is used to define the overall space within the margins of which the content exists
- `content`: It is the white background, thin bordered box that contains the content for the main page

- **firstHeading**: It is the class of the heading tag at the top of every page
- **bodyContent**: It actually contains the main page content within the content box
- **contentSub**: It defines the style of text that indicates the name of the wiki immediately underneath the main heading, but above the body text

The portlets section is a block with the ID column-one, containing portlet blocks with the IDs p-cactions, p-personal, p-logo, p-nav, p-search, and p-tb. At the bottom of the page is a block with the ID footer, containing the f-poweredbyico and f-list blocks. The portlet.css class is the style used by all the div blocks around the main content. The following is a list of blocks using the portlet.css class:

- **p-cactions**: It is the ID for the list of tabs above the main content
- **p-personal**: It is the ID for the list of links that include the login or logout link at the top of the page
- **p-logo**: It is the ID for the block that contains the logo (on the top left)
- **p-nav**: It is the ID for the block that contains the navigation links on the left of the page
- **p-search**: It is the block that contains the search buttons
- **p-tb**: It is the block that contains the toolbox links

The footer at the bottom of the page includes blocks with the following IDs:

- **footer**: It is the block that contains the overall footer
- **f-list**: It is the list for all additional links in the footer section except the copyright and powered-by icon

Now that we have an idea about the layout and style properties for the skins, we can start to explore by changing the layout and then modifying the CSS to change the look of the site even more.

Pop quiz – understanding blocks

I know, you are anxious to get started with the exercises. Before we start, let's make sure that you have a good understanding of the different blocks used in the skins that MediaWiki installs by default.

1. Which ID would have information regarding the site's logo?

    a. logo

    b. image

    c. p-logo

    d. logo ID

2. The block identified as `p-tb` contains links for the:

   a. top navigation

   b. toolbox

   c. links in text

   d. links in the navigation box

3. The main content is identified by the block named:

   a. p-caction

   b. p-caption

   c. p-main

   d. bodyContent

If you answered all three questions correctly, then you are good to move on to the exercises. If you answered any of them wrong, go back and review what the different blocks are responsible for before moving on. After all, we don't want you moving the footer when you think you are editing the main content area.

Time for action – changing the footer

There are many different reasons why we would want to modify the footer for our wiki. We may need to add a link, delete a link, change the wording, and so on. One change that we will be making in this exercise is to remove the text that tells when the site was last modified.

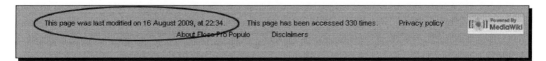

1. Using your file manager or FTP program, open the `MonoBook.php` file for editing. It can be found at `\public_html\skins\`.

2. Locate the following lines of code:

```
<div id="footer">
<?php
   if($this->data['poweredbyico']) { ?>
      <div id="f-poweredbyico"><?php $this->html('poweredbyico')
?></div>
<?php }
   if($this->data['copyrightico']) { ?>
      <div id="f-copyrightico"><?php $this->html('copyrightico')
?></div>
<?php }
```

```
   // Generate additional footer links
   $footerlinks = array(
     'lastmod', 'viewcount', 'numberofwatchingusers', 'credits',
'copyright',
     'privacy', 'about', 'disclaimer', 'tagline',
   );
   $validFooterLinks = array();
   foreach( $footerlinks as $aLink ) {
     if( isset( $this->data[$aLink] ) && $this->data[$aLink] ) {
     $validFooterLinks[] = $aLink;
     }
   }
   if ( count( $validFooterLinks ) > 0 ) {
?>    <ul id="f-list">
<?php
     foreach( $validFooterLinks as $aLink ) {
       if( isset( $this->data[$aLink] ) && $this->data[$aLink] ) {
?>       <li id="<?php echo$aLink?>"><?php $this->html($aLink) ?></
li>
<?php     }
       }
?>
     </ul>
<?php }
?>
   </div>
```

These lines provide information about the footer section of our wiki.

3. Now, we need to remove `'lastmod'` from the links section:

```
// Generate additional footer links
$footerlinks = array('lastmod', 'viewcount',
                     'numberofwatchingusers', 'credits',
                     'copyright','privacy', 'about', 'disclaimer',
                     'tagline',
                     );
```

4. After `<ul id='"f-list">` hit *Enter* and insert the following lines:

```
<li id="f-top">
  <a href="#top" title="Return to the top of this page">
  Top of the page
  </a>
</li>
```

This will add a link to the footer that will take you back to the top of the page.

5. Save your changes.

The following screenshot shows the changes made to the footer:

What just happened?

In order to modify the footer, we learned that we need to open the PHP file associated with the skin we are changing. In the previous exercise, we modified the `MonoBook.php` file so that the last modified date no longer shows up on the wiki. We also added a line of code that creates a link taking us back to the top of the page. To add a link, we need to add HTML to the file similar to the following:

```
<li id="f-list">
<a href="http://www.link.com" target="_blank">Link Text
</a></li>
```

Of course, we would change the link to something we wish to link to such as another website or a page in our wiki. The link text would reflect where we are sending our visitor.

Have a go hero

By default, MediaWiki places a small graphic file in the footer of every wiki that runs its software. While it is considered common courtesy to leave the "Powered by MediaWiki" image link on your site, there are times when the administrator may want to remove it.

The name of this image is `poweredbyico`. With this information, see if you can remove this icon from your skin's file. If you really want a challenge, replace the icon with something that better suits your wiki.

Time for action – changing the navigation links

Well, we decided to work backwards from here. As we modified the footer in the last exercise, it is only appropriate that we edit the navigation box in this one. This task is significantly easier than the last one because site navigation is something that almost every website administrator wants to customize. For this task, we won't have to work with any PHP or CSS, just plain, old-fashioned wikitext!

1. Open your wiki and log in using the sysop account.

2. In the title field of your wiki's URL, add the text `MediaWiki:Sidebar`. For example, in the sample we have been using, the URL would show up as `http://www.flosspropopulo.com/index.php/MediaWiki:Sidebar`. After you hit *Enter*, you will see a page similar to the following screenshot:

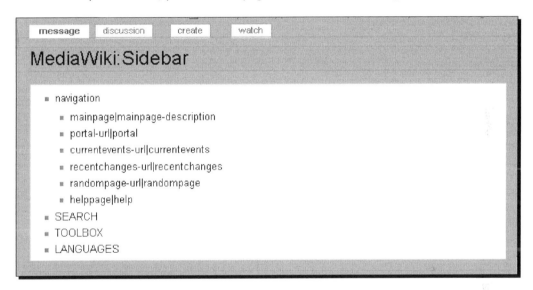

3. Normally, you would click on the **edit** tab at the top of the page. However, the first time you edit this page, you may have to click on the **create** tab if the **edit** tab is not present.

4. Add a new navigation link to the list. Links are listed in the format: `**target|caption`. In our example, we are going to link to a new page called **Tutorials**, so we would add `**tutorials|Tutorials`. If you wish to link to another website, you can use a URL as your target as well.

5. Also add this line, `**Special:listusers|User List`. Notice that to link to a special page, we need to include `Special`, a colon (:), and then the page title.

6. Save your changes. As this is a major edit, you may want to include a comment!

Now, the navigation box found on the left-hand side of your wiki should have the newly-created links as shown in the following screenshot:

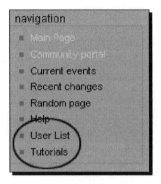

What just happened?

With a bit of added wikitext, we were able to add a new link to our navigation box on the side of the screen. To do this, we navigated to the **MediaWiki:Sidebar** page and added a bit of syntax. We can use this to add new pages, links to Special pages, and links to other websites as well. If we wanted to delete an existing link, we could do that here as well.

Have a go hero

I couldn't let you get away that easy so here is your challenge.

Did you notice when you were adding the **Tutorials** link to the navigation box that there were entries for SEARCH, TOOLBOX, and LANGUAGES as well? Using what you have learned, move the search box so that it is directly above the navigation box.

Time for action – moving sections on a page

You probably found the last two exercises to be a breeze. After all, we are almost all the way through the book. By now, you know your way around MediaWiki well enough to make changes by adding a bit of code here and a snippet of wikitext there. So let's tackle something a bit more challenging. Most websites post their search box towards the top of the page. What if we want to go by this standard for our visitors as well? After all, we want them to be comfortable with our site, right? So can we move the search box up to a spot above the navigation box? Well, we are about to find out.

 It is important when moving a section to be sure that it does not overlap with any other section on the page. If the section is not moved properly, it may overlap the page layout and render an awful-looking page to your visitors.

1. Open up the PHP file for the skin you are modifying. We will stick with MonoBook. php for now as we are used to the layout.

2. Locate the following code section that is responsible for the search box on your page:

```
<div id="p-search" class="portlet">
 <h5><label for="searchInput"><?php $this->msg('search') ?>
      </label></h5>
 <div id="searchBody" class="pBody">
  <form action="<?php $this->text('wgScript') ?>"
       id="searchform"><div>
   <input type='hidden' name="title" value="<?php
      $this->text('searchtitle') ?>"/>
   <input id="searchInput" name="search" type="text"<?php echo
        $this->skin->tooltipAndAccesskey('search');
    if( isset( $this->data['search'] ) ) {
     ?> valuc="<?php $this->text('search') ?>"<?php } ?> />
   <input type='submit' name="go" class="searchButton"
        id="searchGoButton" value="<?php
        $this->msg('searcharticle') ?>"<?php echo
        $this->skin->tooltipAndAccesskey( 'search-go' ); ?> />
        < ?php if ($wgUseTwoButtonsSearchForm) { ?> 
   <input type='submit' name="fulltext" class="searchButton"
        id="mw-searchButton" value="<?php
        $this->msg('searchbutton')
        ?>"<?php echo $this->skin->tooltipAndAccesskey
        ('search-fulltext' );?> /><?php } else { ?>
   <div><a href="<?php $this->text('searchaction') ?>"
        rel="search">
        <?php $this->msg('powersearch-legend') ?></a>
   </div><?php } ?>
  </div></form>
 </div>
</div>
```

Remember, when you are making large changes to the code, you should make a backup of the file you are modifying. Save a copy, if you have not done so, of MonoBook.php called MonoBook2.php. If you mess up, you can revert to the original file.

3. Cut the code from your MonoBook.php file.

4. Locate the following code in `MonoBook.php`:

```
<div class="portlet" id="p-logo">
 <a style="background-image: url(<?php $this->text('logopath')
    ?>); " <?php ?>href="<?php echo htmlspecialchars($this->data
       ['nav_urls']['mainpage']['href'])?>"<?php
  echo $skin->tooltipAndAccesskey('p-logo') ?>></a>
</div>
```

5. Insert the search box code you just cut from your file directly under the `</div>` tag. You can hit *Enter* a few times first to make some space in the code.

6. Save your changes.

If you did everything correctly, when you open your wiki, you should see that the search box is now directly under your logo and right over the navigation box, as shown in the following screenshot:

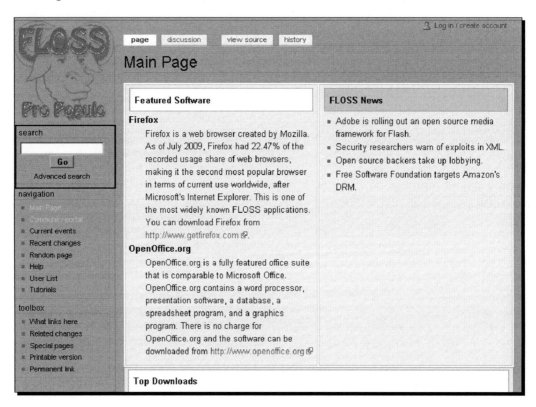

What just happened?

By moving the placement of the code that drives the search box, we were able to move the placement of the search box when the page renders in a web browser. When we did this, the search box was relocated so that it is directly beneath the logo on our page and right above the navigation box.

When we change the order in which the code for our skin file is parsed, we change the appearance. If we wanted to move other sections around, we could do so by moving the code just as we did here. Remember though, we have to make sure that the section we are moving doesn't overlap an existing section or our page will not be displayed properly. If you wish to make major changes to the layout of the skin, I would suggest you pick up a copy of *MediaWiki Skins Design* by Richard Carter. This book will take you through the ins and outs of designing your own skins to use on your site.

Have a go hero

Some of you may have found the last exercise a bit challenging, as it involved tearing through the code. If you are one of those people who want an even greater challenge, give this a try.

Knowing that moving the location of the code in the file will move the sections around, try your hand at moving some other sections. Don't worry if your page doesn't look right. If you overlap, just revert to the original file. This will teach you which sections can be moved without problems. Remember, you can learn quite a bit from taking something apart.

Of course, you can go in to the other skin's PHP files and move sections around there as well.

Customizing user capabilities

We have seen in previous exercises how we can use the `LocalSettings.php` file to define what users can see and do on our wiki through permissions. The ability to define what users can see and do is extremely important, especially if the wiki you are building contains information that may be sensitive or restricted.

Yet, sometimes we just want to disable certain features of our wiki because it makes the user experience better. As we will see in the next exercise, the `LocalSettings.php` file is not the only one we can modify to customize how our wiki functions.

Time for action – disable the ability to change skins

Let's say that you have spent quite a bit of time customizing how your wiki looks to your visitors. You have made the changes we covered in the book, have risen to the challenges, and even went off on your own to learn more about MediaWIki skins and applied this to your MonoBook skin. Your wiki is looking great!

Now suppose you have a user who logs in and changes the skin to *Simple*. All your hard work is now lost on this user, or any others who change their skins on your site.

Luckily, if you wish for a consistent look across your wiki, you can force this by making a few changes to a little file called `SpecialPreferences.php` that can be found in `../public_html/includes/specials/`.

1. Using your file manager or FTP program, open the `SpecialPreferences.php` file for editing.

2. Locate the following lines of code:

```
# Skin
  #
  global $wgAllowUserSkin;
  if( $wgAllowUserSkin ) {
   $wgOut->addHTML( "<fieldset>\n<legend>\n" . wfMsg( 'skin' )
                    "</legend>\n" );
   $mptitle = Title::newMainPage();
   $previewtext = wfMsg( 'skin-preview' );
   # Only show members of Skin::getSkinNames() rather than
   # $skinNames (skins is all skin names from Language.php)
   $validSkinNames = Skin::getUsableSkins();
   # Sort by UI skin name. First though need to update
   #validSkinNames as sometimes the skinkey & UI skinname differ
   # (e.g. "standard" skinkey is "Classic" in the UI).
   foreach ( $validSkinNames as $skinkey => &$skinname ) {
    $msgName = "skinname-{$skinkey}";
    $localisedSkinName = wfMsg( $msgName );
    if ( !wfEmptyMsg( $msgName, $localisedSkinName ) ) {
     $skinname = $localisedSkinName;
    }
   }
   asort($validSkinNames);
   foreach( $validSkinNames as $skinkey => $sn ) {
    $checked = $skinkey == $this->mSkin ? ' checked="checked"'
                                        : '';
    $mplink = htmlspecialchars( $mptitle->getLocalURL
             ( "useskin=$skinkey" ) );
```

```
        $previewlink = "(<a target='_blank'
                        href=\"$mplink\">$previewtext</a>)";
        $extraLinks = '';
        global $wgAllowUserCss, $wgAllowUserJs;
        if( $wgAllowUserCss ) {
         $cssPage = Title::makeTitleSafe( NS_USER,
                    $wgUser->getName().'/'.$skinkey.'.css' );
         $customCSS = $sk->makeLinkObj( $cssPage, wfMsgExt
                                ('prefs-custom-css', array() ) );
         $extraLinks .= " ($customCSS)";
        }
        if( $wgAllowUserJs ) {
         $jsPage = Title::makeTitleSafe( NS_USER,
                        $wgUser->getName().'/'. $skinkey.'.js' );
         $customJS = $sk->makeLinkObj( $jsPage, wfMsgHtml
                                ('prefs-custom-js') );
         $extraLinks .= " ($customJS)";
        }
        if( $skinkey == $wgDefaultSkin )
         $sn .= ' (' . wfMsg( 'default' ) . ')';
        $wgOut->addHTML( "<input type='radio' name='wpSkin'
             id=\"wpSkin$skinkey\" value=\"$skinkey\"$checked />
             <label for=\"wpSkin$skinkey\">{$sn}</label>
             $previewlink{$extraLinks} <br />\n" );
      }
      $wgOut->addHTML( "</fieldset>\n\n" );
    }
```

3. Comment out this code by placing a /* before the line that reads # Skin and a */
   after the last bracket, } as shown in the following code:

```
/*
# Skin
#
  global $wgAllowUserSkin;
...
  $wgOut->addHTML( "</fieldset>\n\n" );
  }
*/
```

   Alternately, you can use a # before each line to comment out the code as well.

4. Save your changes.

Now, when your users try to change the skin under **my preferences**, they see this:

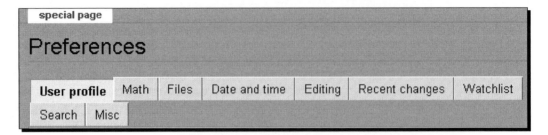

Notice that there is no longer a **Skins** tab so the user cannot change this option.

What just happened?

In order to protect the aesthetics of our page, and to make sure that everyone sees the same thing when they visit our wiki, we used the `SpecialPreferences.php` file to disable the ability for our users to change skins. What we did was comment out the section that defines this in the file. Doing so causes MediaWiki to ignore the code and thus, the function is disabled and our wiki still looks good.

Hacking MediaWiki

Hacking is a term that is still misunderstood. When we speak of hacking, we are talking about making modifications to something. In this case, we are talking about making modifications to our MediaWiki installation to suit our needs. A **hacker** is a person who creates and modifies, or *hacks*, software. This is done by employing a series of modifications to exploit, and/ or extend, existing code or resources. Though the word hacking has negative impact in various societies, most hackers do not have bad intentions. A positive meaning of "hacker" can be someone who knows a set of programming interfaces well enough to write software rapidly and expertly. We will take this definition for our purpose. We will learn how to modify or add features to MediaWiki rapidly by understanding the internal structure and interfaces. We are not going to learn how to damage or deface a wiki through any **malicious hacking** techniques.

The file structure

We already know that MediaWiki is built on PHP and MySQL. So in order to add or modify anything in MediaWiki, we need to have sound knowledge of PHP and MySQL. So far we have applied our basic PHP knowledge in the `LocalSettings.php` file, but now we need to apply more of our knowledge to edit the existing code base, and also a bit of patience to work on it. Let's look at the core MediaWiki files, some of which will be modified as required:

Filename	Description
index.php	This is the main entry point to the application. This page redirects to other pages based on the passed parameters.
Article.php	This page contains code for viewing, deleting, watching, and unwatching a page. It also contains basic functions responsible for a part of the editing functionality, such as fetching a revision and saving a page.
	When we edit a page, all article-related information such as article name, article contents, and so on are provided by the Article.php file. Database and text operations are done through the Article.php file as well.
EditPage.php	This page contains code for editing a page. A part of the editing, however, is handled by the Article.php file.
Parser.php	This page contains the code for parsing wiki syntax to HTML tags.
Linker.php	This page contains code for generating HTML code for links and images.
Database.php	This page contains all the functions for separate database operation.
OutputPage.php	This page is used as output buffer. All the text is sent to this class before being shown on screen or in other media.
Title.php	As the name suggests, this page is solely responsible for displaying and saving page titles.
User.php	This page contains the user-related code—especially code sections for user preference and permission.
Setup.php	This page initializes all variables used in MediaWiki. A part of the initialization also involves the global variables and objects.
DefaultSettings.php	This page contains the default values for all the variables used in MediaWiki. If some values need to be changed or redefined, they are defined in the LocalSettings.php file.

Now we know which files exist and what they do. So it is better to study these files very well before making any changes. Though the code is not very well organized, you can still make out some meaning by reading the contents.

Time for action – making your wiki private

One of the biggest concerns about wikis is that anyone can edit them. In fact, most wikis encourage the community to create and edit content and suggest that if you don't need all of a wiki's functionality, a **Content Management System (CMS)** may be a better choice.

However, there may be times when you want the functionality of a wiki, but you only want certain people to be able to log in to access your content.

In this exercise, we are going to use some of our prior knowledge to hack MediaWiki so that we can prevent people from creating accounts. Once we have done this, we are going to lock down our wiki so that unless you are given a username by your sysop, you cannot get in to read any of the content.

Using your FTP program or your file manager, open up the `LocalSettings.php` file so that you can edit it.

1. At the bottom of the file, add the `# Lockdown our wiki`. This will be the comment that lets us know later on that the following code will be used for this hack. If you wish to open up your wiki at a later time, you can remove the code we enter here.

2. Add the following line of code:

    ```
    $wgGroupPermissions['*']['createaccount'] = false;
    ```

    This removes the **create account** from your login link as shown in the following screenshot. Visitors will not be able to create accounts; the sysop user still has this ability.

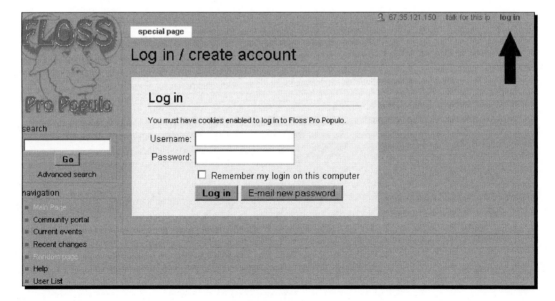

3. Now add the following code below the last line we just added:

```
# Disable reading line, for anonymous (not-logged-in => * ) :
$wgGroupPermissions['*']['read'] = false;

# Enable anonymous to read the followings pages :
$wgWhitelistRead = array( "Main Page", "Special:Userlogin", "-",
"MediaWiki:Monobook.css" );
```

This gives visitors access to the **Main Page** and the **Log in** page, but nothing else.

4. Save your edits.

Now, whenever a visitor who is not logged in tries to access a page other than the **Main Page** or the **Log in** page, they will be greeted with a message as shown in the following screenshot:

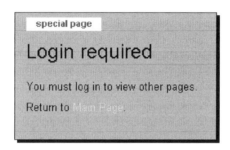

What just happened?

By using the skills we have learned in this book, we were able to hack the MediaWiki `LocalSettings.php` file to make our wiki inaccessible to anyone who does not have a username and password.

As MediaWiki was built to allow even visitors the opportunity to create and edit pages, our modifications tailored the software to fit our needs. By hacking the software, we altered the way it performs. Our hack was not done to damage the software or the site in any way.

Time for action – enhancing custom namespaces

We learned back in Chapter 7 that namespaces are used to organize content that have a similar purpose. MediaWiki provides us with 18 built-in namespaces. As we determined that we needed an additional namespace for our tutorials, we created Tutorials and Tutorials_Talk.

However, now that our skill set with MediaWiki has grown, let's enhance the functionality of the Tutorials namespace. We can give this namespace the ability to have subpages created for all tutorials so if we want to organize a tutorial by operating system, we can use the Subpage feature. Also, we will make this namespace searchable because, by default only pages in certain namespaces are searchable. Others need to be selected from the Search page. Also, this hack allows content in the Tutorials namespace to appear when the **random page** feature link is clicked.

So, if you are ready, let's enhance the namespace called Tutorial.

1. Open the `LocatSettings.php` file with either the file manager or the FTP program.

2. In a new window, open your favorite text editor. We will be copying lines of code here to transfer to our `LocalSettings.php` file. (Remember, any edits to the `DefaultSettings.php` file will be overwritten when we upgrade our MediaWiki software.)

3. Locate and copy the lines of code that read:

```
$wgNamespacesWithSubpages = array(
     NS_TALK                 =>true,
     NS_USER                 =>true,
     NS_USER_TALK            =>true,
     NS_PROJECT_TALK         =>true,
     NS_FILE_TALK            =>true,
     NS_MEDIAWIKI_TALK =>true,
     NS_TEMPLATE_TALK        =>true,
     NS_HELP_TALK            =>true,
     NS_CATEGORY_TALK        =>true
   );

$wgNamespacesToBeSearchedDefault = array(
     NS_MAIN                 =>true
   );
```

These lines can be found starting around line number 1949. Once they are copied, paste them to your text editor file. Once all the lines of code have been copied to the text editor, you can close the `DefaultSettings.php` file.

4. Edit the file so that it looks like this:

```
$wgNamespacesWithSubpages = array(
     NS_TALK                 => true,
     NS_USER                 => true,
     NS_USER_TALK            => true,
     NS_PROJECT_TALK         => true,
```

```
          NS_FILE_TALK         => true,
          NS_MEDIAWIKI_TALK => true,
          NS_TEMPLATE_TALK    => true,
          NS_HELP_TALK         => true,
          NS_CATEGORY_TALK    => true,
          TUTORIALS            => true,
          TUTORIALS_TALK       => true
        );


$wgNamespacesToBeSearchedDefault = array(
     NS_MAIN              => true,
     TUTORIALS            => true
     );
```

Of course you can substitute `Tutorials` for the title of the custom namespace of your wiki where ever it occurs in this file.

5. Open up the `LocalSettings.php` file for editing.

6. Copy the code from the text editor and paste it into the `LocalSettings.php` file.

7. Save your changes.

What just happened?

The hack we just performed gave our previously created Tutorials and Tutorials_Talk namespaces the ability to be searched by default—users no longer are required to select them from the Search page—and their content will appear using the **Random page** link in the navigation box.

We also provided this namespace with the ability to house subpages. Let's say we are creating a tutorial on installing OpenOffice.org. Now, the tutorial can be created in the Tutorials namespace and we can create three subpages—for Microsoft Windows, GNU/Linux, and one for Macintosh users. Using this, we can avoid having one huge page that covers the installation process for all three operating systems.

Most importantly, we learned that there are many different ways to extend the functionality of our wiki. As we grow more comfortable with our wiki administration abilities and our PHP programming skills, we can hack the MediaWiki core even further to make our system perform exactly the way we want it to!

Have a go hero

If you are ready for an even greater challenge when it comes to hacking MediaWiki, then step up to the plate, because here it comes!

When we created the `Tutorials` namespace, we intended it to be available to all visitors to our site. Since then we have changed our minds and decided that only registered users will be able to access this feature. In our situation, we can encourage visitors to register for our site by offering them content that they would not be able to see otherwise. However, the applications of this hack can prove to be extremely useful in a corporate setting as well.

We have seen ways to limit access to our site in previous exercises, but in this particular challenge, you are going to learn how to prevent unauthorized access to a namespace, the `Tutorials` namespace.

To do this, visit `http://sourceforge.net/projects/hiddenwiki/` and download the **Hidden namespaces patch**. When you extract the files, there is a README file included that will help you with the appropriate configuration settings to the `LocalSettings.php` file.

This hack requires you to be able to install the patch to your server so you may need the help of your hosting provider.

Summary

This chapter was especially important because we learned how to modify the look and functionality of our wiki so that it not only has the appearance that we want, but also the functionality.

We started this chapter by learning about ways we can change the wiki's appearance. First we looked at the different skins that users can apply to the wiki when they log in. Then, we moved into locating the skin files so we could learn how to make changes to the skin file that are reflected across the wiki.

When working with the skin files, we covered CSS and saw how these files are responsible for the layout, text, and color scheme that our wiki's skins follow. By changing the CSS files, we were able to change background colors, background images, text, and any other aesthetics we may wish.

As we moved along, we learned how to go about modifying the footer. In the sample, we added a link that took us back to the top of the page, removed some text, and we were challenged to use the same techniques to remove the "Powered By MediaWiki" icon from the footer. With this knowledge in hand, we took on the task of moving the search box so that it appears above the navigation box, and then we learned how we can move the different content sections around the page as well.

After we learned how to make our wiki look the way we want, the task of keeping these changes consistent came next. We learned how to disable the user's ability to change skins so that all of our hard work in creating the perfect-looking wiki was not thrown out the window should a user select a different skin.

Finally, we learned some hacks we could apply to MediaWiki that would extend its functionality even further. For starters, we applied a hack that would make our wiki private. Once this was in place, only the sysop could create new users for our wiki. Next, we looked at a way we could increase the functionality of the namespace we created back in Chapter 7.

We have spent a lot of time over the last few chapters learning how to get our wiki looking, and working the way we want it to. In the next chapter, we are going to learn how we can maintain our wiki so that it continues to run smoothly.

11
Maintaining MediaWiki

Throughout the course of this book, we have installed MediaWiki on our server, configured and customized it to our liking, and added pages of content for our visitors. However, our work is not yet done. Actually, the work of the MediaWiki sysop is really never done because he or she should always be working to maintain their site and its software, so it continues running smoothly and providing its audience with the content and service they expect.

This chapter is dedicated to teaching you how to perform certain tasks that can help keep your site running efficiently and effectively even in the event of a disaster. Specifically, in this chapter we will cover:

- How to run maintenance scripts
- How to back up your wiki
- How to restore your wiki from a backup
- How to upgrade the MediaWiki software

Once you have covered all of the exercises that teach you how to perform these tasks, you will be well on your way to becoming an expert MediaWiki sysop. So, let's get started by looking at some of built-in tools that MediaWiki has that will help with the upkeep of your site.

Maintenance scripts

In the `maintenance` directory of your MediaWiki installation, there are a host of PHP scripts that can be run by the sysop to do various maintenance tasks. While these scripts can be extremely helpful, there are two unfortunate facets regarding them. First, most of these scripts have little to no documentation regarding them, so you are on your own when it comes to learning how to run them. Second, and most important, these scripts are designed to be run from the server's command line or terminal shell. For those of us who are using a hosting provider, we may be out of luck when it comes to accessing this tool as the host company doesn't really want people who don't work for them messing with their server configurations.

Fortunately, someone wrote a neat little extension that will allow us to emulate a command line session so we can run these scripts without ruining the server it runs on.

 For a complete listing of the Maintenance scripts, visit `http://www.mediawiki.org/wiki/Manual:Maintenance_scripts#List_of_maintenance_scripts`.

Time for action – installing the MaintenanceShell extension

As many of the maintenance scripts available to us through MediaWiki perform clean-up and purge tasks, they can be extremely beneficial in keeping our wiki less bloated from garbage. If we don't have access to the command line or terminal of our server, we need to install an extension called MaintenanceShell that will emulate the terminal session for us and run the script on our wiki. In this exercise, we will not only install this extension, but will run a script from it as well so you can see exactly how this will work on your wiki. In order to follow along exactly with the exercise, you will need to have another user in your wiki. While it is not necessary to do so, I would recommend that you create a user called **User**, or a username of your choice. We are going to see how MaintenanceShell works by changing a password and it is not wise to test this, or any, extension against your sysop account. After all, we don't want to make a mistake and lock you out of your own wiki!

1. Download the `.zip` file from `http://www.mediawiki.org/wiki/Extension:MaintenanceShell` by clicking on the `MaintenanceShell.vx.x.x.zip` link in the information box. This appears right after the word **Download**.

2. Using your file manager or FTP program, upload and extract the `MaintenanceShell.x.x.x.zip` file to the `extensions` folder of your MediaWiki installation. This is usually found in the `extensions` directory. If you are extracting the files on the server, this will create a new folder named `MaintenanceShell.x.x.x`. If this is the case, rename this folder to `MaintenanceShell`. If you have extracted the files on your local machine, you will need to move the entire `MaintenanceShell` folder to the `extensions` directory on the server.

3. Open your `LocalSettings.php` file for editing and add the following lines to provide members of the sysop group access to the special page created by the MaintenanceShell extension:

```
#Grant sysop access to MaintenanceShell
$wgGroupPermissions['sysop']['maintenanceshell'] = true4;
```

4. At the very last line of your `LocalSettings.php` file, add the following lines of code:

```
#MaintenanceShell extension
Require_once("$IP/extensions/MaintenanceShell/MaintenanceShell.
php");
```

This line ensures that all the settings are loaded when the MaintenanceShell is run. Make certain this is always the last line of your `LocalSettings.php` file to ensure that everything is included when the MaintenanceShell is run.

5. Save your settings.

If you log into your wiki with a sysop/administrator account, you will see a new page added to the **Special pages** called **Maintenance Shell** as shown in the following screenshot:

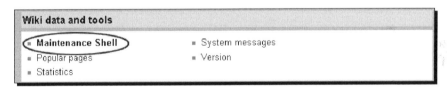

6. Click on the **Maintenance Shell** special page link. When the special page opens, you will see that there is a textbox where you can enter the script you wish to run, a box to add options to the script, links to the Extension's page (http://www.mediawiki.org/wiki/Extension:MaintenanceShell), a link to the MediaWiki page about maintenance scripts (http://www.mediawiki.org/wiki/Manual:Maintenance_scripts), and a complete list of available scripts as shown in the following screenshot:

 You can find out more about the various maintenance scripts from the MediaWiki manual at http://www.mediawiki.org/wiki/Manual:Maintenance_scripts#List_of_maintenance_scripts.

Maintenance Shell

Warning: Use these scripts with care. They are intended for administrators and other advanced users only.

Script name: [   ] .php

Command line options: [   ]

[Run script]

- Manual:Maintenance scripts 🔗
- MaintenanceShell Homepage 🔗

Available maintenance scripts:

addwiki	attachLatest	attribute	benchmarkPurge
changePassword	checkAutoLoader	checkBadRedirects	checkImages
checkUsernames	cleanupCaps	cleanupImages	cleanupSpam
cleanupTitles	cleanupWatchlist	clear_interwiki_cache	clear_stats
convertLinks	counter	createAndPromote	deleteArchivedFiles
deleteArchivedRevisions	deleteBatch	deleteDefaultMessages	deleteImageMemcached
deleteOldRevisions	deleteOrphanedRevisions	deleteRevision	dumpBackup
dumpHTML	dumpInterwiki	dumpLinks	dumpSisterSites
dumpTextPass	dumpUploads	edit	eval

 It is important to note that on your **Maintenance Shell** page, you can scroll down to view more available scripts.

7. In the available scripts, click on the script named **checkUsernames**. Notice that this will populate the **Script name** textbox. Alternately, you can type the name of the script, **checkUsernames,** in this box.

8. In the **Command line options** box, type:`--user User --password newone`

Here, `User` is the username and `newone` will be the new password for `User`.

9. Click the **Run script** button and you will be taken to the following page:

Return to the Maintenance Shell

`/home/flosspro/public_html/maintenance$ php changePassword.php --user User --password newone`

If you log out of your sysop account, you can now log in as **User** with the password **newone**.

The **Return to the Maintenance Shell** link in older versions was not redirecting back to the correct screen and would cause a 403 Error page to display. This has been corrected in later versions of the extension (after December 2009). If you are using an older version, it is recommended that you update this extension. To navigate back to the **Special:MaintenanceShell** page in the older versions, click on the back button on your browser.

What just happened?

As some of us do not have the luxury to run MediaWiki's maintenance scripts on our server, we installed an extension that emulates a shell session for us to run these scripts. By installing the extension, and granting permissions to the sysop accounts, we created a new Special page named **Maintenance Shell**. From this page we have the ability to run a variety of scripts that will help us keep our wiki maintained and orderly.

Additionally, we tried out one of the scripts by entering its name into the **Script name** box and providing additional information in the **Command line options** box. Upon running the script, we were able to change the password for one of the users. This may be useful in a office setting where an administrator, or even a regular user, needs a password reset after they forgot theirs.

It is important to note that some of these scripts may require elevated privileges to folders and files on the server itself. If you do not have the ability to change permissions on these, you may need to contact your hosting provider to see if they will make these adjustments for you.

Backing up your wiki

If you installed your wiki on a server owned by a hosting provider, then odds are it will be backed up for you every night. Should something happen to the server, there will always be a recent copy of your site on file with the company so they can easily restore the site; often times your provider will do this for you.

However, it is always good practice to back up your sites on your own instead of relying on someone else to do it for you. Before we begin, we need to take a look at how everything is stored in our wiki. MediaWiki stores important data in two locations:

♦ The database where pages and their contents, users and their preferences, metadata, search index, and so on are stored

♦ The filesystem where software configuration files, custom skins, extensions, images (including deleted images), and so on are stored

So if you are ready, let's step into the next couple of exercises where you will learn how to back up both your database and your wiki's filesystem.

Time for action – backing up the database

Throughout this book, we have used phpMyAdmin whenever we have had to work with the database. If you haven't been told on how much easier it makes your life by now, this will certainly bring you around.

In this exercise, we are going to use phpMyAdmin to back up the database for our wiki. If you do not have access to phpMyAdmin, then you may need to contact your hosting provider for instructions on how to back up your database.

1. Open up phpMyAdmin for your site and log in.

2. From the upper left-hand corner, select the database that corresponds to your wiki.

3. Click on the **Export** tab at the top of the page. This will open the page as shown in the following screenshot:

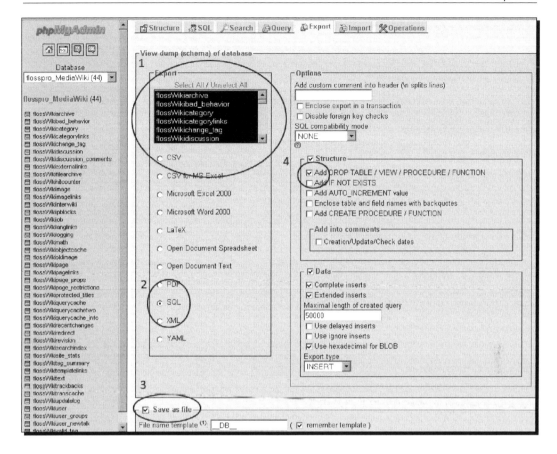

4. On the export page, we need to check for the following:

   ❑ That all of the tables are selected (**1**).

   ❑ That **SQL** is selected as the export type (**2**).

   ❑ That **Save as file** is checked (**3**).

   ❑ That **Structure** and Add **DROP TABLE** (**4**) is selected to add the drop table functionality if the table already exists in the database backup.

5. If you wish to compress the backup file, select **zipped** or **gzipped**.

6. Click on the **Go** button. This will save your file to the location you determine. This is based on your browser settings, so if you are using the Firefox default, the file will be saved to your desktop.

What just happened?

Using a third-party tool, phpMyAdmin, we were able to back up our database using the Export tool. This tool generates a `.sql` file that we can later import should our database become damaged or corrupted. As this is only half of what we need to fully restore our wiki, we need to look at how we back up the filesystem next.

Time for action – backing up the filesystem

Unlike the database, the filesystem does not require any third-party tools to perform the backup. All we need to do is copy selected files from our server using either our FTP program or our file manager.

1. Navigate to the MediaWiki files and folders on your server using the file manager or FTP program.

2. Select the files you wish to back up. These usually are:

    - Configuration files such as `LocalSettings.php` or `DefaultSettings.php`
    - Folders that contain image files
    - The `extensions` folder
    - The `skins` folder

    Any other files or folders that contain important information should be selected as well.

3. Copy the files/folders to your local computer. It generally helps if you keep all of these files and folders in one folder so they reside in the same place.

4. Compress the folder that houses everything you copied down from your server.

What just happened?

That last exercise was so easy that I wouldn't blame you if you were still looking for the next step. All we have to do to back up our wiki's files is save them to a storage location. Saving them on your local computer is fine for now, but if you have a large wiki, you may need to invest in some sort of attached storage device to hold everything.

Have a go hero

We saw how easy it was to back up both the database and the filesystem for our wiki. Now, we are going to combine our first exercise in with our backup as well.

One of the maintenance scripts—dumpBackup.php—will create what is called as an XML dump of all the content of your wiki, without the site-related data. When you run this file, you have the option of creating a full dump of everything in the page's history, or you can opt for just the current contents. You can also select all pages, as well as choose selected pages to include in the dump. As the dump creates an XML file, you can share your content with anyone.

Go ahead and run this maintenance script. Once you are done, open the file to see how the page content is organized. In order to get the file, you will need to specify where you want the dump sent. More information can be found here:
http://www.mediawiki.org/wiki/Manual:DumpBackup.php.

Restoring from a backup

Again, if you are using a hosting provider, the chances that you will have to restore your wiki due to a natural disaster are slim. However, if your wiki is defaced or vandalized, you may be on your own when it comes to restoring files and content.

While MediaWiki has many countermeasures in place that allow you to undo vandalism, there may be a time where damage is too severe, or too widespread, and it would be easier to just restore the content from a backup you know is void of any damage.

For those of us who are creating a wiki for personal reasons, or for a hobby, a well-developed backup schedule can save a great deal of heartache. However, if you are developing a wiki for your company or business, it is imperative that not only you keep best practices in mind when it comes to backing up your wiki, but also test the restore process. Nothing is worse than a false sense of security from thinking that your backup is working fine. Unless you test it out by restoring the data, you never know until it is too late.

There is one word of advice regarding backups that you should be aware of. In this exercise, we will be writing directly over our existing database to test out our backup. In the real world, we would never write over a database that is working perfectly just to test our backups. A better solution would be to run a development server that mirrors your wiki exactly. You can do this on a local machine if you want.

Another solution would be to mirror your wiki in a subdomain on your site. This way, you can test out new extensions, test your backup, see if there are any issues with updates, and so on without interfering with your live wiki site.

Of course, if you are just messing around and learning MediaWiki, feel free to overwrite your database in this instance like I am doing.

Time for action – restoring the database backup

When we backed up our database, we made use of the phpMyAdmin export tool to save a copy of all the tables in our database. If you guessed that we will be using the import tool to restore the data, then you are absolutely right!

If you are one of the few who does not have access to phpMyAdmin through your hosting company, alter the directions so you can restore the data using your own tool. You will be surprised at how easily you will be able to do this after all the experience you have built up over the course of this book.

1.   Open phpMyAdmin for your site.

2.   Choose the appropriate database from the upper left-hand corner of the screen.

3.   From the tabs across the top of the screen, click on the one that says **Import**. When you click this, you will be presented with a screen identical to the following screenshot:

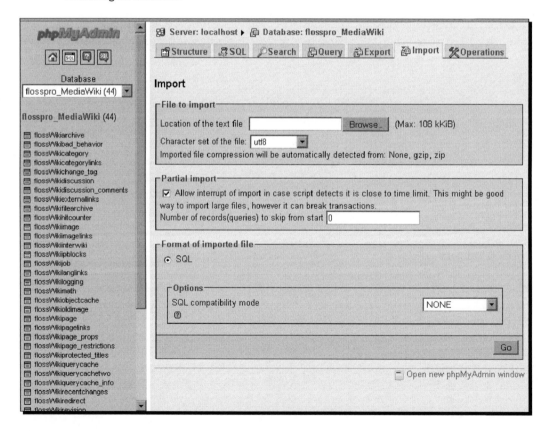

4. In the textbox labeled, **Location of the text file**, you will need to click the **Browse** button and locate your earlier export file.

5. Make sure that the **Format of the imported file** has **SQL** selected.

6. Click the **Go** button. This will now send your backup file to the database where it will populate the tables.

The result of a successful import should look similar to the following screenshot:

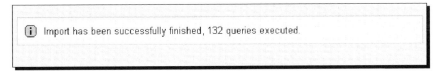

Now, the number of queries that are successful may vary depending on each individual wiki. You may have more or less. Problems arise when you see something similar to the following screenshot:

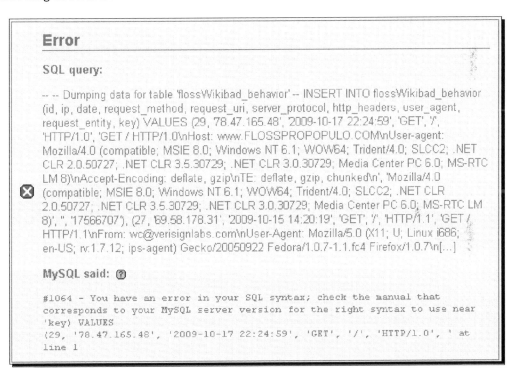

You should be able to see that in this instance, our table for the Bad Behavior extension is causing us a bit of grief. While we won't get into how to configure our database for this in the scope of this book, a quick and dirty work around is to remember that this extension causes a database restoration problem. In the future, we can deselect this table from our export so we don't have this issue.

Don't post for security's sake!

What I just did here is a big no-no in the security world. If you are serious about keeping your wiki or any other site safe, then never post such information on the web. I know that sometimes people ask for this on forums and support discussions, but do you really want all that information about your server out there for anyone to see?

What just happened?

In an earlier exercise, we learned how to back up our database using the export tool in phpMyAdmin. In this previous exercise, we restored the very same database using the import tool. Essentially, we just backtracked. However, we did learn that this is a good practice because there may be times when our database backup may fail. The only way to test if this is working properly is to restore the data from a backup.

We also learned that while we imported data back into our live database, this is something we should not do on a production wiki (one that is live and being actively used). Instead, we should set up a test or development wiki for this purpose.

Time for action – restoring the filesystem on a new installation

You should recall that when we backed up our filesystem, all we did was copy important files from our server to our local machine. To restore them, we simply copy them back. As this needs no instruction, we are going to cover the steps you would take if you were to move these files to a new installation, or new server. As most hosting providers will use an installation script such as Fantastico, which we used earlier, the database and wiki administrator will be created when we install the software. If you are installing this on your own server, you will have to take the necessary steps to create these users and give them full permissions.

1. Import your database to the new server/installation.

2. Copy your filesystem files and folders to the new server/installation using your FTP program or the file manager provided by your web host.

3. Open your `LocalSettings.php` file for editing.

4. Make the following changes to these variables:

   ❑ $IP: Set this to the correct path for the new server or new installation.

   ❑ $wgScriptPath: Set this to the correct path for the new server or new installation.

   ❑ $wgDBserver: Make sure that the database server name is correct. For a new installation, this may not need to be changed. If you have installed on a new server, you will probably have to change this.

   ❑ $wgDBname: Make sure that the database name is correct. Change it to reflect the new database name.

   ❑ $wgDBuser: Make sure that the database username is correct. Change it to reflect the new database user if this is incorrect.

   ❑ $wgDBpassword: Check to make sure that this is the correct password for the database user. If it is not, change this to reflect to right password.

5. Test your site!

What just happened?

Since restoring the filesystem is as simple as moving the old files we backed up to the new installation of MediaWiki, or new server, we went ahead and looked at what variables in the LocalSettings.php file may need to be changed in order for our wiki to function properly. Most of these will change if we moved to a new hosting company, however, if we are working to rebuild these files on a fresh installation of MediaWiki on the same server, not everything needs to be changed.

Pop quiz – backup and restore

1. When moving a wiki to a new installation, a backup and restore of the filesystem is used.

   a. True

   b. False

2. When backing up and restoring the database, we used a tool called:

   a. phpMyAdmin

   b. FileZilla

   c. MaintenanceShell extension

3. When backing up the filesystem, which files/folders should be included?

    a. `LocalSettings.php`

    b. `extensions` folder

    c. `DefaultSettings.php`

    d. All of the above

Upgrading MediaWiki

MediaWiki has a large development community that is always looking to make the software better. As a result, it undergoes quite a few upgrades. It is necessary for you to upgrade the software when new releases are available. Not only does the latest release offer more features, but usually there are security updates included in the upgrade to help keep the malicious users at bay.

Upgrading any software can cause a multitude of problems for you. Before you upgrade, make sure that the release you are using is a stable release and not one that is still in testing. Installing a version of the software that is still in beta testing can cause your site to crash and leave your site open to attack. If you are confident that the latest release is stable, you should still test the upgrade on a development site first if you have that luxury. If you do not test the upgrade first, you could find out the hard way that the latest release doesn't work with certain extensions or third-party applications.

Time for action – upgrading MediaWiki

Currently, MediaWiki is at release 1.15.1. If you recently installed the software, you may not be able to upgrade because a newer version may not be available yet. If you are using an installer such as Fantastico, or one provided by your hosting company, then when you log in you should be alerted when a new release is available for MediaWiki.

When the time comes that you need to upgrade your MediaWiki installation, these are the steps you need to follow. Many people simply click on the upgrade button from their hosting control panel. Failure to upgrade the right way can really cause some serious damage to your site.

1. Check the requirements. Make sure that you are running the correct version of PHP and MySQL, or PostgreSQL. If you are not, you will need to upgrade these first.

2. Read the release notes. These are available to you on the MediaWiki site corresponding to the release you are installing. If everything checks out, then proceed.

3. Back up your files and database. You won't need to use them unless something bad happens. If something bad happens, you will be glad you backed everything up.

4. Run the update script from your installer or control panel.

5. Log in to your wiki and open the **Maintenance Shell** page. From this page, run the script called **update**. This checks the database schema to see if it will work with the upgrade.

6. Check your installed extensions to see if they need to be upgraded as well.

7. Test your upgraded wiki site.

When you upgrade, there is a chance that you will lose some of your configurations. Be aware of this. If this happens, simply reconfigure your wiki or move the backed up file that contains the changes to the server and rewrite the upgraded file.

What just happened?

In this last exercise, we learned what steps we need to take when upgrading MediaWiki to the latest release. We were informed that simply clicking on the upgrade button in our hosting provider's control panel could cause damage to our wiki if we aren't careful. We also learned that it is important to back up our wiki before we upgrade and test the upgrade before we use it on our live site.

Summary

This chapter was short, but it was very important as it taught us how to keep our wiki running smoothly. We learned how to back up our database using phpMyAdmin, and our filesystem by copying important files, so that in the event of a disaster we could restore our wiki back to its functional state. We also learned how to restore our wiki from these backups; most importantly, we saw that we need to test our backups frequently by restoring them to see if everything is working.

We also covered how to install a special extension called Maintenance Shell. This extension gives those of us who don't have terminal shell access on our server the ability to run the maintenance scripts that MediaWiki offers.

Finally, we covered the steps we should take when upgrading our MediaWiki software. While many times, the upgrade is done by the simple click of a button, there are steps we need to take prior to the actual upgrade to make sure we don't damage our wiki.

We are almost done! In the next, and final chapter, we are going to learn how we can integrate MediaWiki with some other web applications such as WordPress and Joomla! to build even more robust sites.

12
Integrating MediaWiki

One of the greatest things about working with free/open source software packages is that the development community works extremely hard to enhance the functionality of the different software packages. The spirit of the free/open source software movement is especially evident in the fact that many of these applications can be integrated so that they work with one another by sharing user accounts and other database information.

Through the use of extensions, MediaWiki can be integrated with other web applications as well. With a few modifications, MediaWiki can work alongside other platforms such as WordPress blogging software, Moodle learning management system, and Joomla! content management system.

As stated previously, the integration works because some of the different modifications made to the applications, through extensions in MediaWiki's case, allow the databases to be shared. By integrating two or more of these programs, users will benefit by either having a single sign-on and/or the ability to easily access content between the various programs.

In this chapter, we will learn how to:

◆ Integrate MediaWiki with WordPress

◆ Integrate MediaWiki with Joomla!

◆ Integrate MediaWiki with Moodle

◆ Apply OpenID signons to MediaWiki

It is important to note that many of these extensions allow the other program access to the MediaWiki database. Although the book will explain what needs to be done to the other program to allow MediaWiki access, the steps will not include how to modify or hack the code of the shared program that will allow MediaWiki access to the companion program's database. In order to maximize the integration between the two programs, you will have to take on the Have a Go Hero challenges that help you create a bi-directional integration. While the steps are not provided, you will be given enough information to use the techniques learned throughout this book to make this happen.

For some of the examples in the following exercises, I will be using fresh installations of each software package instead of referencing the Floss Pro Populo wiki that we have created throughout the book. The reason for this is that in many cases of integration, both the wiki software and the companion software it will be integrating with need to be installed on the same server in the `webroot` directory. The emphasis here is to make sure that the integration works before taking it live. You would never want to install another software package into the root of your working wiki as that could cause huge problems if not done correctly. Instead, we will concentrate on creating working installations of the software packages. If we need to move our wiki content, we can always use the steps outlined in Chapter 11, *Maintaining MediaWiki.*

If you are ready, let's begin.

Integrating MediaWiki with WordPress

The largest social web tool to hit the Internet is by far the introduction of blogging software. Many companies make use of blogs so that they can promote products, educate their customers, or even provide their employees with a forum on which they can express themselves. Huge companies such as BlueCoat and IBM make use of blogs in these exact scenarios.

If your company is already using a blog, or perhaps you are planning to start one, then integrating the blog with MediaWiki can allow you to display comments made on a WordPress blog into your wiki or allow newly-created wiki pages to appear on the blog.

In order for the following exercises to work, you will need to install WordPress onto your server. The WordPress installation should be in a separate directory, in our example I installed it to `www.flosspropopulo.com/blog`. The blog and wiki will need to share the same database. As our database already exists, we will continue using the existing wiki database. If you cannot chose a database during the installation of your blog, then you can change the name of the database by modifying the `wp-config.php` file of WordPress. Visit the site `http://codex.wordpress.org/Main_Page` for more help with WordPress.

Time for action – install WordPress comments

This first extension will allow comments from WordPress to be displayed on a MediaWiki page. The basic use of this extension is to help ease users into using a wiki for discussion. As most users are more familiar with blog comments than they are with a talk page, the developers created this extension to help ease users into an unfamiliar setting. Of course, this only scratches the surface of how you can make use of this extension.

For the purpose of this demonstration, I have gone into Wordpress and created a post titled **Best software**. Additionally, I created a quick comment related to the post.

To get started, we need to copy the PHP file from `http://www.gizmogarden.com/` `index.php/Wordpress_comments_to_wiki#WordpressComments.php` and save it as a file named `WordpressComments.php`. The code is rather long and can be downloaded from the online companion to the book.

1. Using your FTP program or file manager, upload the `WordpressComments.php` file to your `extensions` directory.

2. Open your `LocalSettings.php` file and add the following line of code:

    ```
    #Wordpress Comments
    require_once("$IP/'extensions/WordpressCommets.php"');
    ```

    Remember, if you are using the MaintenanceShell extension, make sure to add any new extensions, such as Wordpress Comments, above this call in your `LocalSettings.php` file or when MaintenanceShell is run, these extensions will be left out.

3. Save your settings.

4. Add a post to your newly-created blog. The post I created talks about a page titled **Best software**.

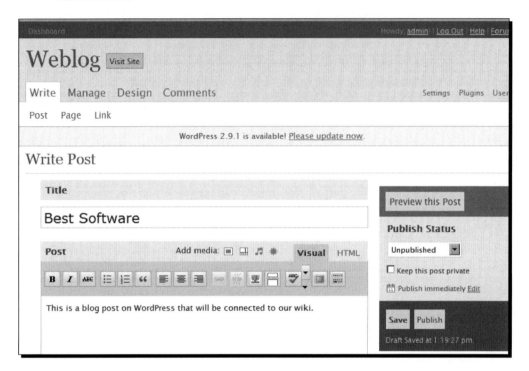

5. Open the MediaWiki page where you want the comments to appear. In this case, we will have them appear on the **Best software** page.

6. Edit the page by adding the following lines:

```
<wp:comments>
wp_post_title=title_of_your_comment_post
wp_url=url base of your wordpress install
</wp:comments>
```

Change `title_of_your_comment_post` to the title of the blog post you created. In the example, this would be **Best Software**. Also, change `url base of your wordpress install` to the appropriate URL. For the example, the lines added would read:

```
<wp:comments>
wp_post_title=best_software
wp_url=http://www.flosspropopulo.com/blog
</wp:comments>
```

7. Save your changes.

Once you have edited the wiki page, you should see a comment box appear much like you would in a blog as shown in the following screenshot:

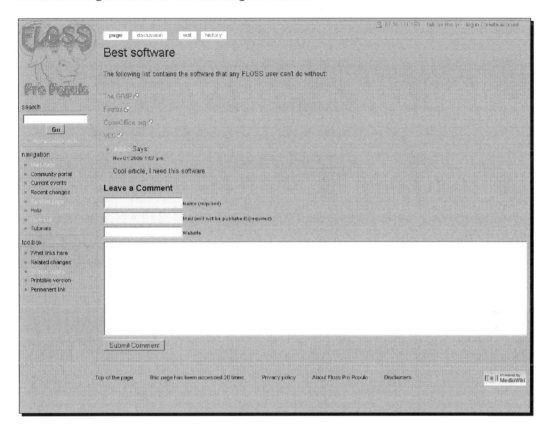

Not only can you read comments left on the blog, but you can add comments as well. If you do submit a comment from MediaWiki, you will be redirected back to the blog page, however, your new comment will appear on both the blog and wiki.

What just happened?

In order to show a basic integration between MediaWiki and WordPress, we shared a database between the two and uploaded a new extension to MediaWiki that allowed us to display blog comments on a page in our wiki. We learned that not only will this extension show us comments from a blog, but we can also submit comments of our own from our wiki page.

You may ask, what can we do with this? Well, we have already discussed how this can be used as a substitute for a talk page, but we can also use it to draw attention to specific articles in our wiki. For example, if we want to draw attention to our **Best software** page, we may write a blog post on it. This blog post could spark enough discussion among visitors and drive more people to the original wiki article. WordPress users can then add directly to the discussion without having to log out of the wiki and back into the blog.

Have a go hero

While it's nice of WordPress to share the comments of certain blog posts with our wiki, we should reciprocate by providing access to our wiki's content and sharing it with the WordPress administrator. With the popularity that blogs have, allowing articles from our wiki to be posted on a popular blog can really do wonders for driving traffic to our wiki.

Installing the extension from `http://www.mediawiki.org/wiki/Extension:WikiToWordPress#Code` will allow us to accomplish this with an added bonus. Included in the extension is the ability to set the `$SearchString` to scan newly-created articles for specific keywords that we want to have blog postings created for.

Because this process involves creating a plugin for WordPress and configuring WordPress files, it is being issued to you as a challenge. You can find much of what you need to get this working from the link in the previous paragraph but it is important to note that the information for the WordPress plugin is listed under the **discussion** tab on the extension's page, so be sure to read that as well.

Pop quiz – WordPress Comments

1. Where does the WordPress Comments extension pull comments from?

    a. Directly from a blog's page

    b. From the blog's database

    c. From the user's local computer

    d. From the MediaWiki site

2. When the WordPress Comments extension is in use, a user that posts a comment directly on a wiki page is redirected to the blog that is connected to the page.

    a. True

    b. False

Joomla! integration

We have made references to Joomla! throughout the book because the developers rely on MediaWiki as a way to deliver the user manual to users. Ironically, there are components (software that enhances Joomla!'s functionality) that have been created to give Joomla! sites some of the features found in a wiki. However, the development team knows that while Joomla! is great for content management, MediaWiki is the choice for wikis!

As there are over 20 million instances where Joomla! has been installed on websites, the odds of you working with this application are quite high. In the event that you wish to integrate Joomla! and MediaWiki, we are going to cover the installation of an extension called AuthJoomla that will allow authentication between the two.

 Install Joomla! with the sample content so you can easily test out this extension.

Before you begin the next exercise, you will need to have an installation of Joomla! and MediaWiki on the same host. For the following exercises, we will be working with a fresh installation of MediaWiki and not the Floss Pro Populo site. The code for the AuthJoomla extension is too long to include here and can be obtained from the online companion to the book.

Time for action – installing AuthJoomla

Installing AuthJoomla is pretty straight forward. What we need to do is visit `http://www.mediawiki.org/wiki/Extension:AuthJoomla#AuthJoomla.php` and copy the PHP code listed on the page. Once we have copied it, we need to paste it into our text editor and save the file as `AuthJoomla.php`. Once we have our file ready, let's begin.

1. Using your FTP program or file manager, upload the `AuthJoomla.php` extension to the `extensions` folder of your MediaWiki installation.

2. Now, open your `LocalSettings.php` file for editing and add the following lines of code. Remember, if you have MaintenanceShell running, that's right; add the lines above it so when you run the scripts, AuthJoomla will be included.

```
// Add AuthJoomla
// Joomla! MySQL Host Name.
$wgAuthJoomla_MySQL_Host      = '';

// Joomla! MySQL Username.
$wgAuthJoomla_MySQL_Username = '';
```

```
// Joomla! MySQL Password.
$wgAuthJoomla_MySQL_Password = '';
// Joomla! MySQL Database Name.
$wgAuthJoomla_MySQL_Database = '';
// Joomla! MySQL Database TablePrefix.
$wgAuthJoomla_TablePrefix        = "jos_";
// Joomla! Absolute path.
$wgAuthJoomla_Path               = '';

require_once("$IP/extensions/AuthJoomla/AuthJoomla.php");
$wgAuth = new AuthJoomla();
```

Make the following changes to the above code:

- Add the host for your Joomla! database between the quotes next to $wgAuthJoomla_MySQL_Host.
- Add the database username database between the quotes next to $wgAuthJoomla_MySQL_Username.
- Add the password for your Joomla! database user between the quotes next to $wgAuthJoomla_MySQL_Password.
- Add the name of your Joomla! database between the quotes next to $wgAuthJoomla_MySQL_Database.
- Leave the $wgAuthJoomla_TablePrefix as jos_ if you are using a default installation. If you have changed the prefix for tables, make sure it is reflected here.
- Add the absolute path for your Joomla! database between the qt to $wgAuthJoomla_Absolute_Path.

3. Save your edits.

   Now, let's go over to our Joomla! site.

4. Create a new user from the home page of your Joomla! site by clicking on the **Create an account** link at the bottom of the left-hand side of the page.

5. Once you have created your account, browse to your MediaWiki site and log in using your newly-created account from Joomla!

If everything was installed correctly, you should be able to link to pages in your wiki directly from your Joomla! site and your users will be logged in seamlessly.

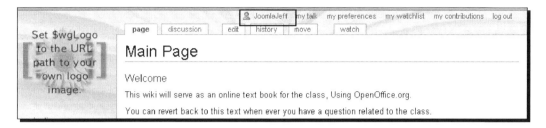

The AuthJoomla extension has a known bug that causes MediaWiki to add the prefix `mw_` or `wiki_` to the `jos_users` table when querying the users credentials. If you receive this error, try the fix found on the Discussion tab for the extension at: `http://www.mediawiki.org/wiki/Extension_talk:AuthJoomla`. This is a rather complicated fix and is outside the scope of this book.

What just happened?

By pointing your MediaWiki site to the Joomla! user database table, `jos_users`, we are able to tell MediaWiki to look there for username and password combinations. Unfortunately, you cannot create usernames in MediaWiki when this is used because the application cannot write to the jos_users table, it can only read from it.

Pop quiz – AuthJoomla

1. Why do you need to add the AuthJoomla code above the MaintenanceShell extension code?

    a. So that the code is easier to read

    b. To enhance the functionality of AuthJoomla

    c. Joomla! does not work well with MaintenanceShell

    d. So that the AuthJoomla extension is included in the maintenance scripts

2. In order for AuthJoomla to work, the MediaWiki software and Joomla! software need to be installed on the same server.

    a. True

    b. False

MediaWiki and Moodle

We have seen in Chapter 1 how MediaWiki can be used to deliver course material, when we discussed how it is used in `http://www.ecgpedia.org`. While MediaWiki does a good job of delivering an online learning course, the real powerhouse when it comes to learning management online is Moodle.

However, what if you took a course built on Moodle and coupled it with an online textbook written in MediaWiki that also served as a collaboration repository? This could provide you with a great platform to deliver your content.

Have a go hero

To create a seamless environment between Moodle and MediaWiki, an extension called MoodleSSO (Single sign-on) was created. This extension allows you to log in to your Moodle course and should you be redirected to MediaWiki via a link in your course, you will already be signed on to the wiki.

The installation of this extension requires some configuration on the Moodle installation and the code involved with it as well. As it is beyond the scope of this book, you are issued with the challenge of not only installing this extension, but configuring everything to work properly. If you have issues when it comes to getting this to work don't fret, later in this chapter we will learn how to integrate MediaWiki with OpenID. OpenID will let you authenticate against Moodle as well as do what OpenID and LDAP can do for our environment.

The Single sign-on approach

One of the most frustrating things for visitors of websites is the need to register for a site before they can read, or in MediaWiki's case edit, the content hosted on the site. Registering for another site means time spent filling out forms, another user name to remember, another password that will probably be forgotten, and more e-mail cluttering up their inbox with login details, forgotten passwords, and other junk.

To help alleviate some of these issues, OpenID was created to help people manage their online identity. OpenID is an interesting tool because not only will it help you populate ridiculously long registration forms, but sometimes, it will allow you to forego the entire registration process as your OpenID can serve as your authentication to the site. OpenID is a highly-touted technology as well with organizations such as VeriSign, PayPal, AOL, and Yahoo! making use of this service for their visitors and clients.

OpenID does not share user credentials with the sites that use this service. This means your information is not stored on the databases of the individual sites, only on OpenID's servers. Should one of these websites have their security compromised, your login information will be safe. However, if your OpenID is compromised, then any site using it can be accessed.

Have a go hero

Using OpenID on your wiki has quite a few prerequisites that you must have in place for things to work properly. Unfortunately, if you are not running your own web server, you will have to request your hosting company do this for you. If you are on a shared hosting plan, odds are you will not be able to complete this task. If you are using a dedicated server, you may have a bit more control over what you can install on your server and what permissions you have. Those using a dedicated server may be able to complete this challenge, but check with your hosting provider first.

In order to successfully get OpenID running on your wiki, you will need to download the **PHP OpenID Library** from `http://www.openidenabled.com/php-openid/`. Once you have this successfully installed and running according to the instructions, you will need to install the OpenID extension from `http://www.mediawiki.org/wiki/Extension:OpenID#Installation`.

Follow the instructions carefully with this one, this challenge is definitely not for the faint of heart!

Summary

Well, here we are at the end of the book! In this last chapter, we saw how MediaWiki can be integrated with some of the leading web applications to build powerful sites for your visitors. Specifically, we saw how extensions allow us to display WordPress comments on a related wiki page, and authenticate to our wiki with a Moodle glossary. Integrating with these programs really makes MediaWiki a more robust and powerful application than it was originally intended to be.

As we are at the end of the book, we should have created a fully-working wiki by now. I hope that you build on the foundation from the exercises in this book and continue to learn more about this wonderful tool. In the following appendices, I have included examples of some great extensions you can use, where to find examples of how wikis are used, and where to turn to when you need more help regarding MediaWiki.

The Best Extensions for MediaWiki

Wikis have grown in popularity over the years. Nowadays, you can sign up for a service such as PBWikis.com and they will host a ready-made wiki for you for free. While this may be a great solution for someone who wants to host a small wiki for a few family members or friends to collaborate and share information on, for building a large scale wiki site, it just won't do.

Much of the problems with the smaller wiki applications lie in their limitations. They don't allow for much customization; in most cases, what you see is what you get.

Conversely, MediaWiki takes a different approach. Being a free/open source application, you are encouraged to customize your wiki to make it work best for you. This is why the developers spend so much time creating extensions.

Extensions are a great concept because they allow you, the site designer, to pick and choose what additional functionality you want for your wiki. While it may have been easier if the MediaWiki team had just included all of these extensions into the base installation, this would be extremely taxing on the server's resources and would limit who could install MediaWiki.

Throughout the book, you have installed many different extensions so you know just how easy it is to do this. In this appendix, we are going to look at some of the best extensions available to you. None of the extensions included here are ones we have already installed.

Of course, you may be looking for other extensions as well. As there are over 1000 extensions available to you, we can only list the ones I think are the best. If you wish to view an entire list, you can do so by visiting

`http://www.mediawiki.org/wiki/Category:Extensions_by_category.`

C	I cont.	R cont.
■ [+] Calendar extensions (1 C, 9 P)	■ [+] Interwiki extensions (5 P)	■ [+] Referencing extensions (16 P)
■ [+] Category extensions (30 P)	**L**	■ [+] Revision management extensions (5 P)
■ [+] Conversion Extensions (1 P)	■ [+] Log extensions (11 P)	
D	**M**	**S**
■ [+] Data extraction extensions (50 P)	■ [+] Math extensions (20 P)	■ [+] Semantic Bundle extensions (14 P)
■ [+] Database extensions (61 P)	■ [+] Media handling extensions (2 C, 24 P)	■ [+] Sort extensions (2 P)
■ [+] Discussion and forum extensions (1 C, 19 P)	■ [+] Modifiable variables extensions (3 P)	■ [+] Spam management extensions (11 P)
E	**N**	■ [+] Subpage extensions (3 P)
■ [+] Email extensions (19 P)	■ [+] Navigation extensions (4 P)	■ [+] Syntax highlighting extensions (15 P)
■ [+] Extensions used by XML Database Dumps (1 P)	**O**	**T**
■ [+] Extensions used on Wikimedia (61 P)	■ [+] On-line learning extensions (1 C, 3 P)	■ [+] Task extensions (6 P)
F	■ [+] Output extensions (7 P)	■ [+] Template extensions (19 P)
■ [+] Feed generator extensions (9 P)	**P**	**U**
G	■ [+] Path extensions (2 P)	■ [+] User access extensions (3 C, 3 P)
■ [+] GIS extensions (10 P)	■ [+] Poll extensions (6 P)	
I	**R**	
■ [+] Import Extensions (4 P)	■ [+] Rating extensions (9 P)	
	■ [+] Redirect extensions (9	

Administration

These extensions all help make your job as the sysop easier.

AbsenteeLandlord

Planning a vacation where you can't keep up with changes to your wiki? This extension helps prevent inactive wikis from becoming the targets of spambots and vandalism by automatically locking the wiki database if a sysop has not logged in during a time period defined by `$wgAbsenteeLandlordMaxDays`. With the database locked, no further changes can be made to the wiki. To unlock the wiki database, and the wiki itself, the sysop needs to simply log in to the wiki.

`http://www.mediawiki.org/wiki/Extension:AbsenteeLandlord`

AbuseFilter

Installing this extension creates a special page named **AbuseFilter** where privileged users can set controls to the user activity on the wiki. These users can also define how the wiki reacts to certain behaviors.

This extension requires the AntiSpoof extension to be installed as well.

```
http://www.mediawiki.org/wiki/Extension:AbuseFilter
```

AccessControl

This extension is used to restrict access to specific pages based on a user's group. After installing this extension, you can control both the viewing and editing of a page. This extension also allows you to grant access to multiple user groups. You can also block access to read certain pages by group or individual users.

Users who have been forbidden to view a page cannot use the search feature to view protected pages.

```
http://www.mediawiki.org/wiki/Extension:AccessControl
```

TitleBlacklist

This extension allows the administrator to create blacklists for page titles and usernames that they deem inappropriate.

```
http://www.mediawiki.org/wiki/Extension:TitleBlacklist
```

BrokenLinks

This extension is meant for smaller wikis. What it does is collect URLs from a table named **Manual: Externallinks_table** and check each URL for a successful server response. Any links that have a failed response are reported to you on a special page named **BrokenLinks**. This report also tells you about the page on which this broken link appears.

```
http://www.mediawiki.org/wiki/Extension:BrokenLinks
```

Google Analytics

Using this extension places a Google Analytics tracking code into each page on the wiki. To keep the statistics more honest, users with bot privileges and sysops are not counted in the statistics. You have the option of keeping logged in users out of the statistical counts as well.

```
http://www.mediawiki.org/wiki/Extension:Google_Analytics_Integration
```

ImportUsers

If you are in charge of implementing a wiki for an organization with multiple users, you would normally have two options when it comes to creating users. First, you could let the users create their accounts individually. While this takes the workload off of you, and any other administrator, it is a given that some of your users will not follow your directions when it comes to creating appropriate user names, using strong passwords, or entering the correct e-mail address. The second option alleviates any issues with inappropriate registrations because it requires you and your fellow administrators, if you have any, to create each account yourself.

The ImportUsers extension gives you the best of both worlds. If you can get all of your users into a spreadsheet, or other file that can be saved as a CSV, then you can easily import the list right to the wiki's database through a special page called **ImportUsers**. Not only will this save you time, but you can be sure that the accounts will reflect exactly what you want.

```
http://www.mediawiki.org/wiki/Extension:ImportUsers
```

MaintenanceShell

We saw MaintenanceShell in action in Chapter 11. This extension gives the sysop access to the wiki's maintenance scripts if they don't have access to the command line of their web server.

```
http://www.mediawiki.org/wiki/Extension:MaintenanceShell
```

ManageCategories

For the beginner MediaWiki user, categories may seem a bit intimidating. This extension allows you to easily define what category you want an article to be a part of and even define new ones if needed.

ManageCategories extends the edit area of the page to include three new parts:

- A menu box where you can choose from all current categories
- A text field to assign the article to a new category
- Checkboxes that represents the currently assigned categories (optional)

```
http://www.mediawiki.org/wiki/Extension:ManageCategories
```

StalkerLog

This extension can be a great help if you need to keep track of user activity on your wiki. StalkerLog creates a log of user logins and logouts. By default, anyone can view this log but by customizing the permissions, you can set it up so that only certain groups or users have access to the logs.

```
http://www.mediawiki.org/wiki/Extension:StalkerLog
```

UserLoginLog

In Chapter 8 we saw UserLoginLog in action. This extension displays the IP address of users who logged in, or attempted to log in, and displays them on the special page **Special:Logs**.

```
http://www.mediawiki.org/wiki/Extension:UserLoginLog
```

UserRightsList

Managing user rights in MediaWiki can be a bit of a chore. Granting extra permissions means you have to search for the user by name and then add the permissions. To make this job a bit easier, you can install the extension, UserRightsList. This extension creates a special page that lists all of the users registered with the wiki. With a simple checkbox, you can grant or revoke additional privileges to your users.

This extension also comes with a filtering system so you can search by group or username and even employ SQL wildcards.

```
http://www.mediawiki.org/wiki/Extension:UserRightsList
```

Content

The following extensions were designed to provide alternate ways to display content and to help make contributing easier on your authors.

PdfBook

For large wikis, your categories may be loaded with content that you wish to share via a print medium or digital reader. This is where the PdfBook extension can come in handy.

This extension extracts your articles from your wiki and creates a PDF file out of it. Each article takes the role of a new chapter and the extension even creates a table of contents for your newly-created book.

```
http://www.mediawiki.org/wiki/Extension:Pdf_Book
```

Cite

When writing, it is common to use outside sources to support your work. However, it is also necessary to cite these sources when you use them.

Cite is an extension that allows you to create footnotes so your visitors can provide credit to anyone else's work they use when writing articles for your wiki.

There are multiple files that need to be installed to get this extension working. If you are installing `Cite.php` on an older version of MediaWiki, you may have issues with HTML parameters and parser functions. However, Cite is in use by Wikipedia so it is considered a stable extension. When used with versions after 1.11, there have been no reported issues.

`http://www.mediawiki.org/wiki/Extension:Cite`

DocumentApproval

If you are using MediaWiki in a corporate or educational environment, there is most likely going to be content that requires the approval of someone else before it is posted. After all, the HR department doesn't want Joe in accounting declaring every Friday to be Hawaiian Shirt day without approval!

The DocumentApproval extension allows the article's author to insert a tag that creates a **Sign** tab to be displayed. The appropriate user can then use this to approve or sign the document certifying its accuracy.

`http://www.mediawiki.org/wiki/Extension:DocumentApproval`

EditOwn

Need to protect pages against edits from your visitors? The EditOwn extension provides security against any user, other than privileged users, editing a page created by someone else. Users can make any changes to pages they create, but the collaboration benefit of MediaWiki is no longer in place. This can be a good extension to use if you are creating your website with MediaWiki or for an online textbook.

`http://www.mediawiki.org/wiki/Extension:EditOwn`

EmbedPDF

Installing the EmbedPDF extension provides you with the `<pdf>` and `</pdf>` tags. Placing the name of an uploaded PDF file or a link to a PDF file hosted elsewhere will create a 700pixel by 600pixel box on the page to display the PDF referred to. Remember, if you are going to host PDF files on your server, you need to tell MediaWiki to allow their uploads.

`http://www.mediawiki.org/wiki/Extension:EmbedPDF`

EmbedVideoPlus

Earlier we saw how we can embed Flash files into our wiki. The EmbedVideoPlus extension allows us to embed videos from popular video sharing sites such as YouTube. The extension doesn't limit your control of how your videos are displayed. You have the option to define parameters such as alignment, width, and height.

This extension does not require you to upload videos to your server. Instead, you define the service and provide the ID of the video and EmbedVideoPlus goes out to the server and pulls the video for you.

```
http://www.mediawiki.org/wiki/Extension:EmbedVideoPlus
```

Flash

This is another extension we saw in action back in Chapter 6 when we learned how to embed Flash movies into our wiki. Flash extensions can leave your wiki vulnerable to a cross site scripting exploit, so use these extensions carefully.

```
http://www.mediawiki.org/wiki/Extension:Flash
```

Google Calendar

Quite simply, this extension allows you display a Google Calendar right in your wiki. A separate site from Google, `https://www.google.com/calendar/embedhelper`, allows you to configure how the calendar is displayed.

```
http://www.mediawiki.org/wiki/Extension:Google_Calendar
```

Google Maps

Just like Google Calendar, you can embed Google Maps into your wiki with this extension. Think of what you can do with articles about different locations! This extension also allows you to add a **make a map** link that, when clicked, opens the maps editor.

```
http://www.mediawiki.org/wiki/Extension:Google_Maps
```

GoogleWave

Want the ultimate in collaboration? How about a marriage of MediaWiki and Google Wave? Google Wave has been called the reinvention of e-mail that allows users to create live, social communication documents that can be edited by multiple users in near real-time. This extension provides just that by allowing you to embed Google Waves right into your wiki using the newly-created `<wave id>` tag. While the ID of the wave is required, there are other parameters you can define as well:

- `height`
- `width`
- `color`
- `bgcolor`
- `font`
- `fontsize`

`http://www.mediawiki.org/wiki/Extension:GoogleWave`

Collection

Earlier, we saw how to embed PDF files into your wiki. However, what if you wanted to create a PDF file from an article in your wiki? Rather than printing the page with a PDF creator, install this extension so any of your visitors have the option of turning a page into a PDF file. Don't want a PDF file but you would rather have the page in OpenDocument format? Maybe DocBook XML is the desired output? No problem, the Collection extension allows for any of these formats.

`http://www.mediawiki.org/wiki/Extension:Collection`

OggHandler

Like the Flash extension, we saw OggHandler back in Chapter 6 to embed Ogg audio and video files into our wiki.

`http://www.mediawiki.org/wiki/Extension:OggHandler`

User

Whether you need to keep a closer watch over your wiki's users or you need to raise their privileges, these extensions were built to help manage all things related to the user.

ConfirmAccount

While allowing anyone to create an account may be the nice way to go, sometimes, you may want to limit who has access to your wiki. The ConfirmAccount extension makes it so that any accounts created need to be approved by the sysop/bureaucrat accounts before they are activated.

This extension has quite a few configuration options available to you, from determining the minimum word count for a user's biography to how long an inactive account can exist before it is automatically rejected.

```
http://www.mediawiki.org/wiki/Extension:ConfirmAccount
```

EditOnlyYourOwnPage

If the EditOwn extension gives your users too much freedom, then EditOnlyYourOwnPage is the extension for you. With this installed, users can only edit their user page, talk page, and subpages of them. That's it.

Of course, your sysop isn't prevented from editing pages.

```
http://www.mediawiki.org/wiki/Extension:EditOnlyYourOwnPage
```

SocialRewarding

Everyone likes to be recognized. So if you are not one of those wikis with EditOnlyYourOwnPage installed, you may want to bring attention to those users who contribute quality content to your wiki.

This extension comes with a great piece of documentation that explains how to use the four reward techniques:

- Amount of References
- Most Viewed Articles
- Rating of Articles
- Recommender System

```
http://www.mediawiki.org/wiki/Extension:SocialRewarding
```

Communication

Wikis are all about communication and collaboration. These extensions help enhance the communication functionality of your wiki.

AIM

The AIM extension provides a tag, `<aim>` and `</aim>`, that displays a button with the user's AOL Instant Messenger status (the AIM username is placed between the tags). Clicking on the button opens an AIM chat window as a pop up.

`http://www.mediawiki.org/wiki/Extension:AIM`

ContactPage

The ContactPage extension creates a special page, called **Contact**, that allows visitors to contact the sysop via a form. While it is similar to **Emailuser** special page, the Contact extension allows for anonymous submissions. Captcha can be enabled in this extension to prevent spam.

`http://www.mediawiki.org/wiki/Extension:ContactPage`

ICQ

Just like the AIM extension, ICQ allows you to place your ICQ number between the `<icq>` and `</icq>` tags. When this is placed on a page, a button with the user's ICQ status is shown.

`http://www.mediawiki.org/wiki/Extension:ICQ`

IRC Chat

Unlike the AIM and ICQ extensions, this one is rather complex as it requires you to modify the database through phpMyAdmin, and make adjustments to the skin. Once you have all of the configurations out of the way you will be happy with the results because now, you can open **Internet Relay Chat (IRC)** right in your MediaWiki interface using PJIRC.

Something like this can be great for a developer wiki, a MMORPG wiki, or a wiki that coincides with a popular IRC topic.

`http://www.mediawiki.org/wiki/Extension:IRC_Chat`

QPoll

Want to include multiple polls on your wiki pages? Or maybe you want to chain a few polls together. In either case, the QPoll extension gives you many more features than the Poll extension.

Installing the extension is not complicated, but setting up the polls requires a great deal of reading. If you are looking for something easy, try the Poll extension. If you want robust polls and don't mind the extra work, stick with QPoll.

`http://www.mediawiki.org/wiki/Extension:QPoll`

Skype

AIM and ICQ have extensions so why should Skype users be left out? With this extension, you can include your Skype username between the `<skype>` and `</skype>` tags to show your online status to wiki visitors.

```
http://www.mediawiki.org/wiki/Extension:Skype
```

WebChat

Want to enable chat in your wiki without having to use the complex IRC Chat extension? If so, look no further. This extension creates a special page named **WebChat**. Visitors can navigate to the page and chat with other wiki users.

This is great if you wish to keep your chat internal, for instance at a work place or school. Keep in mind though, this does not create a chat room on your wiki itself, rather it sets up the client to connect to the freenode IRC server on channel #freenode.

```
http://www.mediawiki.org/wiki/Extension:WebChat
```

Discussion

The Discussion extension lets you place a discussion panel on articles in your wiki with just a small bit of wikitext. The discussion panel mimics that of a blog's comment box. Check back in Chapter 9 to refresh your memory about how this extension looks.

```
http://www.mediawiki.org/wiki/Extension:Discussion
```

Security

Protect your content and data from spam and vandalism with extensions designed to help better secure your wiki.

AuthorProtect

In the EditOwn extension, the sysop made the decision that only authors could edit their own work. AuthorProtect leaves this decision in the hands of the individual authors. They can choose to protect a page that they create by blocking everyone but themselves and the sysop from editing the page, or they can leave the page alone and let any user make edits.

The option to protect a page is done on a page-by-page basis. Installing this extension does not protect every page on the wiki by default.

```
http://www.mediawiki.org/wiki/Extension:AuthorProtect
```

Check Spambots

When it comes to bots spamming your wiki, you can never be too safe. CheckSpambots is an extension that checks the IP address of an editor, their e-mail address, and name against databases that list known spammers. The blacklists are all hosted on external servers and include:

- FSpamlist - `fspamlist.com`
- Stop Forum Spam - `stopforumspam.com`
- SORBS - `sorbs.net`
- Spamhaus - `spamhaus.org`
- SpamCop - `spamcop.net`
- Project Honey Pot - `projecthoneypot.org`
- BotScout - `botscout.com`
- DroneBL - `dronebl.org`
- AHBL - `ahbl.org`
- Undisposable - `undisposable.net`
- Tor Project - `torproject.org`

This extension does not check the body of the edit and does not check external links to see if they are spam. Other considerations include the fact that there is no whitelist so every edit is checked against these external servers. Because these servers are hosted elsewhere, the edit process will be noticeably slower.

`http://www.mediawiki.org/wiki/Extension:Check_Spambots`

EnforceStrongPassword

More and more IT departments are requiring users to have strong passwords for their accounts as a way to protect against brute force attacks. This extension, EnforceStrongPassword, allows the sysop to define minimum password requirements for all users.

If you have users already registered for your wiki, notify them of the requirements. Once the extension is installed, they will not be able to log in if their password does not meet the minimum requirements.

`http://www.mediawiki.org/wiki/Extension:EnforceStrongPassword`

PasswordProtectPages

If the author wishes to protect specific pages using a password, for both viewing and editing, then this extension should be installed. PasswordProtectPages creates a **protect** link on the page that redirects the author to a page to set up the page password. After doing this, anyone wanting to read or edit this page has to unlock it using the predetermined password.

```
http://www.mediawiki.org/wiki/Extension:PasswordProtectPages
```

Bad Behavior

We saw Bad Behavior in Chapter 8 when we learned how to keep spam comments. This extension not only helps prevent spam, but it will help keep e-mail harvesters from stealing e-mail addresses from your wiki.

```
http://www.mediawiki.org/wiki/Extension:Bad_Behavior
```

Monetization

Is it in your plans to make money from your wiki? If so, these monetization extensions will help get you on your way.

AmazonAssociates

With the AmazonAssociates extension, you display Amazon books on your wiki using **Amazon Web Services** (**AWS**) and an Amazon Associates account. When a visitor clicks on a link to make a purchase, the account associated will be credited with a percentage of the sale.

```
http://www.mediawiki.org/wiki/Extension:AmazonAssociates
```

Google Adsense & Google Adsense2

Have an AdSense account with Google? Using these two extensions you can include AdSense ads across the top of the wiki, using Google Adsense, and in the sidebar, using Google Adsense2. This is the easiest solution for monetizing your wiki, however, it does require you to set up an Adsense account with Google before installing this extension.

```
http://www.mediawiki.org/wiki/Extension:Google_Adsense
```

```
http://www.mediawiki.org/wiki/Extension:Google_AdSense_2
```

PayPal

If you plan on selling anything through your wiki, such as an e-book, a subscription, or even a donation, the PayPal extension will give you the means to collect money from your customers. Originally written in German, a few modifications to display information in English and all you have to do is use the `<paypal>` and `</paypal>` tags to create a button and text description for Paypal.

```
http://www.mediawiki.org/wiki/Extension:PayPal
```

Cool

These extensions were just too cool to leave out of the list.

AnyWikiDraw

While there are some security considerations related to the enabling of cookies and JavaScript in order to get this extension to work, it is really a cool addition to your site.

AnyWikiDraw runs a Java applet in your wiki that allows the editing of SVG, PNG, and JPEG images directly in the wiki. For sites where kids are a primary audience, this extension can be a great addition.

```
http://www.mediawiki.org/wiki/Extension:AnyWikiDraw
```

Balloons

Tooltips are a great way to teach people how to do something. For educational wikis, or wikis that attract a great deal of new users, the addition of tooltips can really give your wiki some pop.

The Balloons extension provides the magic tag `<balloon>` that allows you to add pop up tooltips to images and text in your wiki.

```
http://mckay.cshl.edu/wiki/index.php/MediaWiki_Balloon_Extension
```

CSS MenuSidebar

Wikis don't have to be boring. With the CSS MenuSidebar extension you can jazz up your site a bit with some CSS. You can create additional sidebar elements as a menu with dropdown items.

Along with the extension, you will need to copy a CSS file to your server as well so you can style your menus.

```
http://www.mediawiki.org/wiki/Extension:CSS_MenuSidebar
```

CategoryCloud

Category clouds are extremely popular on blogs thanks to a simple plugin made available from WordPress. With MediaWiki, an extension called CategoryCloud creates a tag cloud for every subcategory in the category.

Each word can be resized based on the number of children, both category and articles, in each subcategory.

`http://www.mediawiki.org/wiki/Extension:CategoryCloud`

Flickr

Wikis are all about collaboration and sharing, so why not share your Flickr images with your wiki's audience.

Using the Flickr extension has some advantages over uploading and embedding files. First, you don't have to store them on your server so resources such as storage and bandwidth aren't being used.

Second, you can keep the comments from Flickr so that they can be shared as well.

`http://www.mediawiki.org/wiki/Extension:Flickr`

MediaWikiPlayer

We saw earlier in the book how to playback Flash and Ogg files with separate players. The MediaWikiPlayer encompasses many different file types and allows you to play them back over your wiki.

By adding the URL of the file between two tags, `<mediaplayer arg=value >` and `</mediaplayer>`, you can play the following file types:

- FLV
- MP4 (H264/AAC)
- MP3
- Youtube
- Various streaming servers
- Various XML playlists

`http://www.mediawiki.org/wiki/Extension:MediawikiPlayer`

SendToTwitter

Want to send a tweet when you wiki is updated? SendToTwitter is an extension that will do just that. You can customize your message and the extension will automatically shorten the URL for you.

```
http://www.mediawiki.org/wiki/Extension:SendToTwitter
```

More on extensions

You can find out more about MediaWiki extensions from the **Category: Extensions** page at: `http://www.mediawiki.org/wiki/Category:Extensions`. You will find links to the extension matrix that lists every possible extension for MediaWiki, information on how to request an extension, and how you can contribute your own extensions to MediaWiki.

The Best of MediaWiki in Use

Throughout this book, we have seen some pretty good examples of how MediaWiki is used to power a wiki solution for many sites. Specifically, we have seen how Wikipedia and Joomla! use this software quite successfully.

Over the next few pages, we will see some other examples of MediaWIki in use to give you some ideas as to what MediaWiki can do.

Collaboration

Remember how back in Chapter 1 we introduced you to the early days of the wiki? It was used as a collaboration tool for programmers, right? Well, Facebook developers have created a wiki of their own to help other developers write and share applications for the Facebook platform.

```
http://wiki.developers.facebook.com/index.php/Main_Page
```

The following screenshot shows the **Main Page** of this wiki:

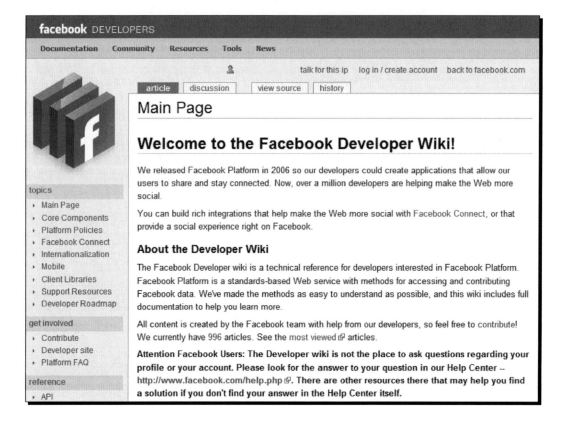

Support

The University of South Florida's Information Technology department created this site to help students access, use, and troubleshoot technology issues around campus. This helps provide quick answers to simple questions so students can find what they need without having to assign someone from the support team to answer the question.

`http://wiki.it.usf.edu/index.php/Main_Page`

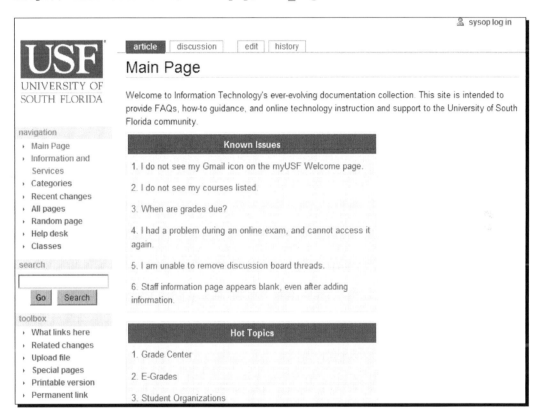

Project management

Because of a wiki's collaborative nature, building a site to coordinate projects is an excellent use of MediaWiki's capabilities. Mozilla Wiki is a perfect example of this. On their site, they list the project schedule, roadmaps, and even meeting information for different sub-projects.

```
https://wiki.mozilla.org/
```

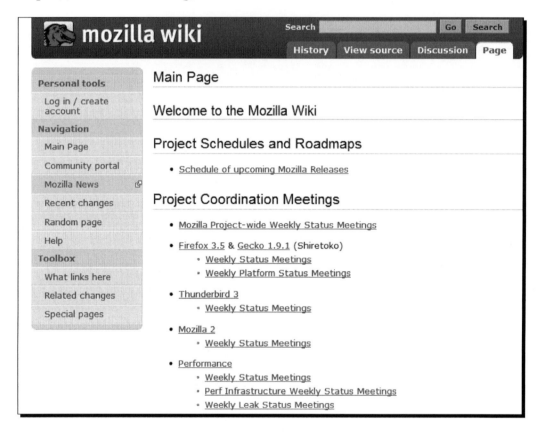

Online learning

Dedicated to biological research and engineering, OpenWetWare also allows professors to upload their courses to this online educational portal. Those interested can view courses from MIT, University of California, Berkley, the Imperial College London, and many others.

```
http://openwetware.org/wiki/Main_Page
```

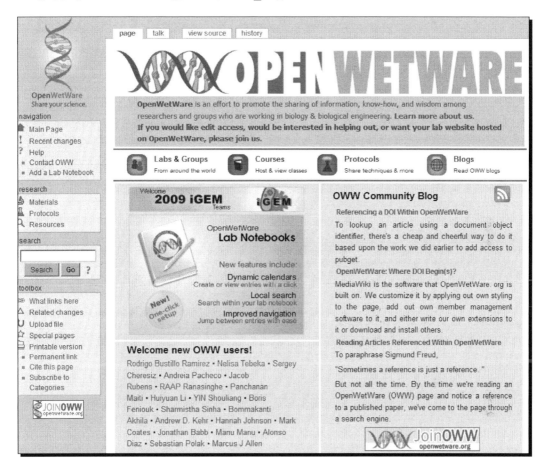

In addition to being a great example of an online learning community, OpenWetWare is a great example of what you can do when customizing an existing MediaWiki skin!

The complete site

There are few sites that make use of everything MediaWiki has to offer, and no one makes use of this software better than the **Open Web Application Security Project (OWASP)**. They have updates on their various projects, a mass collection of tutorials, user manuals, articles, and much more. For an example of what you can really do with MediaWiki, this is the best place to visit.

http://www.owasp.org

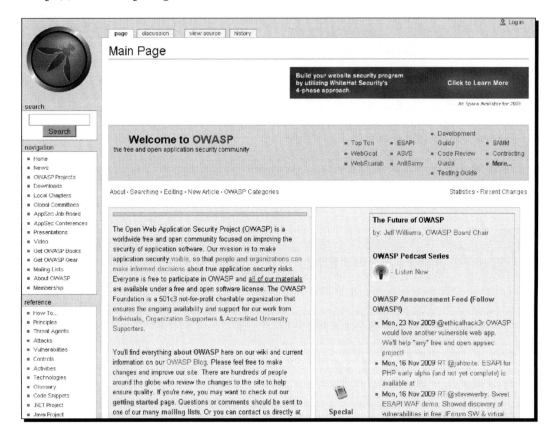

C
Where to Turn to

While I hope you find the information in this book extremely helpful, there are times when you will need to look elsewhere for help. Maybe you need help with moving your wiki, or your extension just won't work right. Whatever the case may be, know that as one of the largest open source projects, MediaWiki has a cadre of community members who are more than willing to help you with any issue you may have.

Before we look at some of the sites where you can turn to, understand that when dealing with online support you are turning to other people who have jobs, families, and other activities in their lives. While it can be frustrating to post a question and have to wait for a response, the people answering your questions are not being paid to do so. They are helping you and it is important to treat them as such.

Another point to remember is that it is up to you to do your research before asking a question. Look through the different support forums and websites to see if anyone else has had the same issue. Extension not working? Check the discussion page to see if there is any information there. The point is, do your research, don't expect someone else to do it for you.

Official MediaWiki support

The developers of MediaWiki have put together a few avenues for users to find help and support on a variety of different issues. Many people may opt for these as a first choice as all fixes are approved by MediaWiki developers. However, even MediaWiki suggests looking to other forums for help as well.

Project:Support desk

The **Support desk** special page was built for users to post questions regarding MediaWiki. There is a warning here that questions may take several days to be answered, and there is a chance they will not be answered at all.

```
http://www.mediawiki.org/wiki/Project:Support_desk
```

Chat

Made up of volunteers, this is the real-time support channel for MediaWIki. If you are in need of immediate support, this is the best place as you can chat with someone regarding your problem. It is important to note some specific rules regarding the IRC channel:

- Check the FAQ page and the Manual before asking your question.

- Post your question and wait for a response. Don't ask, "Is anyone there?" If you are not receiving a response it may because:
  - There are no volunteers on at that time. Come back later and try again
  - No one has an answer to your problem
  - The question you are asking can be found in the Manual or on the FAQ page

- Expect to wait before getting an initial response. You may need to provide more information, so have this ready as well.

You can use the #mediawiki IRC channel.

```
irc://irc.freenode.net/mediawiki
```

Help:Contents

This is the User help page that covers topics from editing a page to how to block a range of IP addresses. In addition to the page that was created for each topic, you can find a great deal of information in the discussion page as well. All of these pages are considered to be in the public domain so do not post anything that you may wish to keep a copyright on.

```
http://www.mediawiki.org/wiki/Help:Contents
```

Manual:FAQ

Just as the title suggests, this is the **frequently asked questions (FAQ)** page for MediaWiki. While a great deal of questions are answered here, you can also look to the old Meta wiki FAQ page found at: `http://meta.wikimedia.org/wiki/MediaWiki_FAQ`.

```
http://www.mediawiki.org/wiki/Manual:FAQ
```

Manual:Contents

This is the official technical manual for MediaWiki. The manual is broken into three sections, one for users, another for system administrators, and a third for developers. Like other pages, the **discussion** tab holds as much important information as the article itself.

If you feel you are ready to help out with the MediaWiki project, you may be able to contribute to the manual by checking out the **to do** list.

```
http://www.mediawiki.org/wiki/Manual:Contents
```

Mailing list

Using your newsreader, you can subscribe to the mediawiki-l mailing list and request support here as well. You can also view mailing list archives by typing `http://dir.gmane.org/ gmane.org.wikimedia.mediawiki` in your browser's address bar to visit the Gmane directory dedicated to MediaWiki.

```
news://news.gmane.org/gmane.org.wikimedia.mediawiki
```

 Gmane is a site that archives mailing lists into news groups. Unlike other indexing services, Gmane is bidirectional so you can post to some of these mailing lists without being subscribed to them. It is up to the individual mailing list as to whether or not they allow this.

Outside support

MediaWiki, being a popular software application, has many other outside sites dedicated to supporting the software. While these are not official MediaWiki sites, they offer a great deal of help to novice users. Most likely, the community surrounding these sites will be able to address your question more quickly than if you posted it to the pages dedicated to support on the MediaWiki site.

MediaWiki Users

This is the unofficial forum dedicated to all types of MediaWIki issues from building your community to monetizing your wiki. Users can also post information regarding projects where they will pay others to help them. While this is a third-party site, even the developers at MediaWiki recommend this site for support.

```
http://www.mwusers.com
```

SiteGround

SiteGround is actually a web hosting company that provides MediaWiki as one of their supported applications. To help their customers, they have created a series of knowledge base articles and tutorials regarding MediaWiki. These tutorials cover some of the basics and don't get into some of the more complicated issues you may face, however they are a nice starting point.

```
http://kb.siteground.com/category/MediaWiki_issues.html
```

Pop Quiz Answers

Chapter 2

MediaWiki requirements quiz

1	2	3
c	a	d

Chapter 3

the navigation box

1	2	3
b	a	c

the toolbox

1	2	3	4
b	b	d	b

the body

1	2	3	4
a	a	b	d

Chapter 4

creating pages

1	2	3	4
a	b	d	a

Chapter 5

tables

1	2	3	4
a	c	a	b

Chapter 6

multimedia

1	2	3
b	b	a

Chapter 7

namespaces

1	2	3
b	c	c

Chapter 8

user groups

1	2	3	4
b	c	a	b

Chapter 9

Recent changes

1	2	3	4	5
b	a	d	a	d

edits

1	2	3	4	5
a	b	c	a	b

Chapter 10

understanding blocks

1	2	3
c	b	d

Chapter 11

backup and restore

1	2	3
a	a	d

Chapter 12

WordPress Comments

1	2
b	a

AuthJoomla

1	2
d	a

Index

D

Database.php 261
DefaultSettings.php 261
definition lists
  creating 115, 116
developer group 177
Discussion extension 307
  installing 228-231
DocumentApproval extension 302
DokuWiki 20

E

EditOnlyYourOwnPage extension 305
EditOwn extension 302
EditPage.php 261
edit summaries, administrative tools 218
edit toolbar
  about 91, 92
  text, editing 92, 93
Emailconfirmed group 177
EmbedPDF extension 302
EmbedVideoPlus extension 303
EnforceStrongPassword extension 308
extensions
  about 188, 297
  AbsenteeLandlord 298
  AbuseFilter 299
  AccessControl 299
  AIM 306
  AmazonAssociates 309
  AnyWikiDraw 310
  AuthorProtect 307
  Bad Behavior 309
  Bad Behavior extension 188
  Balloons 310
  BrokenLinks 299
  CategoryCloud 311
  Check Spambots 308
  Cite 302
  Collection 304
  ConfirmAccount 305
  ContactPage 306
  CSS MenuSidebar 310
  Discussion 307
  DocumentApproval 302
  EditOnlyYourOwnPage 305

  EditOwn 302
  EmbedPDF 302
  EmbedVideoPlus 303
  EnforceStrongPassword 308
  Flash 303
  Flickr 311
  Google Adsense 309
  Google Analytics 299
  Google Calendar 303
  Google Maps 303
  GoogleWave 304
  ICQ 306
  ImportUsers 300
  IRC Chat 306
  MaintenanceShell 300
  ManageCategories 300
  MediaWiki Player 311
  OggHandler 304
  PasswordProtectPages 309
  PayPal 310
  PdfBook 301
  QPoll 306
  SendToTwitter 312
  Skype 307
  SocialRewarding 305
  StalkerLog 301
  TitleBlacklist 299
  URL 298
  UserLoginLog 301
  UserRightsList 301
  WebChat 307
external links
  about 99
  creating 100
  fixing 101, 102

F

Fantastico
  used, for installing MediaWiki 31-34
featured software table 126
file structure, hacking
  about 260, 261
  custom namespaces, enhancing 263- 266
  wiki, making private 262, 263
files, uploading
  cPanel used 36-38

M

Thank you for buying
MediaWiki 1.1: Beginner's Guide

Packt Open Source Project Royalties

When we sell a book written on an Open Source project, we pay a royalty directly to that project. Therefore by purchasing MediaWiki 1.1: Beginner's Guide, Packt will have given some of the money received to the Mediawiki project.

In the long term, we see ourselves and you—customers and readers of our books—as part of the Open Source ecosystem, providing sustainable revenue for the projects we publish on. Our aim at Packt is to establish publishing royalties as an essential part of the service and support a business model that sustains Open Source.

If you're working with an Open Source project that you would like us to publish on, and subsequently pay royalties to, please get in touch with us.

Writing for Packt

We welcome all inquiries from people who are interested in authoring. Book proposals should be sent to author@packtpub.com. If your book idea is still at an early stage and you would like to discuss it first before writing a formal book proposal, contact us; one of our commissioning editors will get in touch with you.

We're not just looking for published authors; if you have strong technical skills but no writing experience, our experienced editors can help you develop a writing career, or simply get some additional reward for your expertise.

About Packt Publishing

Packt, pronounced 'packed', published its first book "Mastering phpMyAdmin for Effective MySQL Management" in April 2004 and subsequently continued to specialize in publishing highly focused books on specific technologies and solutions.

Our books and publications share the experiences of your fellow IT professionals in adapting and customizing today's systems, applications, and frameworks. Our solution-based books give you the knowledge and power to customize the software and technologies you're using to get the job done. Packt books are more specific and less general than the IT books you have seen in the past. Our unique business model allows us to bring you more focused information, giving you more of what you need to know, and less of what you don't.

Packt is a modern, yet unique publishing company, which focuses on producing quality, cutting-edge books for communities of developers, administrators, and newbies alike. For more information, please visit our website: www.PacktPub.com.

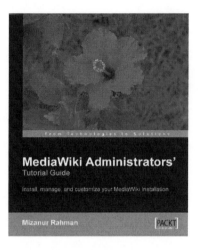

MediaWiki Administrator's Tutorial Guide

ISBN: 978-1-904811-59-6   Paperback: 284 pages

Install, manage, and customize your
MediaWiki installation

1. Get your MediaWiki site up fast

2. Manage users, special pages, and more

3. Customize and extend your MediaWiki site

4. Create new, attractive MediaWiki themes

MediaWiki Skins Design

ISBN: 978-1-847195-20-3   Paperback: 248 pages

Designing attractive skins and templates for your
MediaWiki site

1. A practical, clear guide to building custom
   MediaWiki skins

2. Extensive guidance on adjusting the layout and
   design of your MediaWiki's appearance

3. Attractive examples and design tips for using
   JavaScript and dynamic CSS to enhance your
   wiki's design

4. Change every aspect of MediaWiki's
   appearance to produce a wiki that's fully
   tailored to your requirements

Please check **www.PacktPub.com** for information on our titles

MediaWiki 1.1: Beginner's Guide

ISBN: 978-1-847196-04-0   Paperback: 350 pages

Install, manage, and customize your own
MediaWiki-based site

1. Install and administer MediaWiki to build a
   successful wiki site

2. Master the many administrative tasks
   associated with running and securing your wiki

3. Clear focus on beginners with lots of
   step-by-step instructions and clear explanation

4. Up-to-date with version 1.15 of MediaWiki,
   released in June 2009

Joomla! 1.5x Customization: Make Your Site Adapt to Your Needs

ISBN: 978-1-847195-16-6   Paperback: 288 pages

Create and customize a professional Joomla! site that
suits your business requirements

1. Adapt your site to get a unique appearance,
   features, and benefits of your choice

2. Save on development costs by learning how
   to do professional work yourself and solve
   common problems with a Joomla! site

3. Step through how to build an effective
   subscription-based business with Joomla! and
   market a site effectively

4. Understand and customize modules, plugins,
   components, and templates

Please check **www.PacktPub.com** for information on our titles

1117955R0

Printed in Germany by
Amazon Distribution
GmbH, Leipzig